The Crisis of American Labor

Operation Dixie and the Defeat of the CIO

The Crisis of
American Labor
Operation Dixie and the
Defeat of the CIO

BARBARA S. GRIFFITH

TEMPLE UNIVERSITY PRESS
PHILADELPHIA

Temple University Press, Philadelphia 19122
Copyright © 1988 by Temple University
All rights reserved
Published 1988
Printed in the United States of America

The paper used in this publication meets the minimum
requirements of American National Standard for Information
Sciences—Permanence of Paper for Printed Library Materials,
ANSI Z39.48-1984

Library of Congress Cataloging-in-Publication Data

Griffith, Barbara S.
　The crisis of American labor.

　Bibliography: p. 213
　Includes index.
　1. Congress of Industrial Organizations (U.S.)—History
2. Trade-unions—Southern States—Organizing—History.
I. Title.
HD8055.C75G75　1988　　　331.88'33'0975　　　87-9998
ISBN 087722-503-6

For my family

Acknowledgments

This examination of the CIO's postwar Southern drive was aided considerably by a number of people, some of whom must be singled out for the extra effort they went to on my behalf. Sharon Estes Knapp of Perkins Library at Duke University initially catalogued the Operation Dixie Archives and made my searches in that complex collection extremely productive. Leslie Hough and Robert Dinwiddie at the Southern Labor Archives at Georgia State University also provided a great deal of help at numerous points throughout the process. Jim Roan of the National Museum of American History Library went out of his way to locate material that was essential during the final months of the project.

Throughout, Keir Jorgensen, associate research director of the Amalgamated Clothing and Textile Workers Union, provided me with documents from files of the Textile Workers Union of America, along with names and addresses of retired TWUA organizers. He also put the manuscript into circulation among a large network of retired textile organizers and officials. Among them, I received especially valuable suggestions and additional help from Lawrence Rogin, Sol Stettin, Solomon Barkin, Donald McKee, and Lewis Conn. They are in no way responsible for the interpretations herein, some of which differ significantly from their own. I am all the more appreciative of their cooperation in light of this fact.

Robert Korstad of the University of North Carolina at Chapel Hill provided important information from his own work on the Food, Tobacco, Agricultural, and Allied Workers (FTA) and its Local 22 in Winston-Salem, North Carolina. Janet Irons of Duke University gave me advice and

perspective from her work on the 1934 textile strike, helping me a great deal. Allison Porter provided me with valuable insight on organizers, the work of organizing, and the
labor movement in general. I also extend special thanks to
Nelson Lichtenstein of Catholic University, who gave the
manuscript a sophisticated reading from which I profited
enormously. The interviews so critical to this study would
have been impossible without grants from Duke University's Department of History and Graduate School, the
Duke University—University of North Carolina Women's
Studies Research Center, and the Rieve-Pollock Foundation.
My editors at Temple University Press, Jane Cullen, Doris
Braendel, and Charles de Kay, have been extremely gra-
cious and have made this a very positive experience.

There is a paragraph found in most acknowledgments devoted to those who moved the product from hand-written
notes to a completed manuscript. Those to be thanked are almost invariably women; and they are never thanked
enough. Many of my interviews would be locked away on
audio tape had my mother, Sue Griffith, not volunteered to
type transcripts for me. Without complaint, Dorothy Sapp
typed every word of this manuscript at least once.

Lawrence C. Goodwyn supported this project, and its author, from start to finish, first as a resilient and determined
dissertation advisor and later as a colleague and friend.
Nell Goodwyn's friendship, support, and advice were critical, as well. Scott Ellsworth, Stacy Flaherty, Marjolein Kars,
and Carolyn Stefanco were staunch allies and patient
friends. Mickey Tullar made sure I lived through the process. And, not least, there is George Reed, who lived
through it with me. He read drafts of the manuscript,
learned to read my face, held on through some fairly heavy
weather, taught me many important things, and helped sustain my hope that I might be doing more than simply adding historical minutiae to the written record.

Finally, there are the retired organizers I interviewed and
about whom I wrote. It is through their eyes that we can
see something of the grim underside of industrial life in the
postwar years, labor organizing in the American South,

and the dynamics involved in attempting to build a mass-based movement. Each of them took risks in talking to me. To spend many months or years at great personal cost and sacrifice, fighting something that in large part turns out to be a losing battle is no simple matter. To allow a stranger access to the most personal details surrounding such an experience adds an emotional dimension that is, I think, appropriate to the historical reality of Operation Dixie. These men and women went where the stakes were the highest, where the opposition was most implacable and the workers were most in need. I wanted to set down as complete an account as I could, recording what I took to be their mistakes and weaknesses as well as their achievements. One cannot, after all, honor people by romanticizing them. This, then, is the story of their effort.

Contents

Preface

By the end of World War II, it was clear to many in the Congress of Industrial Organizations that a Southern organizing drive had to be undertaken, both to consolidate the impressive gains labor made during the war and to remove the South as a non-union haven for "runaway" Northern businesses. The task of organizing the North could not be completed until the South was organized. Thus began Operation Dixie, a drive into twelve Southern states from 1946 to 1953.

Inasmuch as the American South had a long-standing reputation as a region particularly unreceptive to organized labor, Operation Dixie was not a challenge for which union activists had anything approaching unbridled enthusiasm. Everyone knew it was a great gamble. Operation Dixie would in fact become a delicate balancing act for a labor organization increasingly beset with internal tensions and conflicting priorities, and confronted by an aggressive business community and a rightward shift in the national political climate.

The CIO also confronted problems posed by the peculiarities of the South. A cultural and economic insularity characterized the region, with relatively little in-migration to the area since the Civil War, a rigid caste system based on a hierarchy of race, class, and gender, and a level of economic development that in many ways more closely resembled the nineteenth than the twentieth century. In addition, textiles, the South's largest industry, was even more resistant to unionization than its counterpart in New England; it was especially competitive in the South, resulting from the relatively small units of production, chronic shortages of operating capital, recurrent cycles of overproduction and low prices, and a large pool of unemployed and underemployed workers from the mountains and marginal farms of the South. Even beyond these factors, the South had fostered a set of closely interwoven relationships between industrialists, politicians, law enforcement officials, religious leaders, and the press—all of which could be mobilized in concert, quite beyond the level of cooperation commonly found among the same sectors of society in the North.

My purpose in this study is not so much to "wrap up" the many social and cultural threads that intertwine in Operation Dixie, a task that would require a number of community studies. Rather, my intent is to open up the topic by setting in place the broad historical framework, both national and Southern, within which the men and women of the CIO and their corporate opponents lived through the daily realities of the struggle.

At the heart of the narrative is, quite simply, a story: the unfolding drama of planning for conflict, the conflict itself, and, rather abruptly, defeat. This story is told primarily through the organizers who staffed the drive, from their correspondence with workers, their peers, and superiors, and from extensive interviews with retired organizers who were active in Operation Dixie. It is through them that one can see how this massive organizing campaign played out on a daily basis in the towns and factories of the region. And it is through them and the cultural context into which they intruded that the responses of Southern workers take on tangible historical meaning.

A word about the place of women in Operation Dixie. Although women workers were a central factor in the textile industry, the industry most critical to the campaign's success, most of the organizers sent South by the CIO and its member internationals were men. Though such unions as the Textile Workers Union of America (TWUA) and the Amalgamated Clothing Workers of America (ACWA) hired some women organizers, CIO organizers did not challenge the inherited "place" for women in the work force and within organized labor to the same extent that they challenged racial barriers and prejudice. A notable exception was the Food, Tobacco, Agricultural, and Allied Workers (FTA), which had a number of black women on its organizing staff. This is not to say that women were not instrumental in the success of certain organizing campaigns; it merely attests to the fact that women and their problems did not hold a distinctive place either in the minds of most male organizers or within the administrative echelons of organized labor. So in looking at Operation Dixie through the eyes of its organizers, it is through a predominantly male perspective that one sees.

Considering their generation, it is not surprising that the women interviewed for this study did not complain of their isolation within organized labor. In their view, all organizers were there for the same reasons. They negotiated contracts with wage differentials for men and women, because, in the words of one woman, "It never occurred to us to do it any other way."

Several women noted that perhaps they had had a better understanding of what motivated women workers than did male organizers; for example, they were more likely to account for the demands of a woman worker's "double day" in her decision to attend or not attend a nighttime union meeting. Beyond that, however, they stopped seeing themselves as different from their male counterparts. Scholarly studies of women in textiles, tobacco, and the automobile industry have begun to acquire a place in the historical literature. It will have to be in their capacity as workers in those industries, rather than as active participants in Operation Dixie, that the history of Southern working women will be written.

With these emphases in mind, what follows is a broad overview of a complex organizing campaign waged over a twelve-state region. Strategic decisions made by the CIO's Executive Board in Washington and by CIO international unions in a dozen locales, and tactical decisions made by the CIO's Southern Organizing Committee at the drive's headquarters in Atlanta—all had an important bearing on the outcome. But the ultimate decisions were made by organizers, on the ground each day in the South. In a sense, they know best what happened to Operation Dixie, for they lived through it as no one else did.

Operation Dixie happened at the juncture of a number of significant American historical developments: the tide of conservatism that is often the aftermath of American wars; the erosion of the New Deal coalition; the wave of anti-communist hysteria; the social change stimulated during the war, particularly among women and minorities due to wartime labor shortages; and the wartime growth of business and organized labor. Had Operation Dixie succeeded, the later course of American history might have been quite different. Clearly, the CIO's purge of its own left wing brought it into closer political alignment with the AFL and paved the way for their merger in 1956. This brought to an end the tradition of aggressive organization among those who previously fell outside the bounds of craft unionism, i.e., minorities, women, and semi- or unskilled workers. Further, a CIO victory in the South might have hastened the civil rights movement by at least a decade. A successful Operation Dixie could have dramatically altered the predominance of conservative Southern politicians in state and national legislatures. And certainly, union membership for Southern workers would have created the potential for shifts of economic power to those in the South who had never known any.

What follows is an analysis of the process through which Operation Dixie intruded upon the politics and culture of postwar America, and then disappeared. For the nation, it was but a moment; for organized labor it was a decisive juncture whose long-term meaning is only now becoming clear.

The Crisis of
American Labor

Operation Dixie and the Defeat of the CIO

I

An Uncertain Model

The question was simple: how to crack the South? How to organize the workers in the most anti-union region of the nation? This problem was at the core of "Operation Dixie," the name given the organizing campaign launched by the Congress of Industrial Organizations in twelve Southern states in 1946. The stakes, as informed people in and out of the labor movement all understood, were very high. Operation Dixie was the culmination of a long search to find a way to organize the nation's skilled, semiskilled, and unskilled workers under one huge institutional umbrella that covered the entire country. The dream of "one big union" was an old one, first nursed along by individual labor spokesmen in the first half of the nineteenth century, shaped further by the Knights of Labor in the 1880s and by the Industrial Workers of the World in the first decades of the twentieth century. After more than a century of experimentation, a breakthrough was finally achieved in the Northern mass production industries in the 1930s with the introduction of the sit-down strike. The lessons learned throughout this long struggle, and how those lessons were interpreted in the immediate postwar period of 1945–1946, determined in decisive ways the shape of the CIO's Southern organizing campaign.

As it had come to exist in the opening decades of the twentieth century, the American working class was a diverse conglomeration of ethnic groups. There were "old stock" British Americans whose roots were in the artisanal trades of the colonial era or who, in the South, formed a yeoman

3

class of smallholders on the land. There were, in addition, the earliest immigrants who had come to dominate certain trades, such as Irish carpenters or the German and Bohemian cigar makers who shaped the formative years of Samuel Gomper's experience. And finally, there was the flood of "new immigrants," the earliest dating from the Irish potato famine in the 1840s, but vastly augmented by the surge of Italian and other southern and eastern European immigrants who came to America in huge numbers between 1870 and the outbreak of World War I. These new Americans and blacks not only predominated in the emerging mass production industries, they had the meanest jobs in those industries. They stoked the furnaces in the steel mills, labored in the searing heat of the paint shops of the new auto industries and, in general, worked where the physical tasks were the hardest and the pay the lowest. They spoke a different kind of English, in Italian, Slavic, and Yiddish accents, lived in the most teeming ghettos, and otherwise were separated—and separated themselves—from the rest of American society. Socially and culturally, as well as economically, they suffered countless variations of American prejudice.[1]

The American Federation of Labor under Samuel Gompers could not address the needs of this pivotal section of the American working class. An historical segmentation divided the growing millions of workers in the mass production industries from the skilled workers in the traditional crafts. Workers named Higgins, Hopewell, and O'Connor labored as carpenters, electricians, and painters; the steel, auto, rubber, and electrical industries were full of Kowalskis, Bialics, and Barzinis; and a good percentage of the Browns and Harrises in their ranks tended to be black. As historian Herbert Gutman pointed out, the new American working class of the industrial era was overwhelmingly composed of immigrants, children of immigrants and blacks.

The structure of the AFL effectively sidestepped the ethnic problems inherent in the composition of the twentieth-century American working class. The combination of the emphasis on organizing the crafts and the tradition of "autonomy" for each trade effectively codified racial, ethnic, and class prejudice within the trade union structure itself. One therefore had to be somewhat free of these inherited prejudices even to contemplate industrial unionism, in which all the Kowalskis and O'Connors and Barzinis would amalgamate in "one big union."

One path that could lead to this conclusion was ideological. As ideology would come to be a divisive issue in Operation Dixie, both within the ranks of organized labor near the end of the 1940s and within the larger society at the onset of the cold war, it is appropriate to review briefly the internal tensions that had long been at work in the American labor movement. The same interpretations of American capitalism that induced a worker to be a socialist also provided explanations as to why the working class was divided and why employers routinely pitted strikebreakers of one ethnic group against striking workers of another. In this sense, to be a trade union Socialist was to be an advocate of a world view that went beyond questions of wages and working conditions to include broad social and cultural attitudes as well. Those working-class institutions such as the IWW that saw ethnic divisions as fatal to the unity of workers warred consciously against prejudice as a prerequisite to successful organizing and strike actions. In their songs that characterized prejudiced workers as "scissorbills" who acted as their own worst enemies, the Wobblies were engaged in a kind of cultural war to redefine social relations throughout the whole society. Ideological beliefs were a potentially powerful force not only against the AFL as an institution, but against the racial, ethnic, and class prejudices that were imbedded in the very foundation of the AFL's structure.[2]

But workers could dissent against the Gompers philosophy on narrower, tactical grounds as well. One did not have to be a Socialist to see that a work force that was only marginally organized could never amass the political authority to change the existing ground rules governing labor-management relations. One did not have to be a Socialist to see that most American workers were not skilled craftsmen who had mastered old-line trades. One needed only to be

able to count in order to grasp that the industrial future lay
in the mass production industries and in their variegated
work force, which lay beyond the reach of the traditional
craft unions.

Advocacy of industrial unionism, therefore, was not restricted to labor radicals. The political and economic weakness of the AFL, grounded in its narrow craft base,
translated into a lack of effectiveness in the organizing and
bargaining process itself—a weakness that a growing number of AFL partisans themselves could see with increasing
clarity in the 1920s. After the first great surge of labor consciousness had peaked in the 1880s and 1890s, organized
labor in America counted over 5,000,000 workers in its
ranks—4,000,000 in the AFL and the bulk of the remainder
in the craft-oriented railroad brotherhoods. But by 1930, it
was evident that two generations of unsuccessful attempts
to penetrate the mass production industries not only had
kept the majority of American workers out of the ranks of organized labor, but had left the crafts themselves more vulner-
able to corporate opposition. By the time of Franklin
Roosevelt's election in 1932, AFL membership had shrunk
to little over 2,000,000. One of the AFL's nearest approxima-
tions to an industrial union was the United Mine Workers.
By 1929, mine worker membership had shrunk in the face
of intense corporate opposition to 84,000 dues payers—20
percent of the work force.[3]

It is not surprising, then, that a great many working-
class advocates felt that Gomper's federation was hopeless
and attempted to build independent unions. They ran afoul
not only of their corporate opponents, but also faced the
kind of cultural isolation to which socialism itself had been
confined. If organizers had to convince American workers
to become Socialists as a first step in freeing themselves
from the narrow organizing tactics of the AFL, the history
of 1900–1935 indicated that the task lay far beyond their capacity.[4]

As a result, a great amount of energy was directed toward reforming the AFL from within by persuading the organization to transcend its craft orientation and adopt the

industrial union approach necessary to unlock the mass production industries. Indeed, efforts in this direction dominated the interior life of the AFL in the 1920s and 1930s. Years of resolution-passing and jockeying over semantics induced the AFL under intense pressure in 1933 to agree to the chartering of federal unions, in which workers were organized outside the jurisdiction of particular internationals. Thus they were "federated" directly to the AFL.[5] That experiment, designed to offer a rudimentary path around craft jurisdiction problems so that organizers could approach workers in the mass production industries, had ended in utter disaster in the abortive strikes of 1934. Desperate organizing campaigns in the automobile industry in the Midwest, textiles in the South and Northeast, and steel and other basic industries in the East had all failed. In the course of these often massive efforts by the progressive wing of the AFL, militant workers in hundred of mills and factories—the backbone of future organizing efforts—had been identified and fired by management. The federal unions themselves had been reduced virtually to empty shells populated more or less equally by bruised and intimidated workers and by watchful company spies.[6]

The organizing failures of 1934 seemed to verify the beliefs held by both factions in the AFL: to old-time traditionalists, the failed strikes revealed conclusively that the federal union concept was as unworkable as they had always said it was. Labor's progressives had never really liked the federal union approach either, but experimented with it as a step in the long campaign to induce the AFL leadership to accept responsibility for the great majority of American workers engaged in mass production.

As a practical matter, organizers familiar with America's mass production industries knew that union status could never be won without long and probably desperate recognition strikes that would fully test the internal cohesion and group solidarity of the strikers themselves. Should victory be achieved, the thought of breaking up the instrument of victory—the local union the workers themselves had created in order to stand against management—seemed an insane proposition. The dismantling of the federal union meant dividing the workers into dozens of new groupings, under the control of people they did not know, had not fought alongside, and who sequestered themselves in far-off headquarters of "brotherhoods." The idea might harmonize with the institutional habits of encrusted twentieth-century craft structures, but it simply did not speak to the organizational demands of the industrial age. So felt labor's progressives in 1935, and so they had felt for the better part of two generations. Corporate capital commanded big production units; only a big union could contest such centralized power.[7]

The creation of the Committee for Industrial Organizations in 1935 addressed the institutional prerequisites, but it was the successful "sit-down" movement that began against General Motors in 1936 that provided labor with the tactical means to challenge corporate power in the mass production industries. Even more to the point, the organizing experience of the late 1930s provided the CIO's leaders with the dominant ideas that were to govern Operation Dixie at war's end.

The breakthrough sit-down strike—at the General Motors Fisher Body Plant in Flint, Michigan—had an electrifying impact on the nation's mass production workers. In the immediate aftermath of the General Motors settlement, sit-down strikes erupted not only throughout the automobile industry, but in the steel, rubber, and electrical industries as well. The number of workers involved in sit-downs multiplied into the tens of thousands, hundreds of thousands, then millions. Recognition followed: the United Rubber Workers, the United Electrical Workers, the United Steelworkers. Almost overnight, it seemed, the CIO had become the major force in American labor.[8] This breakthrough was— in its operative feature of the sit-down strike—more a tactical triumph than an ideological one. It is important to keep this distinction clear, as it bears directly on the strategy the CIO attempted to implement in Operation Dixie.

The sit-down tactic countered the one continuing management weapon that had for over a century defeated workers' attempts to gain union recognition. Indeed, for workers, the scenario of labor-management conflict had long been both familiar and disillusioning: workers nursing grievances sufficiently overcame their fear of being fired to form a trade union to bargain for them; management refused to bargain; the workers struck and threw up picket lines; management hired strikebreakers; the strikers guarded the plant gates and forcibly prevented strikebreakers from entering; management appealed to political authorities for National Guard troops to "restore order" and "prevent violence"; management additionally obtained court injunctions against the pickets; the troops and injunctions cleared the path for strikebreakers to enter the plant; production resumed; the strike was broken; the union was destroyed. Strategically, in defining the balance of forces between American management and American labor, workers remained without bargaining power. But from a worker's standpoint, the specific problem was tactical—the inability of workers to halt production without bringing the full power of law enforcement down on the side of management. The sit-down strike provided the long-sought tactical answer; it circumvented the picket line and its associated violence, and the excuse for calling in law enforcement officials. Management was reluctant to mobilize troops to storm factories under conditions that might cause damage to the equipment inside them.[9] The sit-down was also a tactic that workers immediately understood and wanted to implement. It offered the prospect of success, whether used by workers who saw themselves as Republicans, Democrats, Socialists, or Communists. After Flint, people believed it would work and, partly because of this belief, it did.[10]

In summary, the sit-down strike was the tool that allowed the CIO to rapidly mobilize millions of industrial workers in the 1930s. It created, in some ways overnight, an enthusiasm that fired workers and organizers with the belief that management's tactics could be overcome. In the end, its effect was as much psychological as organizational

because it created a transforming "moment" that, in many
cases for the first time, indicated to workers that they did
have a measure of control over their work lives.

Yet the CIO breakthrough in the North in the 1930s cannot be neatly summarized as the predictable result of one tactical refinement in labor's approach to organizing. The
breakdown of the economic system was a fact of Depression era life that no amount of free enterprise rhetoric
could conceal from the society as a whole. The political result had been the New Deal, with its avalanche of social legislation, including the National Industrial Recovery Act.
Something on the order of what might be called a suppor-
tive "pro-people" culture had come into being as a result of
the widespread pain caused by the Depression. In ways
not yet predictable, this new circumstance carried a measure of popular sympathy for the plight of ordinary citizens, including mass production workers. Beyond this
general political circumstance, the New Deal's more specific
acts seemed to carry less weight.[11]

The idea of targeting the most powerful corporations—
U.S. Steel, General Electric and Westinghouse, Goodyear
and Firestone—became a cornerstone of CIO belief. The sit-
down era was understood to be the period when the CIO organized all the nation's basic industries save textiles. This
belief was strengthened by the fact that the organization
emerged from World War II with active locals in almost all
the flagship corporations in America's industrial sector. The
organizing reality, however, was much more complicated.
The Ford Motor Company held out for five years, and
equally tenacious opposition was encountered at Westinghouse in the electrical industry and at Goodyear in rubber.
Even in organized industries, the CIO had difficulty building strong locals. Membership withered by the hundreds of
thousands after the renewed economic downturn of 1937,
and 250 organizers in steel had to be laid off, even though
30 percent of basic steel remained unorganized. The CIO,
which boasted 4 million workers in 1938, actually had a dues-
paying total of 1.8 million in 1940.[12]

Nevertheless, an institutional model was in place, propelled by the sheer momentum of post–1936 events, coming as they did after many decades of frustration and defeat. The way to organize in a given industry was to knock off that industry's bellwether corporations: this was the Northern model in which the CIO's tactics, strategy, and organization were grounded as it prepared to take on the South in Operation Dixie.

II

Postwar Realities

A curious paradox confronted the American working class at the end of World War II. On the one hand, a great many workers had made significant gains in income since the low point of the Depression. For example, average weekly wages in manufacturing had risen 65 percent from December 1941 to April 1945, while the cost of living had increased only some 30 percent. Because of labor shortages, many workers were also able to move into better paying jobs. Additionally, throughout the nation workers had become accustomed to plenty of overtime at time and a half, so that gross income for millions of Americans had doubled and even tripled over anything they had known before the war. When compared with the frightening insecurity of the Depression, the war years represented a giant step forward.[1]

Further, if the status of workers in general had improved, the condition of organized workers had improved most of all. The War Labor Board and the Office of Price Administration, augmented by a host of regulations administered by New Dealers in dozens of federal agencies, had produced a fundamental shift in the tri-lateral relationships among business, government and labor. If workers still remained the least of equals in this arrangement, and if businesses still remained first, the domination of the economy by corporations was at least modified by the cultural authority that the government had obtained in exercising its mandate to win the war. To all appearances, "Dr. Win the War," whom Roosevelt had announced as the replacement for "Dr. New Deal," had not represented quite the retreat from social progress that many ardent New Dealers feared.

Aside from the very real economic gains made by American workers during the war, the most important change seemed to be structural: organized labor had gained a permanent institutional place in American life. The footholds gained by the CIO in basic industries (and then substantially weakened during the final prewar recession) were almost fully consolidated during the war. Some 80 percent of all workers in basic industries were dues-paying members of organized labor at the end of the war. The dues checkoff itself had become largely institutionalized, providing conclusive evidence for many that American corporations had decided to live with the CIO on a permanent basis. In comparative terms, at least, CIO treasuries were bulging from the monthly contributions of six million members.[2]

No union's change in status seemed more pronounced than that of the long-embattled textile workers' union. Emil Rieve, the president of the consolidated Textile Workers Union of America (TWUA-CIO), had sat on the War Labor Board, a fact that in itself testified to the altered status of the labor movement. But beyond such cosmetic changes, the War Labor Board had real power, and its rulings during three rounds of wartime wage-price adjustments became increasingly prolabor. As a historian of the TWUA has concluded: "During each period, the TWUA's position in the industry improved significantly, to the point where, in 1945, a government ruling was so pro-union that some firms reacted with open defiance of government controls themselves."[3]

At the peak of textile organizing before the war, the TWUA claimed almost a quarter of a million recruits. But the relationship of the union to its members and to the companies with which it had contracts was so fragile that dues collections rarely reflected more than half that figure. This circumstance changed dramatically during the war. The union had operated on deficit financing from the founding of the Textile Workers Organizing Committee in 1937 to the middle of the war, before finally passing into the black. By war's end, however, the TWUA counted 450,000 members, organized in a comparatively well-developed national, regional, state, and local union structure. War Labor Board rulings had played a significant role in this transformation.[4]

If the general situation looked better from the standpoint of the textile union, the stronger and historically more progressive internationals in the CIO arrived at war's end in an even more aggressive frame of mind. The social democrats who had consolidated their position in the United Automobile Workers under Walter Reuther nursed dreams of transforming American society—to be spearheaded by the CIO in the immediate postwar years. The Steelworkers Union, a bit to the right of the UAW, and the Electrical and Rubber Workers, both a bit to the left, all nursed similar expectations. With their organized membership freed from the shackles of the no-strike pledge, the labor movement would lead the way to a new society. After all, they could tell themselves, had they not, in the space of one decade, moved from a beleaguered minority in the AFL to something approaching a position of bargaining parity with the world's largest corporations? Could they not shut down all the nation's basic industries, and the docks, and the trucking industry? Had not the climactic moment for industrial unionism arrived, the moment to usher in the "new America" that progressives had been anticipating since the great strikes of the 1880s and 1890s? As the CIO looked across the postwar landscape, its spokesmen were not timid in their appraisals of their prospects.[5]

It was with some shock, then, that in the war's immediate aftermath, labor found itself thrown completely on the defensive by a surprisingly aggressive business community. As the Truman administration came under steadily mounting pressure from business lobbyists, the labor movement found itself on the defensive inside the Democratic Party as well. When labor economists reported what rank-and-file members had already felt in their pockets—that real wages had declined almost 15 percent in the first three months following the war—dismay extended far beyond those labor progressives who had dreamed of a transformation of American society. Attempts at collective bargaining to gain cost-of-living increases in line with the escalating rate of inflation met stony resistance—in steel, in autos, and, indeed, everywhere. As a result, the great strikes of the autumn and winter of 1945–1946 were defensive strikes, designed to *preserve* the buying power of wages rather than to advance to a higher wage scale.[6]

Yet as denounced by business spokesmen—and, ominously, by some in the Truman administration—labor's actions were viewed by the society as a whole as being impetuous, greedy, or, more simply, radical. Increasingly, business spokesmen called attention to Communists as sources of labor unrest, despite the fact that the most visible and disruptive strikes were in auto and steel, where left-wing elements had been resoundingly defeated in internal battles in the UAW and the USW. But for many Americans, Reuther was not seen as a social democrat who had consolidated his influence over Communists; rather, he was increasingly depicted as the "radical boss" of the world's largest union, the 1,200,000–member UAW. During more than a year of strife following the victory over Japan in August 1945, labor lost battle after battle in its campaign to retain price controls and preserve the purchasing power of union wages. In retrospect, it is clear that inadequate cost-of-living increases were granted only at the cost of excessive price increases. The latter came initially in the cost of steel, and then inevitably, in the price of basic products made from steel.[7]

Thus, at war's end, organized labor was in a peculiar position. Although emerging strengthened in numbers and with a level of cultural credibility it did not possess in the 1930s, it found itself on the defensive in an increasingly conservative society. In addition, its membership base in the North was being seriously threatened by the accelerating flight of companies to the nonunion South. At a time when labor's defensive strikes were commanding a great deal of its attention and resources, it was forced to make organizing the South a top postwar priority and take immediate measures to block the South as a nonunion haven for Northern business. If textile and furniture manufacturers could "run away" to the South, so could a host of other industries. In accepting this challenge, what labor leaders did not realize was the extent to which their strategies were tailored to a Northern, and pre-World War II, society.

In 1946, the reality of social relations in the South did not mesh well with the Northern model. The South had a distinct heritage, disfigured by a time-honored system of racial segregation, and heightened by generations of poverty and provincialism. Above all, the long history of racial and class hierarchy had produced stringent social controls unlike anything that could be found in the North. In the Southern economy, tight cooperation among the owners of industry, the judicial system, and law enforcement agencies was regarded as the natural order of things. It was "normal practice." To be sure, the CIO had encountered police harassment and company thugs in a number of Northern states, and labor had its martyrs to show for it. But the bald hypocrisy and ruthlessness of sheriffs in Southern mill villages went quite beyond the patterns of management-police cooperation common in the North. There really were no Northern "models" that could prepare the CIO for the implacable hostility that awaited textile organizers entering a mill village for the first time.

To have been adequately prepared, organizers and union leadership would have needed an intimate understanding of the decades-long history of Southern textile workers and of the actual day-to-day conditions of life in the industrial hamlets across the South. As a textile worker once explained,

> The company stores took all your money. I've seen plenty of people who didn't draw a cent on payday. It all went to the store. If you wanted to go to a show uptown, you went to the company store and got a pass. But the company store charged you for this and deducted it from your pay when payday came around. Even doctors' bills were paid through the company store.[8]

How could people come to accept such treatment? Actually, for most, such relationships with "the store" had been all they, their parents, and grandparents had ever known. Even before the coming of the mills, as sharecroppers or as rent tenants or as small landowners in the mountains and piedmont of the South, they had gotten their seed and supplies on "furnish" from the "furnishing merchants" who, like the company stores, conducted business wholly on credit. The "rednecks" of sharecropping and the "lint heads" of the mill villages lived so exclusively on credit from furnishing merchants and company stores that they rarely, if ever, saw actual money. The impact of this inheritance was so pervasive that refugees from sharecropping who found employment at mills that actually paid their workers in cash felt they had made a fundamental improvement in their way of life. A mill in a town (i.e., not in its own "mill village") that did not operate a company store was in the position of giving employment to workers who could, as one of them put it, "buy anywhere I pleased." It was a real change, one for which many workers felt grateful.[9]

It would be an error of the first magnitude to pass lightly over this fundamental social circumstance of the postwar American South. Like other people, Southerners had dreams. And like other people, they knew the constraints under which they lived. In this fundamental sense, they were neither "mystified" nor "apathetic." The breath taking speed with which hundreds of thousands of Southern workers had, as one of them put it, "gone into battle" in the great general textile strike of 1934 testified both to the reality of their hopes and to their capacity for collective action.

Nevertheless, in ways that historians and other social observers cannot conclusively "prove" with concrete evidence, these hopes and this potential persisted in a social environment that steadfastly warred against their expression. It was an environment of poverty—of poverty over many generations. It was a culture of dependence, again for many generations, on "the man" who ran the store and whose shelves contained the needs of life. It was, in the end, a culture that could at one and the same time encourage traditional American hopes while confirming an inheritance of poverty and dependence.

The history of organized labor in the South attested to the presence of these contradictory drives in Southern workers. It was an intricate history, one full of dogged determination and violence that on occasion had involved large numbers of workers. Southern workers had, sequentially, been receptive to Knights of Labor organizers in the sugar parishes of Louisiana in the 1880s, to IWW organizers in the lumber industry in Texas after the turn of the century, to Communist organizers in Gastonia, North Carolina, in the 1920s, and, on many occasions stretching over two generations, to the American Federation of Labor. There had even been an interracial general strike in New Orleans in 1902. Textiles, in particular, had long been the center of intense organizing activity. A roster of textile mill towns involved at one time or another in intense labor struggles sounded like a roll call of the industry itself: Cannon, Cone, Burlington, and Erwin in North Carolina; Dan River in Virginia; Comer in Alabama; and Bibb in Georgia. But the large textile chains were by no means the only targets. Some of the most bitter struggles occurred in relatively small mill towns. Several, such as those in Marion in North Carolina and Elizabethton in Tennessee in 1929, attracted national attention. A correspondent of the *Nation* described living and working conditions at Marion as "almost indescribably degrading."[10]

The immediate organizational forerunner of Operation Dixie came just before World War II. It offered sober instruction for the would-be architects of Operation Dixie. In 1937, the CIO's John L. Lewis created the "Textile Workers Organizing Committee" (TWOC) and appointed Sydney Hillman to head it. The ensuing organizing campaign in 1937 embodied an essentially Northern emphasis. Hillman divided the nation into eight regions; only two were located in the South. Some 500 organizers were placed on staff, with 350 of them assigned to the six Northern regions. In effect, the TWOC was assigning organizers on the basis of existing regional membership, rather than on the basis of where its po-

tential members were. In dispatching two-thirds of its organizing staff to Northern states, it was trying to fill a leaking
can. Between 1925 and 1940, for example, one of the great
textile centers in the nation (Fall River, Massachusetts) had
lost three-quarters of its production capacity, seventy-three
mills totaling $60,000,000 in capital investment, to the
South. If the union was to have a future, it lay in the
nearly 500,000 textile workers below the Mason-Dixon line.
The union did, however, take the precaution of disassociat-
ing itself from the 1934 strike by hiring all new organizers,
transferring the 1934 veterans "to regions where they are
less well known." A victory was won quickly at the Coving-
ton Mills in Virginia in March, the first of many that would
come once the full organizing staff was deployed in June.
But "again and again, mill hands voted in favor of the
TWOC only to be suppressed by mill owners and local governments."[11]

During the opening phases, 64,000 textile workers signed
up, 50,000 of them in cotton mills. In North Carolina alone,
workers outside Asheville turned in 20,000 pledge cards.
Nevertheless, by October 1937, the specifics were quite ominous: the North Carolina staff possessed only a single contract covering 450 workers at the Edna Mills in Reidsville.
The total for the *entire* South was seventeen contracts, totaling 21,000 workers. At its peak in April 1937, the TWOC deployed 650 organizers nationwide; eleven months later, the
union could afford to have only 249 on the job.[12]

Undaunted, the TWOC won enough elections in the
North to increase its duespaying membership in the region
to 135,000 by 1940. Together with the 21,000 in the South,
the union had doubled its 1937 strength and stood on the
threshold of reorganizing itself as a permanent institution.
The Textile Workers Union of America (TWUA), CIO, formally came into being in 1939, with Emil Rieve elected president and George Baldanzi vice president. The TWUA then
stood in official opposition to the rump UTW (AFL), which
counted a grand total of 1,500 members nationwide.[13]

Meanwhile, the leading textile firms in the South stepped up their aggressive personnel policies and defeated re-

peated organizing efforts through what can perhaps best be
described as legalized armed repression. In Greensboro,
North Carolina, 6,000 workers walked out at Cone Mills to
protest a 12.5 percent wage reduction in July 1938. They
won an NLRB election in August and a second election in
March 1939. But through what one historian described as
"continued harassment and discrimination," Cone not only
avoided signing these contracts, but also beat back organizing attempts at every other mill in the chain's empire. Similarly, the TWUA won six elections at Burlington in
Greensboro; but even when these were augmented by favorable NLRB rulings forbidding company harassment, the
union failed to achieve "even a foothold." The same pattern prevailed in the Erwin Mills in Durham, where management prevailed throughout three years of sustained TWUA
effort.[14]

Recalcitrant management was not the CIO's only problem in the final prewar textile drive. The AFL joined management in criticizing the CIO's efforts. The federation's
Southern representative, George Googe, a classic race-
baiting craft union conservative, issued frequent statements
regarding the Communist menace represented by the CIO.
All received wide press coverage in the South. It was a hint
of things to come in Operation Dixie.

The importance of organizing the textile industry in the
South increased during World War II. The long decline of
the industry in the North accelerated during the war. By
1945, there were 250,000 fewer textile workers in Northern
mills, and 100,000 more Southern textile workers, than at
the start of the war. Simultaneously, the steady increase in
Southern spindles continued. The balance was tilting
decisively—a majority of the nation's million-odd textile
workers would soon be found in the South, and the figure
could be expected to increase in the postwar years.[15]

In sizing up this challenge, on the eve of its Southern campaign in 1946 the CIO could look to substantial wartime
gains, made not so much on the picket line as through government resolutions of labor-management disputes that
threatened the war effort. These government decisions ena-

bled the CIO to consolidate its membership and achieve a
dues checkoff in the nation's basic industries. One of the reasons the TWUA was able to contribute $125,000 to the cost
of Operation Dixie was traceable to its wartime membership gains—to 400,000.

As it prepared for its Southern drive, its gains since 1936
indicated the CIO had achieved an historic breakthrough in
the nation's mass production industries. If the CIO was not
the nation's "one big union," it was, undeniably, a big
union. Industrial unionism had come to America. Whether
it would attain permanent status, or how healthy it would
be, would depend in no small measure on how well Operation Dixie progressed.

The CIO's organizational model, derived from its Northern experiences, now confronted the unique challenges of
the South. Whatever the odds, however, the CIO leadership had high hopes. They were not alone. Some had had
their sights set on the South long before 1946. Among them
was a delegate to the TWUA's first convention in 1939,
who would become the South Carolina director during Operation Dixie.

> We, too, are going to have some of the good things of
> this life. We are going to get rid of the mill villages
> and company stores. We are not going to send our chil-
> dren to the company schools in order that the boss
> might teach them what he wants them to know. We
> are going to live like free, decent people.[16]

III

The "Holy Crusade"

The specific strategy behind the deployment of CIO organizers across the South in May 1946 reflected a high-level CIO decision to create a tightly centralized operation, firmly under the personal control of the campaign's director, Van A. Bittner. The jurisdictional problems inherent in a multi-union drive received a simple, straightforward solution: the CIO Southern Organizing Committee's (SOC) Atlanta office would decide *after* a successful organizing campaign which international union would inherit jurisdiction over the new CIO members. The assignment of organizers to states and, at the outset, even to regions of states was similarly centralized in the Atlanta SOC office. The initiation fees to be collected with each signed union card would be sent to Atlanta; all petitions for NLRB elections would also be forwarded there; and finally, all state directors would report directly to Bittner, separate from any contact with their own internationals. To emphasize the subordinate role of everyone to Atlanta—and to stress, as well, the priority of organizing over political activity—Bittner instructed all state directors to resign from any CIO Political Action Committee to which they might belong. The Southern Organizing Committee, radiating out of Atlanta, was to be a tightly knit, scalpel-clean force of trade union activists, stripped of any preoccupations that did not directly coincide with the task of organizing the unorganized. It was to be a "no frills campaign."[1]

Bittner, a veteran of the United Mine Workers, had been appointed to head the Southern campaign by CIO President Philip Murray one month earlier. Murray had also chosen George Baldanzi as deputy director of the drive. As it turned out, Bittner served Operation Dixie essentially as a civil servant carrying out the strategic wishes of Philip Murray and the CIO Executive Board. Actual direction of the campaign was in the hands of the more energetic Baldanzi. Bittner could perhaps fairly be characterized as something more of a trade union functionary than a labor activist.[2] Throughout 1946, he was to spend much of his time in Washington and New York. While in the Atlanta headquarters of Operation Dixie, he seemed content to push paper. George Baldanzi ran Operation Dixie.

There was an unassailable logic behind Baldanzi's appointment. From his work in the Dyers' Federation and the TWUA, he was familiar with the many branches of the textile industry. He had also witnessed the deterioration of the New England textile industry, the union's original base, and had organized Southern textile workers during the war, including the victory at the Dan River and Riverside cotton mills in Danville, Virginia, in 1942.[3]

Among other key appointments for Operation Dixie were the men assigned as state directors. In the six textile states, Baldanzi named men who, in the aggregate, constituted an interesting cross section of the labor movement. Named as South Carolina state director was Franz Daniel, a college-trained "labor intellectual" who was experienced, personally engaging, and quite capable. Daniel's counterpart in North Carolina was William Smith. He coupled a courteous demeanor with a quiet passion to organize the textile industry. Tennessee's Paul Christopher was a social democrat, with associations that placed him a bit to the left of most textile organizers. More than most of the state directors in Operation Dixie, Christopher could work easily with both ideological wings of the CIO. The Alabama state director, Carey Haigler, was more attuned to Washington than to the Southern rank and file, and was notably cautious on the race issue. Virginia's Ernest Pugh was remembered for his caution, and Charles Gillman, the Georgia state director, was recalled as an unprepossessing and earnest man who had something of the solid citizen about him.[4]

The state directors set up state offices across the South in May and began assembling the diverse assortment of incoming organizers—representing scores of different international unions—into something approximating working teams. Aware of the Southern habit of reflexive hostility to "outside agitators," Baldanzi decreed that Operation Dixie would be staffed largely by Southerners and, if possible, veterans of World War II. Internationals were so instructed in advance. As a result of his wartime organizing experiences in the South, Baldanzi wished to insulate Operation Dixie as much as possible from any charge that the CIO was radical, un-American, or alien to the Southern way of life.

Like Bittner and TWUA generally, Baldanzi was safely insulated from the CIO's left wing and was, presumably, invulnerable to red-baiting—a charge that was almost certain to be leveled at any CIO campaign. In the case of Operation Dixie, however, that accusation came even more quickly than anyone had expected, and from a quarter that was close to home. The assignment of state directors and organizing teams was overshadowed in the public press by the reappearance of George Googe, the AFL's Southern representative, who reminded Southern newspaper editors of the red threat represented by Operation Dixie. The CIO's effort, he said, was in the hands of "broken down left-wingers." Indeed the AFL went beyond press announcements. Alarmed by Operation Dixie, the AFL convened no fewer than 3,300 delegates from twelve Southern states to launch its own Southern campaign in May 1946. AFL president William Green sounded the tone that would dominate much of AFL rhetoric throughout the life of Operation Dixie: "Neither reactionary employers nor Communists in the CIO can stop the campaign of the American Federation of Labor to enroll 1,000,000 unorganized Southern workers in the next twelve months." Green advised Southern industrialists: "Grow and cooperate with us or fight for your life against Communist forces."[5]

George Meany joined in the vituperation by calling the

CIO's National Executive Board "the devoted followers of Moscow." "The workers of the South have their choice," he added,

> between an organization of trade unions and trade unionists who have never swerved for single minute from the principle laid down long ago by Sam Gompers—the principle that you cannot be a good union man unless you are first a good American—and an organization that has openly followed the communist line and is following that line today.[6]

Thus, one of Bittner and Baldanzi's first tasks in Operation Dixie was to defend the CIO's Southern drive against attacks from the AFL.[7] While buttressing its position against the AFL's charges, the SOC worked on refining its organizing strategy. Operation Dixie was to reflect the 1930s organizing model used by the CIO: the largest industries were to be targeted first, and the "toughest customers" in the largest industries were to receive the initial brunt of the organizing assault. The priorities arranged themselves within these premises. Concentration was to focus on textile country—ranging from Virginia through the Carolina piedmont to the outer fringes of the industry in Georgia and Alabama. The top priority would go to North Carolina, where fully one-third of all textile workers in the South resided. Within that state, the bellwether textile chain was Cannon; and within the Cannon empire's central complex—where 24,000 men and women labored—was the sprawling, deeply paternalistic company town of Kannapolis.[8]

In targeting places like Kannapolis, the CIO strategy centered on winning a symbolic victory, one not unlike the sensational 1937 triumph over General Motors at Flint, Michigan. The object was to create a transforming moment that would sweep away fear and mobilize a flood of Southerners into the CIO in much the same way that the epic victory over General Motors had given the CIO an overnight national presence.[9]

The CIO's strategy did not revolve around Kannapolis

alone, of course. Other flagships of the textile industry
were also due for a reckoning: Burlington, Cone, Deering-
Milliken, Bibb, all anchored in the greater piedmont, plus
the massive Avondale Mills in Alabama. Nor was Operation Dixie to be solely a textile campaign. Other industries
featured bellwether plants, too, each possessing both real
and symbolic meaning. The enormous atomic center built
in wartime at Oak Ridge, Tennessee, attracted the attention
of the Atomic Workers Organizing Committee. The United
Furniture Workers focused on such industry leaders as the
Doak Finch plant at Thomasville, North Carolina, while the
Oil Workers International Union, nurturing the breakthroughs in petrochemicals at Port Arthur, Beaumont, and
Houston, targeted the entire upper Texas Gulf Coast. All fit-
ted within the CIO'S circumference of priorities.[10]

Brave pronouncements in the public press notwithstand-
ing, the CIO's resources paled when measured against
such a grand agenda. A million-dollar budget and a cadre
of 250 organizers sounded impressive, but the geographical
dimensions of the South were impressive as well. More
than 1,500 miles separated the mills of Virginia from the El
Paso mines along the Rio Grande River in Texas. Upon in-
spection, the seemingly robust figure of 250 organizers translated into little more than twenty per state in the
twelve-state region the CIO had outlined. In North Carolina, for example, Kannapolis alone swallowed up an organizing team of ten people.[11] Slightly lesser numbers—from
six to eight—dispatched to other top-priority targets routinely consumed half the entire quota assigned to an embattled state director. In addition, the cost of underwriting 250
organizers represented a huge drain on a national CIO organization that faced an aggressive postwar business community throughout the Northeastern and Midwestern
industrial heartland. The monthly checks sent South would
become increasingly burdensome to union treasuries, de-
pleted as they were by struggles close to home. The Dixie organizers would have to move quickly, and attain success
quickly.

This, it turned out, did not happen.

The CIO discovered that it was going to take time to get started. On paper, a half dozen or so organizers constituted a "team." But in reality, the Dixie staff straggled in one at a time from a score of internationals, each bringing different organizing philosophies, experiences, and apprehensions. Indeed, for some weeks, it was not at all certain that all participating internationals would follow through on their pledges. The discovery of Bittner's intention to exercise iron control over jurisdiction alarmed the CIO's left-wing unions. This fear was intensified by Bittner's clearly expressed hostility toward Communists and toward political activity among organizers in general. Even with politics and ideology aside, the jurisdictional tangles were real enough.

As the Southern effort opened, the left-wing Food, Tobacco, Agricultural, and Allied Workers union (FTA) organized a conclave at Highlander Folk School in Tennessee to review the entire issue of participation in Operation Dixie, a meeting that brought the contradictions within the CIO, and within the CIO's left, into full view. Organizing the South was an old dream of labor radicals. In places like Gastonia, North Carolina, and Harlan County, Kentucky, they suffered great losses in premature efforts to realize the dream. Radical support for the *idea* of Operation Dixie was therefore beyond question; but Bittner's terms, which were, of course, Philip Murray's terms and those of the majority of the CIO General Executive Board, could be taken as an implicit attack on the left. The FTA wrestled with such questions at the Highlander meeting, amid genuine anxiety, and eventually decided to participate in the campaign. However, the issues of which new members were to go to which international, and which organizers were to be assigned where, haunted Operation Dixie throughout its life. The immediate effect was to complicate the initial task of assigning, briefing, and assembling the scores of two- to ten-person teams that fanned out across the South in early June 1946.[12]

Other institutional considerations, less threatening in the long run but no less complicating in the near term, burdened Bittner, Baldanzi, and their state directors. Some fifty organizers within the initially available pool were "on loan" and remained on the payroll of their internationals. The Bittner-Baldanzi emphasis on textiles routinely resulted in the assignment of a number of organizers to textile plants who had little experience for the task. They were not familiar with the shop floor work practices in the industry's various branches and thus did not instantly understand the subtleties of the grievances of textile workers. This meant, quite simply, that they did not know how to exploit such grievances and use them as organizing aids. Indeed, their lack of familiarity with textile production processes undermined their credibility with rank-and-file mill workers, who quite naturally wanted to feel they were associating with organizers experienced in the industry and with relevant management practices. The simple fact of the matter was that a veteran with unimpeachable credentials as a successful organizer in steel might well be a flop with textile workers. Operation Dixie, then, got underway amidst a certain amount of administrative confusion, false starts, staff animosities, and personnel reshufflings that extended into the early summer.[13]

One early source of trouble betrayed a deeper difficulty, existing below the level of staff relations with Atlanta—namely, the relations of the staff with rank-and-file workers. The question concerned a matter of seemingly mundane simplicity—the collection of initiation fees from newly signed workers, a fee from which only military veterans were to be exempted. This matter, an absolutely elementary component of the organizing process, was to be handled in an understandably routine manner: workers signed a union card and paid a $1.00 initiation fee as evidence of their commitment to the union. Each week, field staff counted up all signed cards and sent in a comparable amount of money, with the noted exemption for veterans. In June, the first reports began to trickle in from the field staff, but the accompanying sums of money fell far short of the numerical totals reported; it was, it turned out, often difficult enough to sign workers without asking for money at the same time. Bittner ordered his state directors to look into the matter and a flood of correspondence ensued, as organizers on the front lines generated elaborate explanations as to why fees were not being collected.[14]

As every veteran labor organizer knew, the key component in winning over the majority of workers in all but the smallest plants revolved around the formation of an "in-plant committee" (or workers normally selected from among the earliest rank-and-file union advocates) that could carry the union's story to the far corners of the workplace. Organizers could leaflet plant gates, distribute literature, conduct house-to-house canvasses, hold innumerable meetings at all hours of the day and night, and prior to elections even bring out the sound trucks; but only rank-and-file workers could carry the message inside the plant. Outcomes of organizing campaigns turned on the judicious recruitment of this core group of new union members. Their quality was measured by their determination, their prestige among the other workers, energy, and—routinely in the South—their willingness to risk being fired for union activity.

The recruitment of this core group went slowly in Operation Dixie. Some organizers blamed the weather for the slow development of in-plant committees,[15] while others focused on police hostility,[16] the opposition of ministers,[17] the public pronouncements of elected officials,[18] the harshness of company policies that intimidated workers,[19] the graciousness of company policies that made workers grateful,[20] or the Machiavellian nature of companies that were capable of both.[21] As might be expected, recruitment in company towns was considered by organizers to be difficult, but the opposite was also pronounced to be true: workers who were more scattered were also hard to organize.[22] Overall, the field staff of Operation Dixie had begun to encounter unexpected difficulty in enlisting the pivotal hard core of in-plant advocates. To encourage workers to come along, some organizers simply obtained signed cards without asking for the fees. In sum, the initial evidence from the field in the early summer of 1946 indicated that the World War II years had not quite broadened Southern attitudes toward unions as much as the planners of Operation Dixie had hoped. The South was going to be hard for the CIO to crack.

No one, whether in the field or in the leadership, said as much publicly. Bittner instructed his state directors to issue strict orders that the initiation fee must be collected. Indeed, fee collecting had been so inconsistent that it clouded subsequent decisions as to when NLRB elections should be petitioned for; the card count in otherwise promising plans was often large but unreliable because workers had not been forced to commit themselves by handing over the one dollar fee when they signed their union cards. As a result of election defeats in plants where a large number of workers had signed union cards, Bittner also issued instructions that no NLRB elections were to be petitioned for without his permission. "The first job to be done," he said, "is to set up active, operating committees inside of the plant with special emphasis placed on Veterans committees."[23] In one sense, administrative fumblings in June may be seen—and certainly were seen at the time—merely as "bugs" that had to be worked out of the system. Unfortunately, it soon became clear that more was required here than a simple case of fine-tuning. As June turned into July, reports could no longer reasonably focus on the routine chores of field staffers establishing a base, renting an office, "getting the lay of the land," or in the doubly hesitant phrase of one of them, "making preliminary initial contacts." Dixie required numbers verified by accompanying initiation fees, and it became evident in July that the numbers were not there.[24]

Organizing, like any kind of selling, requires good morale. Bad news cannot merely exist; it must be explained away. Field reports across the South began to take on some of the elements of an art form. In their efforts to keep going, organizers unearthed a myriad of signs that they took as indications of progress, signs upon which they relied to such an extent that a special language, even a shorthand, grew up to describe them. "Committee No. 1 is functioning but had no new applications as of today," reported a summary account from Kannapolis. Indeed, the details were more sobering than the summary: Committee No. 1 met "with hardly any attendance." There was not much need, under the circumstances, to report the activities of Committee No. 2, as such a thing clearly did not exist.

As Operation Dixie moved to a new plateau of anxiety, the artistry of report-writing consisted of finding new ways to explain away the absence of signed cards: "No members signed up. Strictly leg work." Vagueness on numbers was one solution: "That place is moving a little slow, but we are still signing up a few each week." But an even better solution lay in discussing other matters: "Gained some good leads and made some progress on build-up." "Things at Firestone seem to be shaping up right nice." "I would call it a good day as reactions are favorable."[25]

New terminology appeared. Organizers began to refer to the "throw-down rate" for leaflets they passed out to workers at plant gates. Thus a low "throw-down rate" became a major item in organizers' reports in textile country where concrete numbers could not be produced. A Virginia organizer passed out 500 leaflets "with less than ten thrown down." The technique could be extended to house-to-house distributions of labor newspapers: "Bill and Red passed out the paper to the homes today and out of some 950 homes only two refused to take the paper." In such ways did Dixie organizers fill up the pages of the reports demanded of them, the absence of bad news inexorably becoming good news.[26]

The chief instrument in the service of morale was not the coinage of new phrases about "throw-down rates," but rather sheer narrative skill as a complementary aid to their commitment to keep going under the pressure of intense opposition. The Alabama State Director for the Textile Workers Union of America, Edmund Ryan, head of a staff concentrating on textile organizing, hit a brick wall early. He made no reports for seven weeks and then managed deft distinctions in emphasis to different constituencies. To his own international's president in New York, he reported, "Our membership gains in textiles still remain about the same as previously. In other words, we are hold-

ing our own." Ryan followed the next day with a report to
the Atlanta headquarters of Operation Dixie in which he basi-
cally tried to change the subject: "The relative slowness of
the drive in textiles in Alabama does not reflect the success
of the drive as a whole in the state. Tremendous victories
have been won in wood, steel, and auto."[27] Buried in the reports of the state directors in the heartland of the textile industry was the awkward, almost unacknowledgeable lack
of progress at the region's largest mills. Avondale in Alabama, and Cannon and Burlington in North Carolina, all
seemed to remain inpregnable. If Ryan showed verbal skill
in Alabama, Dean Culver, the staff director at Cannon, demonstrated a mastery of the evolving style: "Membership returns the past week will reflect the fact that much time has
been spent by the organizers in developing and attempting
to develop active committees among those already signed
up rather than concerted signing by organizers." [28]

There was not yet reason for general disappointment,
however. Some good news did materialize. Aside from textiles, in smaller plants across the region CIO organizers
began to sign enough recruits to warrant NLRB elections.
And the CIO began to win most of them. After six weeks
of concentrated effort, Bittner finally had a story to tell that
was sufficiently promising to pass along to the editors of
the *CIO News* in Washington. The Southern Organizing Committee announced its first twenty-five victories on July 8.
Two weeks later, Bittner was able to report to the CIO General Executive Board in Washington that the victory total
had risen to thirty-six. Putting the best face on events, as
his own organizers had done in reporting to him, Bittner
struck a heartily optimistic pose. He focused on percent-
ages rather than on aggregate numbers. The thirty-six victories in forty elections constituted "top-flight batting in any
man's league." Stretching the evidence a bit, he added,
"The program to date has been much faster than we anticipated." But lest any of his audience conclude that Operation Dixie had begun to resemble the great CIO organizing
sweep of the late 1930s, he added, "Let's not kid ourselves.

None of our organizers have been killed by a mob of people rushing in to sign membership cards." [29]

Bittner's positive assessment received wide play in the commercial as well as the labor press; left unspecified was the nature of the victories. Most came in tobacco, or in Southern branches of highly organized Northern industries—among auto, steel, oil, and packinghouse workers. Organizers in lumber, furniture, paper, pulp, and woodworking were struggling in a half-dozen states. And wood and wood products represented, with textiles, the heart of the CIO's organizing challenge. [30]

Above all else, however, loomed the problem in textiles. The victories there stood at exactly one—at the Borden Manufacturing Company, a 700-employee plant in Goldsboro, North Carolina. Unfortunately, Borden's significance as an indicator of the start of a trend was marred by the fact that it had been organized before, by the AFL, and thus did not qualify as the sought-after breakthrough.

What Bittner, his roving textile ambassador at large, George Baldanzi, and the key Dixie state directors all knew was that the first big test in textiles would come in August. All eyes focused on three North Carolina mills scheduled for NLRB elections in the first half of the month. The first skirmish was to come on August 6 at Caramount, North Carolina, home of the Sidney Blumenthal Company, a mill employing 500 workers. Two days later, the 460 employees of the Pee Dee Manufacturing Company were to vote in Rockingham, North Carolina, followed the next day by the 650 workers at the Hannah Pickett Mills in the same city. In no sense could these three modest mills be viewed in the same class as the sprawling Cannon empire, or Burlington, Avondale, Milliken-Deering, and the other giants of the Southern textile industry. These small plants were, nevertheless, psychologically crucial for the Dixie staff and for the mass of nearby piedmont textile workers who—all knew—would be watching. [31]

On August 6, the TWUA culminated its campaign with an election day mailing to every employee. It betrayed, perhaps a bit more starkly than the organizers knew, the importance they placed upon the outcome.

> Your election comes at the time the big drive in the South to organize all the workers is in full swing. Already the CIO has won 39 out of 43 elections in this big drive. You will be the second Textile Workers to vote under this drive. You are also bringing hope to those who are looking forward to the day when every worker in America will be under the supervision of a government agent. The election will be secret. No one will know how you vote. AMERICANS NEVER STAND STILL. GO FORWARD BY VOTING FOR THE UNION.[32]

The election was close, but the CIO lost. The tally was 260 for "No Union" and 219 for the TWUA-CIO.[33]

Despite this setback, the remaining two mills offered the CIO somewhat better reason for hope. Management was more intransigent at the Hannah Pickett and Pee Dee mills than at Caramount, thus giving CIO organizers more grievances to exploit. In addition all echelons of the CIO staff had taken a hand in the Hannah Pickett and Pee Dee campaigns: Frank Bartholomew, the local organizer in charge; D. D. Wood, in charge of the Southern area of the state; William Smith, the North Carolina state director; and even George Baldanzi. In a special report to Smith two weeks before the election, Wood characterized the overall situation at both plants as "very bright."Admittedly, "some strong company opposition" had surfaced, especially at Hannah Pickett, where the company had decided during the month before the election to grant a wage increase of eight cents an hour. Red-baiting had appeared there, with the company posting anti-union notices in the plant. While there seemed to be "quite a lot of fear" in the plant, he remained optimistic. The Pee Dee plant seemed in even better shape: "probably 90% or 95% of the people signed up."[34] It was with some shock, then, that CIO staff learned they had been decisively crushed in both plants in consecutive elections on August 8 and 9. The vote against the CIO was 315 to 95 at Pee Dee and 496 to 105 at Hannah Pickett.[35]

These numbers sent a wave of gloom through the CIO leadership. Indeed, North Carolina Director Smith was induced to review his entire organizational structure. Not only was the previous work of Bartholomew, the local organizer—and of Wood, his area superior—called into question, but also that of other leaders of organizing teams scattered throughout the Carolina piedmont. In the immediate aftermath of these three textile defeats, Smith reviewed all his organizers' narrative explanations and concentrated on the numerical substance. The exercise was not reassuring. A graceful and urbane man, Smith was incapable of rough language. However, his post-Rockingham admonition to the head of his Wilson, North Carolina, organizing team reflected more than a new realism; it also revealed an edge of panic. Three weeks before the Rockingham debacle, the Wilson organizer had said, in the course of an otherwise optimistic report, that things didn't "look too good" for the CIO in textile plants in Rocky Mount and Roanoke Rapids. The bulk of his report dealt with tobacco—even though that industry had far fewer workers than textiles. Smith wrote in response:

> I realize that you have been having your hands full and I know you haven't had too much time, but I do want to ask you a few questions. We do not seem to be getting any initiation fees in from our textile plants in your area and I am wondering what the devil is happening and what our organizers are doing and the cause of this let down.[36]

The same patterns were evident in Virginia and South Carolina, as well—very slow progress in the bellwether textile plants, clearly insufficient to warrant an election, and crushing defeats in those smaller textile mills where elections had been held.[37]

As the summer wore on, individual setbacks turned into an almost uninterrupted litany of defeat. In Alabama, the giant Avondale Mills proved approachable but unwinnable, while smaller plants were not even approachable. At Geneva and Enterprise, Alabama, police hostility and harassment were augmented by squads of workers—allied with the Klan—who stormed the hotel where CIO organizers had checked in and forced them to leave town. Organizing defeat and physical harassment surfaced in Georgia, Tennessee, and South Carolina as well. In a decisive ninety-day period from early August through mid-November, evidence accumulated from everywhere: the drive to organize the Southern textile industry had been decisively defeated.[38]

For the TWUA itself, the result was a calamity. The international's investment in Operation Dixie was a staggering $95,000 per month, slightly more than the total sum contributed to the Southern Organizing Committee by all the other internationals in the CIO. And the outcome was totally unambiguous; no amount of arithmetic shuffling could explain away the vastness of the defeat. Not only were elections lost in small and medium-sized plants from one end of the textile belt to the other, but a far greater number had not even been brought to the threshold of elections. All the giants were standing untouched. Operation Dixie had collapsed in textiles.

Inevitably, the realities in textiles meant that Operation Dixie itself was in crisis. Whatever the long-term outcome, the evidence was clear by early autumn that the South was not to be transformed. The legions of "Dixiecrat" conservatives the region sent to Washington—a tide of Congressional votes that had made the New Deal coalition a besieged minority in Congress—would continue. Dreams of a giant labor vote to undergird a steadily more progressive Democratic Party would have to be laid aside. Even before the November 1946 elections confirmed the extent of the bad news for labor, the long-term prospects seemed clear from the earlier election returns coming in from NLRB contests across Dixie. It now seemed certain that a new conservative orthodoxy would characterize the postwar politics of America.[39]

How had it happened? Historical memory is a complex phenomenon. In the summer of 1946, CIO organizers tried, in a complex display of human ingenuity and optimism, to put the best possible face on the disastrous events in which they had become entangled. Years later, they could be very candid in their views on Southern workers.

From a textile organizer:

> They would not stop and talk to you at the gate because the bosses are standing off looking, see. Then you'd run into this stuff: "I wish you wouldn't come to my house no more. I got a nosey old neighbor over yonder and they tell their boss everything they know of." That kind of thing. Just scared. Bless their hearts, you just felt so sorry for them.[40]

From a labor lawyer:

> I remember sleeping in a little wooden hotel in one of those towns and someone shot through the hotel one night. I had a great big old steelworker who shared a room with me after that. I was not anxious to be a hero.[41]

In the difficult summer of 1946, a well-known labor progressive, Palmer Weber of Virginia, was sent on a mission to Greensboro, North Carolina. Years later, he recalled playing poker with CIO organizers assigned there—"a lot of nice young fellows from New York, Socialists."

> One of them was saying how hopeless this whole thing was. He said, "I'm beginning to think our problem is to get out of here alive." "What do you mean," I said. Well, a week ago he had been out at Cone Mills, distributing leaflets. Workers came out—wham—hit him, knocked him right down. I said, "You're sure it wasn't company police?" "No. No, it was the workers," he said. "A group of them said to me, 'Don't ever come back around here. We don't need you. You're going to cost us our jobs.'" I said, "Well, what did you do?" He said, "I'm not going back there and distribute leaflets again. They might kill me."[42]

After two and a half months of trying to organize textile workers in Greensboro, the organizer realized that the work-

ers he approached saw him as an enemy, rather than a potential ally in their struggles for a better life. While the news defeated the young man, it hardly surprised Weber:

> These people had just come off of cut-off and cut-over
> woods, and come off of red clay country farms. They
> figured these were the best jobs they had ever had.
> Their brains were soaked in the Depression mentality
> of the 1930s. When they saw a union organizer, the
> union organizer was a threat to their jobs.[43]

None of these judgments, whether related to the ferocity
of the opposition or the depth of "fear" in Southern workers, can be taken at face value. As will become evident, the
complexities of the social realities into which the CIO Southern Organizing Committee intruded in 1946 cannot be easily compartmentalized or neatly summarized. Matters of
race and religion, as well as the historical legacy of poverty
and paternalism, all helped to weave the blanket of resistance that ultimately suffocated the CIO. Similarly, a measure of evidence accumulated that the CIO itself
contributed to the failure. Although each of these ingredients merits attention in appropriate sequence, it seems useful to consider briefly some other concrete, on-the-scene
interpretations.

The demonstrable elan visible in CIO organizers who covered the South in June was sustained through mid-summer
amid a generally shared understanding that "it took time to
get things started."[44] The August defeats in textiles—the industry that had attracted more organizing attention than
any other—sent the first shock through the CIO staff. The ensuing six weeks were traumatic, mounting frustration
slowly ebbing away into despair, silent resignation, and, finally, anger. The judgments that emerged from this variety
of reactions were equally varied. Some blamed the CIO for
placing Bittner and Baldanzi in charge, "Northerners who
did not understand the South."[45] Some blamed the Communists.[46] Some blamed the Communist issue.[47] Some, as we
have seen, blamed the workers, while some emphasized
the incompetence of other organizers.[48] Quite a number

blamed the race issue,[49] and some, boosters to the bitter end, declared the effort a success.[50]

In the aggregate, the shocking defeats of August, confirmed in September, forced the CIO leadership into the deepest kind of soul-searching. Early in October, the CIO organization in the most important textile state, North Carolina, participated in four elections. Two, in small tobacco plants, were won; and two, in textiles, were lost. The state director, William Smith, reacted by writing an intimate and revealing letter to Bittner:

> Frankly, I am worried and heartsick about the loss of these two textile elections this week as I realize only too well that unless we crack some of the major textile mills in the state, the rest will not mean too much. I never wanted to do anything more in my life than to do a real job in the textile industry. The lethargy and disinterest of the textile workers is enough to frustrate anyone and frankly, while I have some ideas, I do not know the answer to it all.[51]

The impasse the Southern Organizing Committee faced in textiles was truly baffling. There seemed to be two distinct ways for textile companies to thwart the CIO. Most common was the adoption of a stance of unrelenting intransigence, a tactic evidenced in the managerial styles of mill executives at Sumter in South Carolina, Elizabethton in Tennessee, Milliken-Deering and Bibb in Georgia and Avondale in Alabama, and in a score of large- and medium-sized plants in the North Carolina heartland of the industry. While the tactics of intransigence varied in style from mill to mill, there were patterns. Local law enforcement authorities often shadowed CIO organizers from the moment they arrived in town, accosting them in public places, arresting them for leafletting or for using a sound truck. Quite frequently, they were detained merely for "questioning." The effect was not merely to impede the process of orderly trade union activity, but, more important, to engage in what might be described as a cultural war to discredit individual CIO representatives and the CIO itself.

Many other ingredients made up the thick mixture of intransigence. Workers showing initial responsiveness to organizing appeals could be called in by the company for a quiet conversation about the implications of worker participation in CIO "in-plant committees," and references made to past employees who similarly allowed themselves to become known for their prolabor sympathies. Such employees, it could be noted, were no longer around. Rumors about the CIO penchant for "race-mixing" could serve to rile some workers—it did not take many—to go en masse to confront and threaten CIO organizers. Should the organizing team make measurable progress despite such hazards, other tactics were available. The rumor could spread that the mill would shut down in response to unfavorable NLRB election results. If necessary, rumor could turn into a public statement to the same effect, offered either explicitly or implicitly by management and duly publicized in the town or mill village newspaper. Employee fear was the mill owners' most useful weapon against the CIO. In apprehension, CIO staffers told one another, "We have to find some way to get the fear out of these people."[52]

Yet the grievances of textile workers were both real and multiple. It was widely understood that Southern mill workers were paid less, often far less, than their counterparts elsewhere. Tight supervision, both in the plant and throughout the mill village, made working conditions oppressive and life itself difficult. Job security was fragile in some plants and nonexistent in most of them. Vacations, sick leave, and health protection were minimal or entirely absent. Safety standards were low and accidents on the job, especially in older mills, were frequent. Workers' grievances were so pronounced and so long-standing in some places that workers essentially organized themselves soon after the first arrival of CIO representatives. NLRB elections, in such cases, could be obtained with relative speed. More often than not, however, what happened after election dates were set demoralized the field staff of Operation Dixie. Intransigence of mill management—even historically rooted resistance going back more than a generation—could suddenly disappear, to be replaced by conciliatory attitudes that mill workers found startling. Union proposals on wages and working conditions around which the CIO had organized could—up to the very eve of NLRB elections—be resisted, but then partially, substantially, or totally accepted by management. The thought accompanying these actions was direct, simple, and appealing to many: "We can settle any problems we might have right here in the family, without outsiders coming in and telling anybody what to do. We don't need, in our town, these _____ coming in and trying to change our Southern traditions." The blank could be filled in with various phrases of description, depending upon the predilections of individual mill executives: Yankees, radicals, Communists, race-mixers, thugs, CIO conspirators, or non-Southerners with foreign-sounding names.

In some mill villages, only those descriptive phrases were necessary in order to dampen union possibilities; in others, the phrases gained cultural authority only after marginal or sweeping concessions were offered by management. As textile organizers knew from past experience (or discovered in the course of Operation Dixie), mill owners could prevail by being aggressive, by being conciliatory, or by being both in sequence. At year's end, the frustration and despair of the Carolina leadership had seeped into every corner of the Southern campaign. Like William Smith, they "did not know the answer to it all." In early December, a statewide meeting of organizers in Tennessee produced a summary judgment so ominous it had to be softened: "There is a certain amount of defeatism."[53]

After only seven months, the "Holy Crusade" had produced results that called for an overall reevaluation at the highest levels of the CIO. The 1946 national CIO convention at Atlantic City heard Bittner's report with outward displays of understanding and occasional reaffirmations of militance. But international presidents, in many cases urgently pressed by their treasurers, placed rhetoric alongside the balance sheet of income and expenditures. It was no contest. Operation Dixie was costing $144,000 a month while the balancing inflow from initiation fees and union dues was not remotely comparable.[54]

In the leading Southern industries—textiles, tobacco, wood and wood products—the results were difficult to believe. In trades allied with wood, some 340,000 potential recruits were available to the International Woodworkers of America, the United Paper Workers, and the United Furniture Workers. Operation Dixie organized fewer than 25,000 in 1946. The Woodworkers gained 3,887 new members in Mississippi. The union added 2,774 in Arkansas, 1,401 in Louisiana, and 1,207 in Tennessee. The Woodworkers' membership in every other Southern state was less than 1,000. The United Furniture Workers of America recruited 1,400 in Tennessee, 1,350 in North Carolina, and 1,000 in South Carolina. The highlight was a dramatic victory at Thomasville, North Carolina, after a protracted strike and a bitter, exhausting boycott. This victory brought 1,200 new CIO members. Sadly, this constituted almost 95 percent of the North Carolina total for the year. The Southwide total in furniture in 1946 was 6,245.[55]

The CIO tobacco workers' union (FTA) performed well, its twenty-three election victories in North Carolina accounting for a statewide gain of 7,582 and a total membership in the state in excess of 20,000. Considerable progress had been made in the cigarette industry as well. Virginia's total of 9,000 organized tobacco workers resulted mainly from the Southern drive. But though the cigarette industry was essentially organized, the number of employees in tobacco was small, as these figures indicate. It was textiles and wood products upon which the fate of Operation Dixie depended.[56]

At the 1946 Atlantic City convention, the national CIO was forced to concede, in its internal discussions, that Operation Dixie had become unaffordable. Almost $800,000 had been spent since the campaign opened in the late spring. The figure was short of the projected budget of over one million dollars; but even at that level, the drain was too much for embattled internationals facing difficult trials in their Northern bases.[57]

Huge staff reductions in Operation Dixie were decided upon at Atlantic City. In November, North Carolina had counted forty-five affiliated staff organizers; Georgia, thirty-eight; Tennessee, twenty-eight; Virginia, twenty-two; Alabama, twenty-one; and South Carolina, seventeen. These organizing teams, spread over the heartland of Southern textiles, represented a majority of the CIO monthly operating investment in the Southern drive. All state budgets were cut in half. William Smith was forced to terminate twenty-three of his forty-five–member team in North Carolina in the first week of December. Reductions were comparable in other states, extending beyond textiles to the other industries in the Southern drive.[58]

The impact of these events on the morale of Southern industrial labor was devastating, although a brave face was put on events by Bittner. Though the ruthless staff reductions reflected a "re-examination of the whole Southern campaign" by the CIO leadership at Atlantic City, Bittner insisted that the action did not mean that the CIO campaign in the South was "being called off or discontinued." However, the long-term political implications of these organizational readjustments were already clear by the first week in December, following as they did on the heels of the Republican landslide the month before. State directors had to summon a new resolve. "The time has come when we must forget the election and everything else except our job of organizing," Tennessee CIO director Christopher informed his lead organizer in Knoxville. "Our union is the only stabilizing force of real consequence in America today."[59]

For those no longer on the payroll, other explanations were called for. Perhaps the most poignant example of what might be called the "termination correspondence" transpired between Jesse Smith, a discharged South Carolina organizer, and George Baldanzi. It also revealed one of the hazards of organizing: the damage done to the CIO's credibility in leaving workers behind, without a union. Wrote Smith,

Mr. Daniel informed us that the entire CIO staff in Spartanburg, S.C., was being laid off . . . which means, as the workers at the Brandon mill will phrase it, that the whole CIO campaign is a flop, and many of them express their regret that they had ever confided in the CIO.

Baldanzi groped for an explanation. As for the Atlantic City decision, "It was felt that we should encourage the international unions of the CIO to provide organizers where at all possible. . . . This naturally meant laying off some of the CIO staff throughout the South." Turning to the immediate organizing crisis, Baldanzi added, "I think you ought to make clear to the workers at the Brandon Mill—or any other mill in Greenville—that the campaign of organization will go on, even though it may not be carried on at the same tempo it has up to this time."[60]

Yet it was precisely here—on the matter of "tempo"—that the tragedy of the American labor movement became incontrovertibly visible. In the North Carolina piedmont, a twenty-eight-year-old Southerner named Dean Culver had headed an organization team of ten. For months they had confronted the sprawling Cannon mill town of Kannapolis. They had been variously ignored, responded to, harassed, and arrested. The staff had been reshuffled and Culver himself replaced. In the course of various struggles, the organizing team had been augmented beyond the ten originally assigned. However, nothing had thus far availed. The number of signed cards had not yet reached 10 percent of the 24,000 work force. In December 1946, it was clear there would never be twenty organizers mounting a concerted effort in Kannapolis; nor would ten organizers maintain a daily presence. Rather, the Cannon Mills would have assigned to it five union organizers.[61]

At the other end of the textile belt, the largest organizing team in Alabama had challenged the huge Comer Mills at Avondale for seven months. After all their efforts, they had fewer than 1,000 signed cards among the 7,500 workers. The issue, after the organizing team had been cut in half in

December, went beyond matters of strategy: how could they achieve with four people what they had failed to achieve with eight, and sometimes with fifteen?

But the collapse of Operation Dixie had other implications, chiefly relating to the balance of forces across the region. This involved the most fundamental questions about the South, about the CIO, and about the entire American labor movement. What had happened in 1946 "down South?" What was the source of the "fear" on the part of workers that had surfaced in a thousand organizers' reports? Where lay the essence of the catastrophic defeat in textiles? Why did workers beat up union organizers? Why were ministers so actively hostile? Where did the race issue fit in? Or ideology? In sum, what was the social reality that derailed the CIO's "Holy Crusade" in the American South? What did the architects and the rank-and-file of Operation Dixie confront and what did their defeat mean?

IV

A Case Study in Textiles
Defeat at Kannapolis

Since the textile industry historically had proven most resistant to unionization, the organizational drive in textile country was clearly the first priority of Operation Dixie. The priority, however, was not merely a Southern one. Textiles constituted the preeminent "runaway" industry; the flourishing mills in the South represented the other side of the coin from the closed plants in the North.[1] The campaign in textiles thus built upon the underlying strategic rationale of Operation Dixie—to protect labor's recently acquired and still fragile base in the North. Unfortunately, the very industry on which Operation Dixie's success depended turned out to be the one in which it showed the least success.[2]

Almost all the hazards the CIO faced in trying to organize textiles were at work at the huge Cannon Mills in Kannapolis, North Carolina. Kannapolis was the largest mill village in America, an unincorporated city of 50,000. Its owner, Charles Cannon, was firmly in control of the town's economic, political, and social climate. Almost every street, every home, even the fire stations and grocery stores were owned by Cannon. The mayor, the police chief, and the ministers were all part of the Cannon "family," as were, of course, the workers. In every way, Kannapolis provided graphic physical evidence of the meaning of the word "paternalism."

The first thing that distinguished textile operations from other industries in the South was their size. Not only were individual textile plants often larger than plants in other industries, they were often part of a chain and clustered together in the same, or a nearby, town. To organize one plant in a company might simply lead to a shift in production to one of the others, causing layoffs and derailing the organizing drive. Thus, all the nearby plants had to be approached by the union at the same time. This situation also increased the number of workers involved, further complicating the task of organizing. In Cannon, Plants 1 and 4 consisted of eleven mills at Kannapolis, and Plants 2, 5, 6, 9, and 10 housed six additional mills in the adjoining village of Concord. The Cannon chain had a total of four other small plants, three of which were in nearby China Grove, Salisbury, and Thomasville.[3] Thus, twenty of Cannon's twenty-one mills were concentrated around the main hub of Kannapolis,[4] employing some 24,000 workers.

The structure of the industry imposed harsh strategic choices upon the managers of Operation Dixie. Sheer size in textiles seemed to force upon the CIO a choice between mobilizing an enormous campaign against all the plants in a given chain or mounting no campaign at all. The alternative would have been a small-plant agenda, first organizing the rest of the industry one plant at a time, prior to beginning any assault on the bellwethers.

Attempting to organize bellwether plants had serious drawbacks, however. One of the most compelling arguments against it stemmed from the fact that bellwether plants were often the only industry in an area and had been built with their own mill towns around them. The level of control that owners of such plants exercised over the lives of their workers was much greater than that found in towns with more than one employer. The peculiar problems posed by the paternalism of textile mill villages added an altogether different dimension to the task of union organizing and more often than not made an organizer's job significantly more difficult.

At the same time, however, any strategic campaign that turned on organizing small plants, plants whose owners exercised less community control than those with their own mill villages, also presented significant obstacles. The most intimidating prospect turned on the probability that a small-plant agenda would be immensely time-consuming. Across the South, small 50-to-500-employee textile plants were so numerous that literally hundreds of organizing campaigns would have to be sustained. This constituted a logistical burden well in excess of the CIO's resources.[5] It made no economic sense. The national CIO could not afford to keep hundreds of organizers in the field while they chipped away for years at hundreds of small textile mills scattered across the South. The trickle of dues-paying members thus obtained could never generate enough funds to offset the organizing overhead: the CIO would go broke trying to support a small-plant agenda.

Moreover, in terms of the CIO's organizing traditions, a small-plant campaign had no "transforming" element that could sweep away fear and help stimulate among workers a new vision of society. A victory at a small plant was . . . a victory at a small plant. It sent no galvanizing signal to the South's long-suffering working class. Without the kind of mobilization stimulated in the North in the late 1930s, the CIO could expect no breakthrough in the huge textile chains that dominated the region.

Reflecting the importance of textiles to Operation Dixie's success, the CIO leadership hedged its bets by choosing a compromise between the large and small-plant strategies. While the drive would concentrate on the giant chains, the most promising of the smaller plants—those with a known history of worker discontent—would also receive a measure of attention. Regional assignments reflected these assessments. Of all the Southern states, North Carolina, as the center of the textile industry, received the largest number. Of the twenty-five organizers assigned to North Carolina in late May and early June 1946, fifteen were assigned exclusively to textiles, with the remainder divided among all other types of industry, most prominently tobacco and wood and wood products. Of the fifteen organizers in textiles, ten were dispatched to Kannapolis under the direction of a thirty-two-year-old organizer named Dean Culver.

The son of a railroad worker and a native of Iowa, Culver had come to North Carolina at the age of twenty-two in 1936. He had found employment in the town of Badin, a company town owned by Alcoa Aluminum. The traditional assortment of control, benevolence, and fear characteristic of company towns was at work in Badin. Yet Culver was able to organize the plant and carry it into the CIO. He was, with some justice, proud of his achievement, one that had brought him to the attention of CIO leaders in the South and had led to his appointment at Kannapolis. A political progressive and an experienced organizer, Culver brought a certain measure of confidence to his assignment as head of the organizing team at Cannon.

None of Culver's initial ten staff members were from Kannapolis. Most, like Culver himself, had caught the attention of Operation Dixie planners through their work during organizing drives in their own plants across the South. Kannapolis itself had been free of such campaigns since the activity accompanying the 1934 national textile strike. Although several staff members on the Cannon drive had had at least some experience in previous mill village campaigns, and some had grown up in mill villages, they were not fully prepared for the elaborate portrait of sophisticated paternalism that they encountered in Kannapolis.

The CIO team's first discovery concerned the prestige of Charles Cannon himself. As president and chairman of the board, Cannon maintained a highly visible level of involvement in the lives of his workers—to the extent that both Cannon Mills and the town of Kannapolis became extensions of his personal presence, influence, and power. In spite of the size of Cannon's mills in Kannapolis, he was able to maintain a bond with his workers that felt relatively "personal" and special to them. A CIO organizer who married a former Cannon employee confirmed the popular impression.

They loved Mr. Cannon. Everybody loved him. He was their daddy. The father, the grandfather, the great-grandfather, all lived here. And everybody looked to Uncle Charlie Cannon. He was a Santy Claus. "He

was good to my daddy. He was good to my grand-
daddy. He was good to my great-granddaddy. He
give us a job, give us a place to live." They'd say, "I
gotta be faithful to him. Long as he likes me, he'll
take care of me."[6]

So pervasive was this view of Charles Cannon among the citizens of Kannapolis that CIO staffers came to call it "the Cannon myth." It was something to be avoided while
organizing. One could criticize hiring practices, work rules,
wage levels, and sparse fringe benefits. But one could not
criticize "Uncle Charlie." To do so would have been counterproductive to effective recruitment. Culver was not de-
terred. Badin was located fewer than thirty miles from
Kannapolis and Culver felt he was in touch with the aspirations that lurked beneath the surface of this public display
of affection and gratitude for Charlie Cannon.

There were, however, certain tangible signs, materializ-
ing out of preliminary organizing efforts in Kannapolis,
that indicated the campaign would be neither easy nor
quick. The town itself contained no motels or rental property, as it was an unincorporated township owned wholly
by the company. The CIO staff, therefore, could find neither housing nor an office there. They secured both in the adjacent town of Concord.[7] The town's physical layout
generated a special psychological impact. Plant 1, the heart
of the Cannon chain, was described by one awed organizer
as "a huge collection of seven different mills, a bleachery
and finishing plant, a machine shop and a powerplant.
This is all enclosed in one area by a high woven-wire
fence." There were eleven gates, seven of which were used
heavily at shift changes. Plant 4 was about one-half mile
from Plant 1 and had ten gates, at least five of which were
used during the three shift changes each day. The number
of gates made it all the more difficult to talk to the 24,000
workers who came and went. In addition, a number of workers parked their cars within the gates—making it nearly impossible for the CIO staff to make contact with them at *any*
point around the workplace.[8]

With interaction at the plant gates reduced below their expectations, the CIO staff printed up a series of leaflets and, with them, began a sustained effort to recruit an initial "in-plant committee" of activists who could assist the organizing staff in contacting other workers in the plant and in planning meetings in workers' homes. This process moved very slowly in the initial organizing month of June. As the CIO staff interpreted the general climate, Cannon's policies generated among many workers "great fear and suspicion of one another." Whatever Cannon could not find out on his own, some worker would tell him. One organizer compared such employees with what he knew of people in Communist countries: "They'd report anything that was going on to the company."[9] Ironically, this "fear," as the staff was soon at pains to explain to the Atlanta office, was as much a function of company benevolence as it was of raw oppression.

> Short-range popular issues are very few, because 1) the workload is comparatively light (compared to other textile plants); 2) employment is more stable; 3) housing is very good in comparison to other textile villages, although most of them lack adequate plumbing; 4) rents are probably below cost (about $5 a month); 5) wages, with a few exceptions, are higher than in other textile mills; 6) the community is neat, clean and comfortable.[10]

The "fear" that organizers frequently referred to was therefore oddly compounded of workers' belief that they were part of Charlie Cannon's family and as such would be protected, alongside a deep anxiety about opposing him. This anxiety seemed to derive not only from what the CIO staff described as an "emotional" fear about being expelled from the fold, but being fired and then evicted from relatively cheap company housing.[11]

In spite of evidence of fear among workers, organizers reported that attitudes were "favorable" throughout the first month of the campaign, even though people were "unwilling to sign." Such euphemisms slowly became almost a way of life; one staffer found "favorable people now more favorable, altho still reluctant to sign up."[12] The "situation with regard to the women" was that "most of them are waiting to see what the men do. Have got some good potential leadership but have been unable to sign many up or move them into activity as yet." Nevertheless, cautious optimism was the predominant theme: "Am sure I can get several to next Sunday's meeting."[13] The staff also contacted veterans, but the immediate response was so light that they felt compelled to report that "at least one" had signed up.[14]

So by the end of the first month of effort, the Kannapolis staff had made some contacts, signed a small number of cards, "met some opposition . . . among lady workers," and "made a geographical survey of the village of Kannapolis."[15]

July brought new information on the campaign. In a lengthy "Initial Report on the Kannapolis Situation," produced early in the month, organizers explained the reaction to their campaign both by the pull that "the Cannon myth" had on the workers, and the prevalence of "fear" that could assume a number of different forms. "The fear of being fired and losing their houses is very strong with them. I think we should go rather slow for a while on putting out [membership] books until we get more of a committee built up."[16] "Did house to house work among women workers without too much selection. Women are plenty scared."[17] "There is more fear at Cannon than I found at Firestone"—a mill in Gastonia, North Carolina, whose employees possessed a tenaciously lingering memory of a disastrous strike in 1929.[18] "If we can get the fear out of these people, I think we will be able to put it across."[19]

The report held out more hope for reaching World War II veterans because they were "less influenced by the Cannon myth." Veterans, it was reasoned, "have had sufficient experience, and have only recently arrived back under the influence of the popular opinion, so that these generalizations are not entirely valid when applied to them." Veterans were deemed not yet "reintegrated into the Kannapolis pattern"[20]

Revealing more than the presence of fear, the report made clear the difficulties involved in formulating concrete solutions to problems that proved hard to identify in more than an abstract way. Among the workers, "the desire to improve present material conditions is almost non-existent. It may possibly be cultivated, but this would require a long period of time and expenditure of much money in an educational program." The author suggested, however, that seniority might be exploited as an important issue: "the desire to feel more secure in their jobs is a factor with most workers, particularly women."[21]

There was a deeper and more puzzling problem that the organizers also mentioned: the workers "can and do read," owned radios and automobiles, and had had some contact with the world outside Kannapolis—far more than workers in "the average textile mill village." Given this relatively low level of physical isolation, the staff struggled to explain why time had stood still for the workers of Kannapolis, and why they had not yet realized that they needed the CIO.

> They seem to be insulated in a different way from liberal ideas than that which exists in the average plant. They have had contact with thinking, liberal sources, but there is a general pattern of rationalization built around the prestige of Charles Cannon, which does the same thing to the mental attitude of these people as physical separation and hard social lines do in the average mill village.[22]

Although this "Initial Report" offered very little in the way of a concrete plan of action, it posed the central dilemma of organizing Kannapolis: how could an organizer—or a supervisor receiving such a generalized summary—plan an assault on a formless "mental attitude"?

In response to such field reports, the CIO leadership at the state level in North Carolina and in the Southern Organizing Committee in Atlanta seemed at a loss for creative solutions. One directive sent to the Kannapolis organizing team at the end of June instructed them to dress up their image. Organizers were to "become part of community life by going to church on Sundays." They were to remain in " 're-spectable' parts of town" and mingle with " 'respectable' people." They were not to "indulge in drinking" and were to "drink 'chocolate sodas' rather than beer." Finally, they were admonished to avoid entering "any home where only the 'womenfolks' " were present, and to "return when the head of the house" was there.[23]

The resistance they encountered gradually induced orga-nizers to keep something of a low profile in an effort to cope with workers' fear of premature exposure as union ac-tivists. In a form letter inviting workers to a staff meeting, Culver instructed prospective recruits to "bring any person with you as our guest and yours, whom you are sure is a friend of yours, but please do not give this little meeting any wide publicity . . . ."[24] Internal staff correspondence re-vealed the CIO analysis: "The reason for using the Hotel con-ference room instead of the hall is the fact that the people may be as yet afraid to come to the Union hall."[25]

During the last two weeks of July, the CIO staff at Kannap-olis struggled hard to maintain morale and energy in the face of very tough going. Against increasingly negative evi-dence, the staff demonstrated a determination to remain opti-mistic: "Only have 5 applications this week but set up machinery that I believe will *PAY OFF* SOON—."[26]

Against this background of minimal progress won at great effort, active involvement of the CIO leadership is diffi-cult to locate. In examining months of internal CIO reports, one searches in vain for decisive action from the North Caro-lina state director, William Smith, or from Baldanzi and Bittner in Atlanta. Only Dean Culver's immediate supervi-sor, D. D. Wood, the "area director" for the Southern re-gion of North Carolina, found a way to talk openly and clearly about the mounting crisis in textiles. In the second week of July, Wood took his team leaders in the Southern area to task for mishandling the collection and submission of initiation fees.[27] He also reprimanded them for the poor quality of reports on contacts made with local officials and ministers in the Southern area: "This is special work and re-quires a special report."[28] Nor did Wood seem to think his teams were working hard enough: "We had lull during the week of the 4th [July] and we must make up for it during the next ten days."[29] Wood worried that the CIO's resources were being squandered. He confronted Culver:

We find that you have several people working in the office most of the time. We feel that there is no need for two people in the office hereafter, with the exception of yourself, and unless you have a mass mailing, no organizers are to work in the office. The National Union can not pay two people salaries to do office work.[30]

By July 19, Wood had lost his patience. "It is not clear in my mind exactly what is wrong in our area." Wood noted that his superiors had been

waiting very patiently for results in this Southern Area and the time has now come for explanations and I feel sure they are not interested in excuses. As I pointed out before, in the other areas they are getting such great results that in comparison it looks as if we haven't even started.

Wood also added that his next meeting with the state director would be most "embarrassing" if he had nothing more to report.[31]

For his part, Culver struggled desperately for a way to break through. "At the Locke Mills we experimented with the device of enclosing several pieces of literature in one envelope, unsealed, and watched the effect very carefully." He suggested that such an innovation would be worth trying at Cannon, even if it were "considerably more trouble." The bottom line was that workers with an envelope were thus less likely to throw the papers away, "finding they had a neat convenient way" to keep them.[32]

On August 8, 1946—the date of the first shocking defeat at the Hannah Pickett Mills in Rockingham, North Carolina[33]—North Carolina state director Smith pleaded with Atlanta for five additional organizers for Kannapolis. Smith wrote that more staff was needed because "we have a long way to go yet and have merely scratched the surface in Cannon." Inexplicably, he added: "The drive is progressing splendidly." He stressed "a spirit of victory over there," and expressed with confidence that "our drive, without question, is cracking." It was, on the contrary, cracking up.[34]

By mid-August, after seven weeks of effort, any residue of optimism slowly seeped out of organizers' reports: "The atmosphere" in Kannapolis was "still too cold" for committees to form or operate "with any real degree of success."[35] Three days later, Culver described a staff session with similar grim brevity: "Meeting was a little depressed."[36] The "still too cold" of August 5 had become the "very cold" of August 20.[37]

And so the Cannon campaign stumbled on into September, amid declining morale that extended beyond the staff of Kannapolis, to Wood and Smith in Charlotte, and Baldanzi and Bittner in Atlanta. The entire Southern effort, meanwhile, was costing the national CIO and its internationals almost $200,000 per month.[38] Culver, meanwhile, had begun to fight to maintain his dignity and to hold on to his job. "No person that I have ever met could have, in my opinion, produced much more organization using the tools available to me and my staff in this particular time. . . . I have made no strategic error of any consequence."[39] He then advised,

What is needed now is accurate, down-to-earth, motivating publicity, unless, of course, the organizing committee anticipates a long-range educational program before great organizational success is won. I am doing the best I can. . . . The make up of my staff in this situation is, as you know, mostly hard working, young, local boys, who do not understand much about the labor movement, or its history. And while they certainly want to organize the Cannon Mills, what is needed is a more crusading spirit, not simply directed toward the obtaining of membership but directed toward the obtaining more of the good things of life for people.[40]

The public announcement of Culver's removal as the head of the Cannon team came on October 23, 1946.[41] His successor, Joel Leighton, was briefly optimistic about prospects for overcoming "the deadness that has been here."[42] However, the enthusiasm expressed by the new lead organizer at Cannon did not last. It could not be sustained in a surrounding climate of despair, an emotion that seeped into every corner of the South where Operation Dixie organizers had mounted campaigns in textiles. From May 15, 1946, through the end of the year, the TWUA participated in forty-seven elections in nine Southern states.[43] The CIO won twenty-one of these elections by an aggregate total of 2,967 to 1,381 votes. Twenty-six elections were lost, with 7,126 "no union" votes, 3,478 votes for the TWUA, and 365 votes for "other unions." Meager as these numbers were, they concealed another dimension of the CIO defeat—namely, the overwhelming percentage of textile workers in plants that, like Cannon, were never brought to an NLRB election. These unorganized textile workers numbered over 500,000.[44] As for Kannapolis, the CIO maintained a presence there throughout the course of Operation Dixie. Sporadic efforts to organize Cannon continued through the 1950s, 1960s, and 1970s, until the first election was held at Cannon mills in 1973, one the Amalgamated Clothing and Textile Workers Union lost. As of December 1986, Cannon Mills was still without a union.

And so, in the end came the organizational retreats that signaled defeat. The Kannapolis staff dwindled, as did the ranks of organizers throughout the rest of the South. The press offices closed down and the membership books full of unsigned cards were folded away. Remaining, amid the wreckage, were the workers—still nursing their hopes and grievances, and their fears. Cautious but watchful, they had weighed the options and, in the end, had decided against taking that final fateful step that would have separated them from the way things were before the CIO came to Kannapolis. At the time (and years later) when they reviewed the decisions they made in the summer of 1946, their thoughts turned to Charlie Cannon. For some, he symbolized safety. As one old-timer put it, "Mr. Cannon didn't fire you for every little thing you done. You felt security, just knowing you had a job and could pay your bills."[45] The thought, turned over in the mind enough times, became the basis for extravagant praise. Charlie Cannon became a man who could be seen as fair and even generous—"a man with a big heart,"[46] as one long-time employee explained. Another veteran of fifty-four years in the mills remembered the Cannon management as "good people to work for. You could talk to them and they'd listen."[47]

Yet the litany of praise concealed many contradictions. Charlie Cannon was "strict," but in a way that was to many, helpful: "If he heard of anybody runnin' around with somebody else's wife or husband, you lost your job," one worker said approvingly.[48] On the other hand, such "strictness" came through to others as simply malicious. One old millworker described the Cannon management as "cruel." But he lowered his voice as he said it, furtively conveying a view he did not want his fellow villagers to hear. Anything that could be interpreted as a disrespectful attitude, he said, "was enough to get anyone fired."[49]

But people who lowered their voices in retirement in the 1980s did not sign union cards in the summer of 1946. "I just saw that it wouldn't be worthwhile to even get your name on [a union list]. Because once you openly come out for the union, you was marked." Such people would "never advance any at all. And I believe if you're going to put eight hours in one place every day that you might as well make the best of it, whether you like it or don't like it."[50] Other workers who felt the same way were even able to put the imposition of piece rates into a benign perspective: "You worked hard, but you worked at your own pace. If you wanted to make good money, you worked harder. If you didn't, well . . . ."[51] In sum, Cannon knew that, for his workers, half a loaf was better than none. This was the primary lesson of the Southern past, one that found expression in the words of a worker who concluded: "Even though it wasn't extra good, it was good."[52]

Clearly, one of the elements at the heart of decision-making by Cannon employees was their sense of the balance of forces between those who ran the world of Kannapolis and those who spoke for trade unionism. A hidden ingredient of Operation Dixie, one that surfaced in hundreds of mill villages that lay far beyond Kannapolis, was the memory of the 1934 general strike. As an event of Southern history, the 1934 strike has received little attention from historians, which is surprising because it was the largest industrywide general strike in American history. Some 400,000 Southern workers walked off the job in 1934. The action, initiated from below by workers rather than at the instigation of union leadership, spread over textile country like a cloud, closing whole districts, whole states. The stories of "united workers" and of "militance" were real, and so were the stories of "desperate picket lines" and, finally, of "desperate hunger." The strike was widespread, it encountered implacable opposition, and it failed. The resulting roll call of blacklisted workers ran into the thousands.[53]

The strike, however, did not engulf Kannapolis. Cannon Mills, in fact, was one of the very few companies in the South that escaped the full brunt of the 1934 uprising, despite the fact that "hundreds of organizers came to Kannapolis."[54] The folklore of 1934 was vivid in 1946, as it remains vivid for many in the 1980s. Bessie Shankle, who worked at Cannon Mills from 1939 to 1970, had an older sister and brother-in-law working there in 1934. The pickets sometimes make it impossible for them to get inside the plant to report for work, she recalled. And even though they had not joined the strike, their family "nearly starved to death" by the time the conflict was over.[55] Even those who had not been directly affected by the strike remembered it. Although textile workers might not have been earning much, "they at least had a job. And they knew that the union in Gastonia and other places did not support the workers and a lot of them nearly starved to death." As a result, "most of 'em were really scared to go for the union."[56]

The Shankle family oral tradition about the 1934 general strike was not completely accurate. It incorporated memories from Gastonia where the searing events of the 1929 strike created vivid stories quite apart from the events of 1934. But in the deepest sense, the tradition is all the more effective as the conveyer of an emotion rooted in historical events, if not always precisely remembered events. The operative memory conveyed by Shankle family tradition was that "the union" brought trouble, picket lines, hungry families, and defeat.

All working classes in all societies have such ingredients buried in their oral traditions. Such memories fortify deference by providing deferential people with a rationale for continued passivity. It was in this sense that the long struggle in textile country in the 1920s and 1930s, punctuated by moments of extreme drama in 1929 and 1934, added up to a powerful barrier for CIO organizers in 1946 (and thereafter).

The "Cannon myth" that CIO organizers found also served to fortify deference among the workers there. Stories of the purported "kindness" of Uncle Charlie persisted, alongside stories of management "cruelty," precisely because they served to justify and explain inaction. The simple fact was that many stories praising Cannon were authored by workers who did not join the CIO for the elementary reason that they were afraid to do so. It was easier to praise "Uncle Charlie" than to talk about one's fear.

"Paternalism" is a word that sometimes conceals more than it reveals. To an extent that remains difficult for outsiders to grasp, workers in company-owned mill villages in the American South lived under the most debasing kind of police tyranny. Uncle Charlie could not only fire a worker, or elect not to fire him, for "runnin' around on his wife"; he could cause people to lose their jobs for other transgressions including, but extending beyond, a "disrespectful attitude." Cannon had access to all arrest records. Indeed, such records were kept in triplicate, one copy for Cannon Mills, a second for the newspaper files, and a third retained by the sheriff's office. The effect of such extreme forms of social control are hard to exaggerate. The resulting "popular attitude," however it might be characterized, was something deep-seated that CIO organizers confronted every day as they passed out leaflets at the gates of Cannon Mills.

The workers wanted help—the low throw-down rates provided certain testimony of this—but they preferred getting it in some way that did not fundamentally threaten them. As the CIO organizer's report affirmed, "We must find some way to get the fear out of these people."

The objective was worthy. However, the means were not at hand in the summer of 1946.

V

Race

Under the general subject of what might be called "race relations," the bits and pieces of social evidence that make up the daily history of Operation Dixie pile up chaotically, a patchwork of contradictory impulses and actions. Whereas some CIO organizers literally were shot at while engaged in interracial organizing, others found, and accepted, a rigid interlocking of membership between unionists and Klansmen. How to sort through such a maze? One way, perhaps, is to visualize the CIO's potential membership for what it was—a simple reflection of the Southern population as a whole. Not only did the CIO rank and file collectively possess many tendencies and urges that were contradictory, but contradictory urges could be found within the same individual. Under different appeals or pressures, an individual Southern worker, whether white or black, was capable of a range of responses to racial stimuli.

A long-forgotten "Southern incident" illustrates the way in which apparent ideological differences or jurisdictional rivalries in the internal life of the CIO could be used to conceal the operative cause of trouble—the race issue.

In New Orleans, a representative of the Communications Workers of America (CWA) complained to his international president, Joe Beirne, about the conduct of "a bunch of Communists" who, in the course of administering the CIO Packinghouse Union in New Orleans, were carrying on "all sorts of activities" that were ruining the entire trade union movement in the city. Beirne forwarded the complaint to Packinghouse President Ralph Helstein at the union's headquarters in Chicago. Helstein promised to investigate, and later discovered that the trouble focused around two segregated pay lines at the American Sugar Plant, across the river from New Orleans. The pay line for white workers was covered with a canopy, while the line for black workers was not. When it rained on payday, black workers got wet.

> After a particularly nasty storm, I guess they got together and decided, "to hell with this silly noise. Let's just break this up." So they advised the company they weren't going to stand for this anymore. The company protested and said, "You gotta." But they started mingling the two lines. And the company tried to make an issue out of it and couldn't make it stick.[1]

That the South had its own particular rhythms when it came to race is beyond question. But the task of measuring these rhythms is necessarily an exercise requiring considerable care. The local CWA official who saw the hand of communism in an integrated pay line expressed an instinctive response against "race-mixing" that was widely shared among the white population. But after covert, internal remedies proved ineffective in putting an end to such activity within the labor movement, he was persuaded to accept the new order of things. If Southern white workers would stand in pay lines with black workers in some places, what else could they be induced to do? Unfortunately, one never knew beforehand the limits beyond which white workers would not go. In the spring of 1946, there were many opinions about "how far to go." These views, while passionately held, were uncertain. It was clear only that a measure of risk was implicit in any action that involved recruiting black and white workers into the same organization.

In any event, imposing statistical realities seemed to impel action of some kind. The tobacco industry employed great numbers of blacks; so did ventures in wood and wood products, packinghouses, and a wide array of other local enterprises in scattered industrial enclaves honeycombing the region. Organizing opportunities and potential racial cataclysms existed everywhere. The CIO's commitment to organizing the unskilled quickly translated into a commitment to organizing black workers. There was no practical way the CIO could build a solid following in basic Southern industries without organizing black workers. Quite naturally, then, CIO leaders found themselves searching for relatively "non-inflammatory" ways to make clear their intentions. A fairly representative approach was Bittner's summation that the CIO was "organizing all the men and women of the South, because they all are God's human beings." Such an effort could only lead to "a better United States."[2]

Throughout the first months of the Southern drive, CIO leaders added more specific references to the importance of the South's black workers to the CIO. In response to the suggestion that the South would remain out of reach of the CIO precisely *because* of the large number of black workers in the region, Bittner reminded his organizers that "a Negro gets just as hungry as a white man," and that from his experience there were "no better union men than the hundreds of thousands of Negro workers already in the CIO."[3] Sherman Dalrymple, the CIO's Secretary-Treasurer, went so far as to assert that "the extension of CIO unionism in the South would encourage the forces of democracy and lead to the ultimate removal of racial prejudice and the poll tax," and added, on another occasion, that mass unemployment and race prejudice comprised "the greatest threat to world peace."[4]

There is evidence that the CIO and some of its internationals took concrete steps to make public their moral revulsion toward racist policies and racially motivated violence. At a Georgia conference of CIO textile workers, held against the backdrop of America's victory over Hitler, organized labor in Georgia took a stand against "industrial dictators in the state." Resolutions against the Klan were passed as well.[5]

Criticism of Southern white supremacy was often openly political, in spite of Bittner's demand that the Operation Dixie staff remove themselves from participation in formal political activity. A National Committee to oust Senator Theodore Bilbo was formed in spite of "violence and intimidation," and promised the people of Mississippi the removal of "an avowed member of the Ku Klux Klan from the Senate" and "a setback for the system of terror, disfranchisement and race supremacy which Bilbo typifies."[6]

On the grounds that their union stood for "complete equality between all races and creeds," all district directors, field representatives, and affiliated locals of the United Packinghouse Workers of America, a left-wing, heavily black union, received a plea from their international in Chicago for contributions to the National Committee for Justice in Columbia, Tennessee. Cochaired by Eleanor Roosevelt, the committee needed the funds to underwrite legal fees for thirty-one blacks who had been arrested there on a variety of charges.[7] The president of the Food, Tobacco, Agricultural and Allied Workers of America (FTA), also a left-wing and heavily black union, issued a similar appeal for funds after a black FTA worker in Arkansas, on strike "against 55¢ an hour and a 12-hour day," was murdered by a strikebreaker in Little Rock. Although having confessed to stabbing the man, the strikebreaker was set free and, in his place, six union members were rushed to trial under charges of "attacking" a strikebreaker. All were black. Philip Murray, president of the CIO, protested what he termed a "whitewash" of the incident by the federal government, and at the same time initiated a petition for a new federal grand jury investigation.[8] CIO leadership, as represented by its Committee to Abolish Racial Discrimination, also protested the murders of two black couples in Monroe, Georgia, by a mob of thirty white men. The CIO's National Maritime Union contributed $5,000 to a reward of almost $30,000 raised as part of one investigative effort aimed at overcoming what the *CIO News* described as the "tied-tongue tradition that makes it inadvisable for white or Negro people in the South to expose lynchers."[9]

In response to such public stances, the CIO received support from organizations such as the Southern Conference for Human Welfare, the National Association for the Advancement of Colored People (NAACP), the National Ur-

ban League, and the National Negro Congress (NNC).[10]
The NAACP contributed to the CIO's general strike fund.
Its secretary, Walter White, joined a national committee set
up to collect funds for strikers at General Motors.[11] In much
the same manner, the NAACP and the NNC also assisted another group of Southern strikers, led by the CIO's Fur and
Leather Workers Union, who had "crippled" laundry service in Winston-Salem, North Carolina, in an effort to win a
recognition strike during Operation Dixie.[12]

Such pronouncements were made and such interracial co-
alitions, however fragile, were formed and deserve to be recorded as part of labor's postwar effort to cope with
centuries of racial segregation in the South. But beneath the
surface of resolution-passing and the rhetoric of brother-
hood, another and far more complicated drama unfolded
within the interior of Operation Dixie. This struggle can be
summarized as labor's war with its own racism.

CIO policy existed on a national level and was expressed
in a variety of ways in Washington; it also was expressed
in diverse forms "on the ground" in the South. Some organizers simply could not bring themselves to go beyond per-
functory efforts to organize blacks. Their understanding of
possible approaches was so limited by their own customs
and experiences that they succeeded primarily in convinc-
ing potential black recruits that the CIO offered no real
prospects for change. Such organizers were described
somewhat elliptically by fellow staff members as "good
people, but not good organizers."[13] They were "overly
cautious."[14] They were "not effective."[15] They were
"Southerners."[16]

More specific descriptions were applied to Dixie organizers who were of a somewhat different mold. There was, for
example, the CWA organizer in Texas, a native of the eastern "old South" part of the state, who remembered a colleague this way:

> He never could get over saying "nigger." But, biggest
> and best champion of civil rights you ever saw. In-
> sisted that we never have a meeting that wasn't inte-

grated. A lot of times we'd have them in the fields because we couldn't get a place to meet; or we'd have it
in a black church or something, hoping we could get a
few whites over there. Usually, we'd have it out in a
field or in a pasture, or something like that, because
that's the only place we could go. Bill was great, but
his whole past was out there on that farm where
every black was a "nigger." Like to never got over it.
I don't know that he ever did.[17]

This is an extreme example of the expression of a long-
standing white supremacist habit coexisting simultaneously
with interracial organizing activity. The general truth was
less contradictory: the CIO organizers who were more progressive politically tended to do more, or to try to do more,
in terms of interracial organizing than did the least progressive staff members. Yet an unconscious aura of white supremacy tended to hang over the great majority of CIO
efforts, however advanced they were, or appeared to outsiders, to be.

It was in this sometimes deeply ironic sense that the organizing differences between the AFL and the CIO became
clear. With many white supremacist assumptions intact, the
CIO tried to organize black workers; in contrast, the assumptions of AFL organizers were such that they often did not attempt to organize black workers at all. A CIO organizer
from Mississippi filled in the distinction that existed as the
bottom line of Operation Dixie: "Any plants with a mixed
work force, the AFL did not try as hard as the CIO. And if
it was an all-black plant, you might see the AFL not fooling
with it at all."[18]

Divergent institutional policies of the AFL and CIO under-
girded these different approaches. In its constitution, the
AFL, too, declared itself open to "all workers," but the white-
only orientation of the organization was maintained by way
of a policy of "local autonomy" that left decision-making capacity in the hands of local AFL functionaries. Whether applied to internationals or to local affiliates of internationals,
the AFL policy of "local autonomy" was, in effect, a policy

of racial exclusion. Everyone in the labor movement knew this and, at plant gates throughout the South, the custom became most visible in what the AFL did not do: it rarely made a concerted effort to organize black workers.[19]

In this general context, the racial record of the CIO has been retrospectively characterized by one participant as "good, but not good enough," by another as being "as good as the times permitted," and by a third as "good by the left-wing unions, much less so by the rest."[20]

Quite obviously, in an effort as expansive in purpose as Operation Dixie, an effort that reached into every Southern state and into the remote countryside as well as into metropolitan centers, plenty of evidence was generated that can be selectively employed to demonstrate, or contradict, all of these judgments. Perhaps a useful way to bring some sense of order to this interpretive problem lies in reconstructing the organizing process itself, so as to determine how matters of race affected each stage of union activity.

Reduced to its essentials, the organizing process required CIO staff people to perform a sequence of actions: (1) they entered a town and found a place to stay; (2) they made contact with individual workers and continued doing so until they had a nucleus of committed recruits; (3) this core group was instructed in what to say to their co-workers inside the plant in order to recruit them; (4) the organizers planned a meeting to which the initial recruits would bring the most responsive of their co-workers; (5) more advanced plans gradually unfolded, involving more meetings, larger meetings, distribution of leaflets, books and union cards, and still more meetings; (6) the drive was successful enough to warrant petitioning for an NLRB election, or it was not. The inherited racial customs of the South intruded upon, and distorted, every step in this organizing sequence.

In the decisive months of Operation Dixie, the mere holding of a meeting quite often became a political act of some magnitude. Black and white workers gathering in the same room constituted a physical violation of the caste system that deeply threatened those in the local Southern establishment. While working in Decatur, Georgia, one organizer held his first meeting in his motel room.

> There was no union hall or anything like that, because there was very little union in Decatur at that time. The manager came in the motel room during the meeting and said, "Blacks don't come in this motel." I guess I may have had more black people in there than there were white people. And I said, "We're just talking." "Not in my motel!" He broke up the meeting. So we went out and met on the grass, you know, right there in public.[21]

Another organizer remembered one of the first meetings he held while working in Louisiana and Mississippi:

> We went over and had a meeting down the railroad tracks with the blacks that worked in the plant, in a little black church, a little wooden church. And we must have had 12, maybe 15 people. And I was sitting on the front or second row. And someone rode around the street there and shot the meeting up. They just shot the little wooden church full of holes. And bullets was coming through the little wooden church and hitting this great big woodstove there, ricocheting off the ceiling and hitting the stove.[22]

That it was difficult and dangerous for labor organizers and interested workers to meet during the Southern drive is hardly surprising. Even when a meeting involved the participation of federal officials, some Southerners still would not cooperate; the NLRB itself was not sufficiently "official" to be able to hold hearings without interference. Although NLRB hearings were usually held in a federal building, officials in one small Alabama town refused to open the post office building for the occasion. The local postmaster "ran them out. He said, 'You're not having no Labor Board hearings in *my* post office!" After a futile search for another suitable location, "some lady who was brave" let them use the tables in the barbecue stand she operated, only to be threatened by her landlord with the cancellation of her lease once

he discovered the nature of the arrangement. The participants finally ended up meeting in "a little old hall the
union had." On top of such difficulties, the town's police
force "insisted on coming in and sitting with their guns on
display. They wouldn't take them off!"[23]

Under such circumstances, organizers developed a certain anticipatory sensitivity. Discretion was not only safer,
it was more practical. Meetings that attracted undue outside attention had prolonged aftereffects: "Sometimes you
lose your people. They won't come back if they feel like
there's no security at all. They may want to be with you,
but, you know, that paycheck—to eat on—is important."[24]

If, as one Mississippi organizer put it, it took "grits and
backbone"[25] to be a union member, it took more to be a
union organizer, and more still to be a black organizer in
the South. A case in point was the occasion of an NLRB election at an Alabama chicken-processing plant employing 490
black workers and ten white supervisory personnel. The
CIO's "watcher" at the election was a black organizer with
the International Retail, Wholesale, and Department Store
Workers Union. The union had won the election "overwhelmingly" and the NLRB officials had left the scene. The
"watcher" happened to look out at the parking lot, only to
see the hood of his car up and a number of whites standing around it. Thinking that the activity in the parking lot
might involve a bomb, and finding local authorities unwilling to offer any assistance, he crawled out a back window
and ran to safety at the house of a sympathetic black minister several blocks away. An official at the federal Justice
Department was finally contacted, who then sent federal
marshals to investigate. A white co-worker of the black organizer remembered the incident quite clearly.

> Henry was a teetotaler. And Alabama had wet coun-
> ties and dry counties. And whites could go into a wet
> county and buy liquor and bring it back, and they
> weren't harassed too much; but blacks were. And [so
> blacks] used to buy liquor and they'd open the hood
> and put it up under the hood. The whites [in the park-

ing lot] had opened Henry's hood and taken a cigar box with the top torn off of it, and in that cigar box was two or three Dixie cups and a pint or half-pint of liquor. And the sheriff was right down the road there. And what they were going to do, apparently, was to stop Henry when he left there and search his car and find that, and then confiscate his automobile and prosecute him for transporting whiskey in a dry county.[26]

One black organizer so deeply imprinted in the minds of his colleagues his courage and skill as an organizer—work that was far more dangerous for him than for his white counterparts—that he acquired a certain fame in the oral tradition of the labor movement. In the folklore, one of this organizer's many talents involved the ability to go into black communities in Mississippi and "get lost."

No white person could go in and find him. And I couldn't even find him—and he worked with me. I'd go into a plant in north Mississippi in one of those little communities and put him out on the street corner. And then he'd have to find me; I couldn't find him. And nobody else could find him. [Black organizers] survived because they were smart.[27]

However, the tentacles of Southern companies had a long reach. "Eventually, you had blacks in there who would tell the sheriff who the organizers were."[28] For retired black organizers, such reminiscences are rife with painful memories that make their recollection an activity to be avoided. Not only did black organizers face the harassment that grew from a Southern public opinion that was generally anti-union; they also, of course, faced the threat of white racist reaction. But beyond these hazards, because most of the black organizers had been hired by the more left-wing unions, they were red-baited as well. In addition, salt was rubbed into those wounds each time the racist or red-baiting attacks came from others within the CIO—whether from rank and file, other organizers, or the leadership.

Forty years after Operation Dixie, some black organizers still do not want to talk about it.[29]

As the surrounding social realities are pieced into an overall context, it becomes clear that "having a meeting" was often a major event in Operation Dixie when it involved workers of both races. For one veteran Mississippi organizer, the biggest problem was finding a place to talk. "We met in the woods, under railroad trestles, railroad bridges, and just anywhere we could get people together. You just could not do anything about the race relations, because that's the way the politicians got elected."[30]

In the course of their activities, white organizers gradually learned what black organizers knew from the basic shape of their daily lives, but what very few white Americans, then or later, understood: Southern black people were highly politicized. Behind the mask of enforced social deference, black people knew an opportunity when they saw one. Even today, after all that has happened to alter racial perceptions in America, white organizers express their hard-won insights on race with a kind of qualified awe. "At this time, blacks were very, very susceptible to unions. All the way through they were. And they weren't afraid to strike."[31] "You got to do some little somethin' to make 'em believe you're with 'em. Then, they'll stay with you until hell freezes over."[32] From a labor lawyer: "Well, many, if not all the people who looked to the CIO for help were black."[33] An Alabama organizer: "Not only was everybody underpaid, but blacks were *more* underpaid. The blacks were given the most disagreeable jobs. And very quickly, they saw that not only everybody had a lot to gain, they had *more* to gain."[34] A North Carolinian added: "Oh, yeah! Blacks was right with ya! They were smarter than the whites, where the union was concerned. They had more to gain. And they knew that!"[35] Black workers definitely "responded more to organization at that time than the white people did. They sure did."[36] And a CWA organizer agreed: "It was true in Texas: the only time you could do very much with low income people was when a large group of them were black."[37]

In placing Operation Dixie in historical perspective, it can be argued that these qualifying phrases surrounding white praise betrayed an unconscious white supremacy. Blacks were not seen so much as being inherently pro-union as they were pro-union "at this time." They were not understood to be politically sophisticated, but, instead, "smart where the union was concerned." Such militance where white organizers expected to see deference could only be accounted for as a series of exceptions—"at this time," or "in Texas," or "where the union was concerned." Black organizers, of course, had to live with such attitudes, and even value (with appropriate awareness of the ironies involved) the relatively "advanced" quality of these white opinions.

The historically relevant point is that these opinions of white CIO organizers *were*, in fact, advanced. Indeed, by making vivid the utter irrationalities of much of daily life in a segregated society, interracial organizing generated experiences that "radicalized" white organizers. While they remained firmly in the grip of many white assumptions, they *were* changed in fundamental ways. They became "different" from other white Southerners.

A generation after Operation Dixie, when the civil rights movement rolled across the South, there would be one group of native whites who understood, and could even anticipate, the ebb and flow of assertion and repression that would characterize the 1960s. The group would include people like Woody Biggs and Jim Touchstone in Mississippi, Barney Weeks in Alabama, Lloyd Gossett in Georgia, B. T. Judd in Tennessee, Dean Culver in North Carolina, and Jim Pierce in Texas. Such people understood. But there was one group of CIO veterans who understood even better— black men and women like Cornelius Simmons, Moranda Smith, and Elijah Jackson who had earned their stripes with Food and Tobacco, Fur and Leather, and the Packinghouse Workers, the unions with the most prolonged experience in interracial organizing.

If Operation Dixie exposed the raw nerve endings left by centuries of racial oppression, it also exposed the damage that segregation had done to both races. Most specifically, it exposed the Klan. The KKK was to be found all across the postwar South. In communities where the CIO was trying to organize, the police belonged to the Klan and so did white union members. To discover that local politicians and law enforcement officers were Klan members was rarely a surprise to organizers in the South; it was simply a fact of life around which they had to work. However, it was less "in character," more embarrassing to progressive forces within the CIO, and more destructive to the work of organizers at the local level to have CIO rank-and-filers involved in Ku Klux Klan activity. And by all accounts, they were. The membership of a large Birmingham local of the Steelworkers was about half black and half white. There was a nice symmetry to their outside affiliations. Most of the blacks belonged to the NAACP, and most of the whites belonged to the Klan.[38] Such a situation was not confined to Birmingham. In Georgia, the local at the Atlantic Steel Plant held separate meetings for black and white workers, at the insistence of those who were Klan members. According to Lloyd Gossett, a long-time CIO organizer, even the international representatives and all the officers of that local were members of the KKK.[39]

Various internationals added a number of inherited racial attitudes and policies to the mix. For example, while certain steelworkers in Georgia and Alabama moved in one direction, certain autoworkers and communications workers in Texas moved in another. "Race was the first hurdle," remembers a Texas organizer. "You crossed that hurdle first. If you didn't cross that hurdle, I wouldn't speak to you; the leadership wouldn't speak to you. Nobody would help you if you couldn't get over that."[40]

But what was true of the autoworkers and communication workers, and even more so of the Packinghouse, Food and Tobacco, and Fur and Leather Unions, was not true of the South's numerically dominant industry: textiles. In the heart of textile country, the North Carolina state director, William Smith, had the delicate problem of balancing the radically different approaches of the two unions engaged in organizing the state's textile and tobacco industries. Food and Tobacco representatives were habitually generating literature that Smith believed could be "deeply harmful," should it surface in textile country. He rejected one FTA leaflet because it raised "a Negro nationalistic approach which could easily prove dangerous to us." In addition, "our campaign in the Tobacco drive is such a huge success [relative to textiles] that we should easily be able to bring it to a successful conclusion without the need of elaborating on the racial issue." The state director was certain that "this material could very easily boomerang on us and be used by the AFL against us, for instance, in the Textile Industry—especially in Roanoke Rapids, where the racial issue in reverse is being played up by the AFL."[41]

In South Carolina, state director Franz Daniel also waged a continuous, and often unsuccessful, rearguard action against the distribution of union literature that was too explicitly integrationist. An organizer for the Paperworkers was chided by Daniel for not showing him copies of all flyers and newspapers before they were printed. "You know, of course, some of the problems we are faced with in organizational work in the South. Many times unions will send in quantities of papers, only to have a picture or story that makes distribution impossible."[42]

The pattern of what might be described as racial defensiveness extended beyond textile country to the CIO's Southern headquarters in Atlanta. Van Bittner, too, lectured staffers on the need to be circumspect. For example, the CIO's racial policies could on occasion win the approval of such anti-discrimination public agencies as the Fair Employment Practices Commission. In response to a suggestion by the head of the CIO-PAC in South Carolina that a meeting be called to publicize a message of support for the CIO recently received from the FEPC, Bittner illustrated the degree to which caution on race issues was considered essential by the Dixie leadership.

I do not know what the FEPC statement would do toward helping our campaign, at this time. We are not

afraid of making anything public that is for the best in-
terests of men and women of labor, but the prime objective of the CIO is to organize unions and bring about
higher wages and better living standards through genuine collective bargaining.[43]

Clearly Operation Dixie became a kind of racial balancing
act. Moreover, though it might not have appeared evident
at the time, it was a balancing act that could not be long sustained among such a variegated assortment of unions and
rank-and-file constituencies. While Packinghouse organizers
endeavored to be "fair to all workers," and CWA organizers tried to be "progressive, but not too progressive" on
the race issue, textile representatives intuitively stepped
around the issue whenever possible. Black Southerners got
many different signals from the CIO.

The irony was, of course, that no public posture could insulate any CIO union from the charge—by local chambers
of commerce, sheriffs, or, for that matter, AFL organizers—
that the CIO was a hotbed of Communistically inclined race
mixers. It was no surprise that race-baiting was coupled
with red-baiting on many occasions, such accusations having been a routine component of the array of obstacles set
up to stop the CIO in the South. Indeed, an interesting "logical" dynamic was at work. Viewed from an orthodox segregationist perspective, anyone—especially a fellow Southerner,
as many of the Operation Dixie organizers were—who
could even *consider* trying to form an integrated union was
so flagrantly bucking entrenched custom and reason that a
truly extraordinary explanation was called for. How to account for such deviant behavior? The logic was both simple
and compelling: Only Communists would seriously try to
mix the races in a labor union. So convenient and suitable
was this explanation that to view it simply as demagogic red-
baiting is to underestimate the grip that traditional Southern racial attitudes had upon a large majority of the white
population. Clearly such explanations were self-serving; but
they were also deeply believed.

The CIO's problem went quite beyond the impact that red-baiting by Southern industrialists could have on the general population. The CIO was not dealing merely with a "public relations" problem. Rather, the fundamental difficulty was the simple fact that Southern workers participated fully in the region's hegemonic racial philosophy. That "race mixing" translated as communism in the view of Southern political and business leaders was a problem. That it translated in precisely the same way for vast numbers of Southern workers was more than a problem: It threatened the CIO's entire undertaking.

While noting that the Communist issue dovetailed neatly with the racial issue in the dynamic manner just specified, it is important to emphasize the power of the race issue when considered wholly by itself. Much has been written in recent years about "hegemony" and about the complicated political process through which beliefs achieve a truly hegemonic prestige within a given culture or subculture. The racial organization of society was the cornerstone of Southern life in slavery, and it remained so with the establishment of fixed patterns of segregation after the Civil War. Sociologists and historians have carefully interpreted the complex process through which a white supremacist racial hegemony was reconstructed in the South, and they help make clear how each new generation of white Southerners could come to regard any action directed against inherited racial custom as constituting nothing less than the subversion of the homeland. In this sense, the CIO was "unpatriotic" because it was anti-Southern to all people who unconsciously used the word "Southern" when they meant "white." While the red issue added a certain weight to the equation, the essential loyalty of Southern traditionalists was to this unconscious definition of racial identity. In its various invocations, the defense against Operation Dixie was hegemonic. The subtleties of ideology, of radicalism, and specifically of the Communist Party all had a bearing on Operation Dixie that are of sufficient importance to warrant consideration in a separate chapter; but Southern white

supremacy, however blended with other issues, had a life
of its own that separated Operation Dixie from any other
major labor organizing campaign in American history.

Certainly, the CIO captains of the Southern drive
thought so, or quickly came to think so. The CIO's awareness of the South's conscious regionalism lay behind the decision to staff the campaign with as many native Southerners
as possible. The clear intent of this policy was to deflect the
charge of "invasion" by "outsiders," a charge that was routinely aimed at interracial organizing. Hiring Southerners
was a public relations tactic, defensive in nature. The practical task was more demanding: to fashion an appeal to black
workers in such a way that the appeal itself did not alien-
ate white workers.

The daily life of Operation Dixie illustrates how this task
came to be addressed. The interracial "commitment" of organizers or of specific unions influenced the initial approach; however, Southern workers themselves played an
important role in shaping the tactics that eventually came
into wide use by CIO staffers, regardless of their individual
predispositions. In essence, organizers of varying styles
and racial attitudes came to apply those things that worked
and gave up on other methods that did not.

In approaching an interracial work force, a CIO organizer encountered a group of people who, in a social
sense, shared little beyond their common time in the workplace. The nonwork time of black and white workers was
spent in separate spheres. Since company opposition prevented organizers from meeting workers in the one place
where they congregated—the workplace—the organizing
task routinely and inexorably became two tasks, a black campaign and a white campaign. Which to begin first? CIO staffers soon learned that one had to organize white workers
first. As a Fur and Leather organizer put it:

> Once we could get among the whites and get them or-
> ganized, [we could] begin to do a little education
> work, a little working out of some understanding that
> "you can't win here unless you get the black people,

too; they've gotta come." If you started with the blacks, it was almost sure that you were gonna have trouble, then, with the whites. At least this is what we found in practically every case. So, normally we started with the whites. And then as quickly as we could, we'd begin to talk to them about organizing the blacks. "You'll have to have them. Otherwise, the boss is going to use them against you. And here, if you ever have a strike, he'll hire some black scabs. And these things will help destroy you." Now, when it was approached properly, you see, it worked.[44]

But organizers had to be careful not to take in blacks "too fast." As a veteran of Alabama's labor wars put it, "If it looked to the whites like you had a black union and you wanted them to join it, you'd be dead. They wouldn't do it."[45]

It would be misleading to suggest that anything approaching a formula evolved. What emerged can be more aptly described as a set of practical guidelines. Given the anxiety levels in the 1940s associated with racial "commingling" in the South, the entire organizing process involving an interracial work force was inherently volatile, if not explosive. The need to be calm and to improvise were two of the guidelines. A certain plateau was reached when workers in both races knew, and accepted, that organizing was going forward on both fronts. "You met with whites, okay; you met with blacks, okay; but the day came when you had to meet together. And that first meeting was touchy. I've had it all fall apart right there. Whites just wouldn't do it."[46] What whites would and would not do depended upon circumstances frequently beyond the organizer's control. "If a guy everybody liked got up and said, 'O.K. we'll do it. We can stand for that,' then it would happen. But if he said, 'We ain't meeting with no niggers,' then it could all blow up."[47]

The sheer irrationality of radial segregation created a tactical climate where subtlety—sometimes subtlety that warred against the best of human instincts—was necessary. The resulting clash of values could produce a complicated organizing situation. For example, an organizer for the Retail Clerks spelled out the lengths to which black workers would go in order to counter company efforts at race-baiting.

> The company would say, "Oh, I saw him shaking hands with"—call a name—"right down there by the county courthouse!" [All because] I shook hands with somebody, a black man! Really! And, really, black people knew [the effectiveness of this tactic, and also wanted] to be your friend; but they didn't want to— it's hard to use the right word—reduce your *effectiveness*. So, they would kind of want to avoid you a little bit, too. They watched where they shook your hand.[48]

And so, in the name of cooperation, black and white CIO members agreed on occasion not to cooperate in public.

Defensive tactics among rank-and-file black workers as well as among CIO organizers clearly took many forms. Indeed, all CIO organizers involved in Operation Dixie were defensive to some extent. Simple intelligence dictated this posture. But an organizer's decision as to what to be defensive about strongly influenced the shape of the campaign. The most effective defense against Southern racism—one that ensured no counterattack of any kind—was to ignore the black workers. The more one attempted, the greater the requirements for poise, subtlety, and, often, physical courage.

The initial problem white organizers faced, however, was their own innocence about the patterns of life in black communities. They had to learn some elementary truths, such as the extent of influence—quite beyond anything in white communities—of the guiding social, political, and economic influence of black ministers. As an organizer explained,

> We had to learn that the black churches were the very center of the black communities. Then that's where *we* went. When we went into a town to talk to the blacks and to try to get a foothold in some of these plants, we went to the black preachers.[49]

The more sophisticated CIO staffers soon learned that more was at work in the structure and function of black churches than just religion. "Generally speaking, blacks are much easier to organize, not just because they are the most downtrodden, but because of the greater sense of organization that they got through churches and all kinds of lodges."[50]

But management, too, soon learned the relevance of the black church. Indeed, the practice of making financial contributions to black churches as a means of cultivating cooperative relations with black spokesmen had been pioneered by Henry Ford. The auto magnate had demonstrated how financial contributions to selected black churches could, where properly followed up, be utilized to mobilize the ministers as employment agents. As one historian has noted, "prospective workers were hired, upon presenting a written ministerial recommendation from their minister to company officials. Negro ministers welcomed Ford's assistance because it increased church attendance, helped keep the church financially solvent, and strengthened their community leadership position."[51]

Similar policies were pursued by Southern industrialists, none with a more institutionalized consistency than tobacco and utility magnate, James Buchanan Duke, who set up permanent endowments for black and white ministers. Duke concentrated his largesse in regions adjacent to his tobacco factories and power companies.[52]

The CIO's Food and Tobacco international won a notable victory in 1943 when it successfully organized the R. J. Reynolds plant in Winston-Salem, North Carolina. The campaign brought to light the organizing talent of a black woman in Winston-Salem, Moranda Smith, who went on to become the Southern regional director of FTA–the highest position any black woman had held up to that time in the American labor movement.

Food and Tobacco also helped pioneer integrated picket lines in the course of Operation Dixie. The possibilities for overcoming entrenched racial custom afforded by such ef- were vividly revealed in 1946 at the American Tobacco ⋅ ⋅. ıpany in Charleston, South Carolina.

Black and white women were walking the picket line in front of the "white" gate, [when] one of the white non-strikers spat at one of the black women as she left the factory in the afternoon. The black woman stepped out of line and slapped the white woman. The police, who were always there, arrested the black woman for assault. At the magistrates' court the next morning, the white woman presented her case; then the black woman presented her case. [But] the magistrate dismissed the case when one of the white women union members said, "I saw the whole thing. This scab spit in this sister's face, and she deserved every slap she got." This new alignment of sympathy reversed what would have been an open and shut case of believing the testimony of the white witness. It also showed a new level of understanding on the part of the white women workers.[53]

A subtle truth about race relations in the South lurks beneath the surface of events in Charleston in 1946. Cooperation between black and white workers could generally reach higher levels *after* a union had won recognition. In the initial organizing effort, company tactics to divide workers through the use of hearsay could (in the absence of previous interracial contact that would contradict such hearsay) prove effective in ways that could be disastrous for the union's cause. A Fur and Leather organizer described the tactic:

The company would go to white workers and say, "You can't trust them Goddamn so-and-sos." And then they would go to the blacks and say, "You know, they've always sold you down the river, those whites over there. You get with them and you ain't gonna get that other nickel or dime we told you about."[54]

A Mississippi veteran summarized, "Companies race-baited constantly, and the workers would fall for that."[55] A labor lawyer added, "The CIO could get [blacks] to join but they couldn't keep them, because the employers would come in with one strategy or another and just flush them out like birds."[56]

But alongside these pessimistic generalizations, Operation Dixie offered specific case histories that provided examples of how the traditions associated with Southern segregation could be overcome. Food and Tobacco, Fur and Leather, and the Packinghouse unions were notable in their ability to achieve such victories. Each possessed the intuition, as a matter both of union policy and the leadership's conviction, that interracial organizing was possible in the South in 1946. The ingredients of success seemed to lie in a judicious combination of close and candid contact with workers of both races and an ability to express in down-to-earth language the choices that had to be made, the costs and benefits of those choices, and a preview of company efforts that would be made to derail them.

The experiences of the Packinghouse Workers in Texas provided concrete illustration. In the meat-packing industry, the union entered a working environment that contained a number of long-standing discriminatory practices. There were "male" jobs and "female" jobs, "black" jobs and "white" jobs, differing rates of pay in Northern and Southern plants, and separate eating facilities and dressing rooms for blacks and whites.[57]

Tension developed in the Armour plant in Fort Worth when, under the terms of the contract, management was to take down the partitions that separated the races in the plant dining room and in all the dressing rooms. The head of the Fort Worth union had been elected by a white segregationist faction in the local. The district director of the Packinghouse Workers Union in charge of the Fort Worth area, A. J. Pittman, was sympathetic to the local union leadership there, and reported to the international in Chicago that union members were "marching on the union hall" to protest the removal of these segregationist symbols in factory life. The president of the international, Ralph Helstein, dispatched two lieutenants, Russell Haisley, a black vice president from Chicago, and "Butch" Hathaway, a Southern white, to Fort Worth to call a meeting of the local. "They were both strong union men," said Helstein. "Haisley was calm and firm and Hathaway was a Baptist who spoke with a strong Southern accent, and I figured these two guys ought to be able to solve it."

Over 1,000 members attended the unusual meeting. "There were knives and guns all over the place. There was screaming and hollering. It was impossible to keep order and they didn't want order; they didn't want to hear anything. The blacks who were there were outnumbered." The two union officials confirmed the seriousness of the situation to Helstein upon their return to Chicago.

The impediments—and the opportunities—that the race issue visited upon labor-management relations were vividly demonstrated by the Fort Worth incident. Helstein contacted Frank Green, Armour's vice president in charge of industrial relations, and told him:

> "You and I got a date to go to Fort Worth. We've got a lot of trouble there." He said, "I understand *you* got some troubles down there, but they're not my troubles." And I said, "Oh, Frank, you're wrong. You've got troubles, too. And you had better *make* them your troubles; or, if you prefer, I'm going to pick up this telephone and I'm going to call every Armour local in the United States and tell them you are reneging on your agreement about eliminating segregated dining rooms." So, he quickly came around and sent his lieutenant—whom I actually preferred to Green, because he was a better man—Dean Hawkins.

Hawkins and Helstein went to Fort Worth, where Helstein met first, alone, with Pittman.

> I said, "Let's get down to specifics. I don't think we can have the kind of union we need unless you do." I pointed out how much this contract provided, and how much of that had come out of the pockets of black people in the North. And I explained to Pittman that he had to tell his union members that they couldn't have it both ways. So, we met with the leader-

ship of the local and they said they didn't give a
damn about a contract. And I said, "Do you want me
to put that to a vote?" Of course they didn't. But they
told me that I didn't understand, that "rape was
going on all the time," and "everybody knows they
[the black union members] all got syphilis. We're not
going to use the same toilets as they do." Well, I lis-
tened to this stuff until I got tired of it. And I said,
"Let me make this clear. You know this union. You
know the rules by which we live. You know what our
constitution provides; and, that it is enforced. You've
got the following benefits out of this last contract."
And I named them. "You will either live by those
rules that got those benefits for you, or you'll be out
on your ear. And you can't go argue with Armour on
your own." And they said, "You don't mean that!"
And I said, "Don't put me to the test."

Helstein, together with Hawkins, then met with the
company's supervisory personnel. Helstein said to the local
plant superintendent:

We have every reason to believe that you people insti-
gated this and spread the word, playing on every prejudice. And I understand that there was fertile soil here,
that the union as well as the company is in this thing.
Now I want Mr. Hawkins—in my presence—to tell
you whether or not this represents Armour policy,
and what you can expect if you continue it.

Hawkins said that the partitions had to come down and emphasized to the Armour supervisors that they were not to vio-
late the conditions of the contract. Helstein told the local
union head, Pittman, to "sit" on the situation, and he
added privately to Armour's Hawkins, "Don't do anything
yet. I'll tell you when the time has come to move."
One of the items in the contract concerned paid holi-
days. To collect, an employee had to work the day *before*
and the day *after* the holiday. Helstein waited until the next

holiday—several weeks—and then called Hawkins on the day beforehand and said:

> "The walls come down tonight." And he said, "You're not giving us much notice. What's the hurry?" And I said, "The men, they have to have a self-interest in it." So, the partitions came down. And there were rumblings. But, after three days, when everybody had worked the day after the holiday, nobody had died, nobody had contracted syphilis. The heat had gone out of it.

The upshot of this affair was a change in the style of the local union in Fort Worth. As Helstein summarized,

> Throughout, black union members conducted themselves with discipline. Two months later, we had an election and the international got actively involved, putting together a black-white slate against a completely white slate. It won by a two-to-one margin. The black membership was about 40 percent. There was a heavy turnout. Of course, the union was much stronger after that.[58]

The conclusion that arises from such case histories concerns the distinctions that can be made between an integrationist policy, on the one hand, and integrationist action, on the other. In interpreting CIO racial policy in the immediate postwar era, Helstein, among other CIO progressives, made this distinction: "The CIO fulfilled its commitment to organize all people, irrespective of race, creed or color; but its concept of organization stopped with their becoming members of the union." Many CIO unions maintained separate seniority lists, black and white, and had differences in terms of participation in decision-making and union office-holding. Said Helstein: "I think it is crucial to understand the distinction that should be made, and was not made, between the CIO's constitutional commitment to organize all workers, irrespective of race, creed or color, and what discrimination means in terms of daily life. Now, we in the Packinghouse Workers Union had become sensitive to that, and were able to make that distinction. But very few other unions ever did."

Helstein added, "And as far as I know, many haven't to this day."[59]

Having specified the pivotal distinctions between pronouncements and performance, it is nevertheless necessary to add that Operation Dixie did not fail because the CIO was "not liberal enough" on racial policy. To the extent that issues of white supremacy bore on the outcome of Operation Dixie—and they bore heavily if not decisively—the racism of the larger society, including the racism imbedded in the Southern work force, seemed to blunt the racial initiatives inherent in the CIO commitment to organize a "big union" of all workers. In terms of institutional commitment on issues of racial equity, the CIO was in advance of the business community, the nation's religious and academic communities, and the white workers of the South.

Yet white supremacy was not the only barrier—nor even the only cultural barrier—to a successful outcome of Operation Dixie. The Southern heritage of poverty and paternalism also played a central role.

VI

"They Went Out to Intimidate the People"

The Mayor, the police chief, the deputy, the business-men, the president of the Chamber of Commerce—everybody was against us.[1]

They mobilized the towns against us. They con-trolled most of the churches in the towns. Even the black churches they sometimes controlled, too, with do-nations. They owned practically everything else. They controlled the educational apparatus. They controlled the police force, the deputy sheriffs and the county clerks. And they mobilized them. They did a real job, in most cases, of mobilizing them.[2]

When a textile plant or a lumber plant or any other kind of plant opened up, the local politicians told them, "You're in the South here. You don't need to worry about unions." They were just told:
"We guarantee you won't have a union." That's what the leadership of the community said.[3]

You had to be awful careful not to provide the com-pany and the local law officials with anything they could arrest you for. I've been arrested for littering. And *I* didn't throw the leaflet down! I handed it to a per-son there that was walking and *they* threw it down. But *they* weren't arrested. *I* was the one arrested for littering. And, of course, the local sheriff was always on their side.[4]

Historians have long struggled with the challenge of defining the "peculiarity" and "uniqueness" of the American South. The paternalism and patriarchy visible in the region have been almost as widely noted as its distinctive racial customs. Southern society has been seen as more highly stratified, with less class mobility, than the rest of the nation. Sharp imbalances of power are highly visible—between blacks and whites, between men and women, and, as CIO proponents were always ready to assert, between workers and employers. A wide variety of evidence supports such conclusions. Department of Labor statistics verify the markedly lower wages that have historically prevailed throughout the region. A solid array of segregation laws demonstrate the stratification of society along racial lines. Cultural stereotypes describe the distinctive character of the region: the "good old boy," the "Southern belle," the "redneck."

As hard social evidence, however, such generalizations are unsatisfying. They do not explain the failure of the CIO's Operation Dixie. In the North, for example, an "imbalance" of power between management and labor also existed prior to the sensational CIO organizing drives of the 1930s. Patriarchy, in workers' families as well as in the society as a whole, had long been a feature of life throughout the country, as had ethnic and racial tensions. And there were certainly "company towns" in the North as well. Yet the CIO's organizing campaign of the 1930s overcame these impediments. Even in the South, Operation Dixie achieved enough local successes in 1946 to give pause to any observer who might name the South's "peculiarities" as the easy explanation for labor's postwar defeat in the region. The task at hand, then, is to attempt to look beneath such generalizations and locate those things in the substance of daily life in the South that, in 1946, affected the CIO drive in significant ways and help explain its ultimate failure.

The highly visible imbalances of power at that time

should be noted as the outset. There was, for example, the matter of resources that could be expended in politics. The CIO's Political Action Committee in Texas in 1946 managed a treasury of $3,500 to contend with a war chest of $3,400,000 mobilized by the Texas Manufacturers' Association in the same year.[5] Similarly, a TWUA official in Louisiana alerted the Atlanta SOC office to the "vicious nucleus" of "bag factory and fibre factory owners" who were financing a broadly gauged anti-union campaign in the state legislature.[6]

Owners of plants threatened by CIO organizers were by no means the only source of anti-union sentiment. Bankers in Georgia distributed a pamphlet entitled, "Preventative Medicine Against Unionism" to textile workers in Columbus.[7] And in Andalusia, Alabama, 132 businessmen joined in a full-page advertisement warning "out-of-town and out-of-state organizers" of the troubles that awaited them. Local strikebreakers in a labor dispute were characterized as "loyal employees." The president of the Commercial Bank in Andalusia told a striker, "I'm going to do all in my power to see the CIO run out of Andalusia."[8]

But if the odds looked long as a result of business influence on the general public and on Southern state legislatures, there were, in every Southern legislature, at least *some* friendly faces—if only an embattled handful. However, such was not the case among local law enforcement officials and mayors in the towns and villages where the CIO attempted to organize textile workers.

In mill villages daily life had a fundamentally different shape. To assess these differences, it is necessary to note some clear distinctions between managerial prerogatives in a wholly company-owned mill village and those available to owners of small plants located in cities which supported other industries as well.

A great many small plants were not "company towns" in the all-consuming cultural sense of the classic Southern "mill village." The patterns of paternalism were thus not as securely in place. The owner of a small plant might be expected to be on friendly terms with the local political, religious, educational, and law enforcement establishment, but he would not "own" them in the exclusive manner that historically prevailed in mill villages. This is not to say that a small textile manufacturer could not count on general agreement between himself and the other sources of authority in a Southern city. But cooperation existed within broad limits— for example, the limits of legality. An anti-union campaign generated by the company could, within the circumference of certain rules, be expected to receive routine support from city officials and from religious and educational leaders who otherwise functioned as independent actors.

But in a mill village, the local mayor was not merely compliant within the constraints of his own self-respect and sense of autonomy; he was wholly subservient because he was either a dependent employee or a part of the management team itself. Similarly, the superintendent of the village schools and the police chief were, in effect, company employees, while local ministers, accustomed to company contributions as an important element of church budgets, were only slightly less dependent.[9] In practical terms, these relationships meant that mill village owners enjoyed a relatively unrestricted range of options in combating a union organizing campaign. More than "cooperation" could be anticipated. Something approaching an intimately shared agenda could be counted upon. While Southern sheriffs could be expected to "enforce the law" and in so doing liberally interpret local ordinances against "distributing leaflets" or "unlawful assembly," mill village sheriffs could go far beyond such limits. They could actively harass and imprison; they could "forcibly restrain." They could intimidate.[10] In mill towns, the will of the company blanketed the universe. "They owned the houses people lived in," as one organizer put it. "They owned the store where they bought their groceries."[11] Elaborated another: "If they wanted to put pressure, they'd go up on the rent, or they'd go up on the water."[12] In mill villages, local merchants were routinely responsive to the mill. In the words of a veteran textile organizer,

They could put so much pressure on, where that
wasn't true of the other industries. If somebody in the
mill wanted to join the union, then the first thing [the
merchants] told them was, "You're probably not
going to be able to get any more credit, because I'm worried about your job."[13]

Southern CIO organizers for industries other than textiles
agreed that special conditions existed in mill villages. A representative of the Amalgamated Clothing Workers, for example, stressed the differences in the organizing hazards faced
in the garment industry as compared with textiles. She emphasized the extent of social control in mill villages.

If you didn't have a job, you had to move out of that
house and you couldn't go to the commissary and buy
groceries. *That* would make it much more difficult to organize in that field. Most of the clothing plants that
came into town just opened up a little building, hired
people, and they didn't control your whole life.[14]

Southern workers tell of mill-owner power that reached far
beyond the limits of social control normally associated with
anti-union employers. Stories about children being taken
out of school and put into the plants were common. A CIO
organizer recalled one woman's story:

The manager of the mill—they lived in the mill village—
told her, "If your daughter don't come to work in the
mill, we're gonna make you move out of the mill village house." At eight years old!! Took her out of
school! And they had a switch up there and when
you didn't mind them, they'd whip you! At the plant,
workin' on the job! The second-hand, the foreman,
the loom-fixer or the doffer—anyone they had over
the section could whip them.[15]

Another organizer told of being summoned, at age four-
teen, to the school principal's office:

He was all smiles and said, "How're you doing,
Lloyd?" And he went on, "Lloyd, you're a big boy

now. Have you thought about goin' to work?" I said,
"No, sir." He says, "Has your mother talked to you
about it?" (You see, my father had been dead about a
year and a half, two years then.) I says, "No, sir." But
I already knew; my brothers had come along before
me, you know. So I knew what he was talking about.
He said, "Here, take this card, and carry it home and
tell your mother to sign it." That's all he told me. I
knew exactly what it meant. I carried it home at
lunch, and I carried it back that afternoon. And if I remember right, it was Wednesday. And he said,
"Now, next Monday morning you go to the plant.
And you go to the weaving shop and tell them that I
sent you; but they know you're coming." And they
did; they knew I was coming. So they put me to
work, filling batteries in the weaving shop.[16]

Such control triggered family arguments—anger alternating
with fear, a sense of being exploited alongside a sense of
needing the job. Said one woman, a survivor of a mill village who later became a textile organizer:

When I first started to join the union where I worked,
times was bad and my sister told me, "You're going
to lose your job if you join the union!" And Mom
said, "What has she lost, if she loses it? She's eating
and sleeping; she'll eat and sleep somewhere. But some-
one in the family had to work in the mill. My dad
would pick up a little job now and then; he was a car-
penter. My brother-in-law was a plasterer. And they
might get a little job now and then. I was the only
one that had a weekly paycheck coming in that house.
And how little it was![17]

For many, time had transformed this experience into rage.
According to some, mill owners wanted "large families
who could populate the mills."[18] "The company expected
'em to raise 'em some more hands."[19] Companies "instructed" workers and "encouraged them to have gar-
dens," so the workers "wouldn't realize how little they

were making."[20] Mill owners were determined to "keep people from an education."[21] "No education and the lowest paid," another escapee from a Southern mill village agreed. He added, in some bitterness, that the textile mills employed "the most ignorant people."[22]

Southern mills workers knew they were held in contempt, knew the outside world regarded them as "lintheads" and "rednecks."[23] They understood—more than did outside observers—the extent of social control in the mill village. The CIO's immediate challenge was to find ways to avoid simply being overwhelmed in mill villages.

Perhaps nothing illustrated the difficulty of this task more than the mundane, day-to-day details revealed by Lucy Randolph Mason in her reports back to the CIO's Atlanta office. An August memorandum from the mill village of Liberty, South Carolina, was typical in tone and substantive detail of the reports from the front lines where the CIO's graceful and Southern-born "ambassador" encountered the representatives of local officialdom in textile country. She found the mayor of Liberty at his gas station and auto parts store. The mayor was "very busy." Denying any violation of civil rights by police, the major said "the truth was the people there did not like the CIO and did not want a union." Mason then located the village's police chief and "talked civil rights" with him. She told him she had heard reports about his driving a car around where organizers were visiting. Although the chief denied any intent "to spy on them," he did admit knowing the "names of all who had joined the union." In Anderson, South Carolina, Mason found a police chief, "obviously much against unions," whose manner "indicated a readiness to help break strikes." The chief seemed unconcerned about violations of civil rights, telling Mason, "I don't hold with all that stuff."[24]

But if Mason's summary of power relationships in mill towns was stark, it soon became apparent that more sophisticated legal machinery in the South had also been mobilized for use against the CIO. Just as one of the first applications of the Sherman Anti-Trust Act in the 1890s had been against unions, rather than against trusts, so anti-Klan measures passed during Reconstruction were dusted off and applied to CIO organizers in Nashville and elsewhere in the South. Such actions kept the CIO's few lawyers in the South busy fighting defensive actions in courts rather than using their legal expertise more profitably to seek enforcement of NLRB guidelines.[25]

One of the many levers in the legal system that companies could exploit involved the use of law firms specializing in anti-union tactics. Such firms provided sophisticated tactical advice. The CIO's Alabama state director Carey Haigler found himself without recourse in the face of one such labor relations consultant whom he confronted in numerous situations in southern Alabama and northern Florida. Petitions for elections were systematically delayed for prolonged periods through legal maneuverings. Haigler's adversary was notorious for insisting on having an NLRB representative present at every certification hearing, "along with a whole lot of unnecessary trimmings."[26] Other key organizers in textiles confirmed the existence of concerted legal efforts to "delay the process wherever possible," in an attempt to ensure that it was "very expensive to organize, and almost impractical." Southern textile manufacturers tried to convince CIO organizers that "every legal ruse" would be employed in hopes the union "would tire and go away."[27] Long organizing campaigns that ended in victorious NLRB elections did not necessarily result in union recognition and contract negotiations, but rather in immediate company-sponsored court appeals for new NLRB elections. Meanwhile, company-worker relations remained as they were during the CIO campaign. Pro-union workers were harassed and fired, intimidating the remainder. Most CIO organizers felt the long NLRB appeals process uniformly worked to the benefit of employers so that, as one organizer put it, "by the time we won, we had no members."[28]

The CIO's only full-time lawyer in the South during the decisive months of Operation Dixie, Jerome Cooper, went to great lengths to describe his frustration in such strike cases. "We were fairly helpless," he said.

They'd picket a plant, and then the company would start advertising for scabs. And scabs started coming in and taking these people's jobs, knowing that whatever was won by the force of the strike would redound to the benefit of the non-strikers, too. Although it seemed to me immoral and wrong, I had on many occasions to tell the strikers, "You can't stop those people from going in and taking your job. The law gives them the right to take your job, as long as you're on an economic strike and not on an unfair labor practices strike." Sometimes we could prove the employer had engaged in unfair labor practices and then we could get our jobs back through the Labor Board.[29]

Anti-union legal tactics were not restricted to federal laws; local ordinances, too, could be activated to impede CIO organizing efforts. In Canton, North Carolina, organizers found themselves up against an ancient city ordinance prohibiting distributing and soliciting on city property. Similar practices surfaced throughout the Carolina piedmont.[30]

While it could be argued—and was, in internal CIO discussions among organizers—that these same tactics had been unsuccessful in thwarting the CIO's organizing drive in the 1930s, a deeper truth was that the basic social climate in the nation as a whole had changed drastically since the CIO had triumphed over General Motors in 1937. Franklin Delano Roosevelt was dead, as was the New Deal coalition's congressional majority; no New Deal governors were to be found in Georgia or Mississippi in 1946, as had been the case in Michigan in 1937. Perhaps most important of all, American business had regained its footing and, after tallying record profits during the war years, was confident and determined in its postwar moves against organized labor.[31]

How did these shifts in national climate translate regionally, in the daily life of Operation Dixie? The Southern establishment was sufficiently confident of its status in the society that its first reactions to the appearance of CIO organizers were often relatively low-key. One example involved what might be called the politics of ridicule. When the CIO attempted to establish its presence in a community, some companies positioned large empty trash barrels at the plant gates, bearing prominently displayed signs: "Put CIO Trash Here." One organizer recalled that sometimes "they'd have it on fire," so that workers could conveniently "drop the leaflets in there and let 'em burn, see."[32] This sort of psychological warfare made life difficult for organizers. But more effective than ridicule was surveillance to persuade organizers to leave town or at least to demonstrate to workers the powerlessness of the CIO staff. Organizational meetings were routinely watched and interrupted, often followed by visits to organizers' rooms and apartments. Organizers also reported attempts to "rabble-rouse you on the telephone."[33] Company supervisors also made a great display of taking down license numbers in parking lots outside union meetings. Organizers in Mississippi were kept under surveillance, while others had their telephones tapped in a number of towns in Georgia and South Carolina. "It all came down to making people afraid," said one organizer who spent most of his organizing career in eastern Tennessee.[34]

Such tactics, demonstrating the vulnerability and relative weakness of the CIO, had the intended effect of making pro-union workers think twice before lining up on what appeared to be the "losing side." In Sumter, South Carolina, the chief of police picked up a CIO organizer and "paraded him all over town in the police car." Although no charges were filed and the organizer was released soon after, the incident so heightened existing fear among the workers there that the organizer reported he was subsequently unable to make any progress at all.[35] One labor lawyer cited arrests over "the right to use pamphlets, loudspeakers, and even the right to use the streets—what Justice Douglas called the poor man's newspaper."[36] Sometimes the police arrested organizers on "John Doe warrants," wherein the official was not required to identify any particular individual beforehand and was thus free to use the warrant to arrest anyone he chose.[37]

And so it was that reports on Operation Dixie in CIO newspapers began containing accounts of bizarre arrests, quick convictions, and harsh sentences. Organizers engaged in passing out leaflets in front of plant gates were arrested for trespassing and sentenced to "terms on the chain gang." In response, CIO attorneys planned to make an appeal challenging the North Carolina law that prohibited jury service to nonowners of property "on the grounds that blacks were systematically excluded from jury service."[38] Similarly, seven striking laundry workers, picked up and charged with nuisance, assault, and resisting arrest, were sentenced "from 3 months to a year." Some were sentenced to serve their time in jail, and others on road gangs.[39]

In Parsons, Tennessee, labor's position became so tenuous that CIO lawyers asked the United States attorney general to investigate charges that a mob had driven union members out of town, that one union member had been threatened with death, and that an outdoor union meeting had been broken up when "Mayor William Long appeared at the head of a mob of 50 men and ordered the organizers to leave town." An insight into what the mayor thought about the CIO was gained when one of the organizers asked him if he was the mayor. Long replied, "Hell, yes, and if you don't believe it, just start something."[40]

Dixie organizers came to understand that even appeals to federal authorities carried a certain risk. In Mississippi, one CIO staff member went to a local FBI office to complain about local law enforcement tactics. Shortly thereafter, he was picked up and interrogated by the local police officers and told that it "wouldn't do him any good" to "run back over and cry on the FBI's shoulders. They're our friends."[41]

But there was an entirely different level of opposition that could be mobilized against the CIO. Company reaction to the appearance of Dixie organizers could be both immediate and violent. The CIO office in downtown Gadsden, Alabama, was the scene of a direct assault. Persons under the employ of a company the CIO was trying to organize broke into the office and took typewriters, desks, and chairs and threw them out the upstairs window onto the sidewalk below.[42] In addition to acts of intimidation against the CIO staff itself, roving squads threatened pro-union workers as well. A veteran organizer assigned to textiles during the Southern drive said: "If the company found that any workers were the least bit in favor of the union, visits were made to their homes. They threatened them in their homes!"[43] In Bibb City, Georgia, the CIO staff made an initial visit to the gates of a textile plant only to find "a mess of goons" waiting. "They ran us away from the gate." Though the organizers responded by increasing their numbers the next day, the initial mob action had been sufficient to undermine their efforts. The organizer conceded: "We really never made any progress."[44]

Another common maneuver involved the transfer or firing of employees engaged in union activities, especially debilitating to a CIO campaign when those individuals constituted the nucleus of the CIO's in-plant committee. One in-plant organizer, working in a dyeing and finishing plant near Linwood, North Carolina, had a job that took him to all the departments in the plant. Thus, he was able to make contact with a large number of his fellow workers, taking along membership books and signing up new union members while on his way through the plant. He was soon reassigned to a job that kept him in one place all day. It had the intended effect. He remembered workers coming up to him and saying, "'Well, you see! That's why they did that! They're gonna get me too if I mess with what you're into!'" The only response the organizer could make was pithy, but something less than persuasive: "I'd say, 'Well, that's alright. We'll eat crow for a while, but we're gonna be eating chicken one of these days!' "[45] An organizer reduced to such retorts had clearly lost in his contest with the company for credibility in the eyes of the workers.

The almost unrelenting abuse that descended upon CIO organizers throughout 1946 is recorded in legal depositions, staff appeals to the U.S. attorney general, Justice Department briefs filed in federal courts, and, rather vividly, in the oral testimony of participants in Operation Dixie. The ritual humiliation enshrouded in such evidence had an understandable effect on organizer morale. This circumstance helps account for another kind of evidence that is also properly a part of the history of the campaign. This evidence constitutes part of what might be called the "oral tradition" of Operation Dixie. It conveys the near heroic determination of certain legendary CIO organizers. That the tradition persists—forty years after Operation Dixie—has its own historical meaning insofar as it verifies the intensity of the struggle that took place in 1946. One such legend surrounds the activities of J. P. Mooney in Alabama.

Mooney was an organizer for the Mine, Mill and Smelter Workers Union, an institution with a long radical heritage dating back to the days of IWW militance in the West. Mooney seems to have been a rather appropriate representative of this tradition, for his encounter with textile company police in Avondale, Alabama, had an apocalyptic flair out of which legends are, indeed, made. As the tradition goes, on Mooney's "first day" at the plant,

The company cops beat him up in front of the workers. He came back the next day all bruised, beat up, black eyes, distributing his leaflets. This time they not only beat him, they stomped him almost to death. They kicked his viscera loose from his spine. He was in the hospital for six weeks. While he was in the hospital, the head of the company police came to see him and said, "J. P. Mooney, you are a very brave man. But look, if you come back again with your leaflets, we're going to kill you. Now, we're giving you notice: you're dead if you come back." The day after he got out of the hospital, by himself he was back at the plant gate with his leaflets. And the next day, he signed every bloody worker in that plant. And two weeks later he had negotiated a contract. And, he put a black man on the board of that textile union, because Mooney had come out of that Mine, Mill and Smelter Workers [tradition]. You see, he had guts.[46]

The story possessed the essential ingredients of myth. Beyond the fact that the story was essentially true was the fact that it addressed a general truth: to be successful in Operation Dixie, organizers had to find ways to overcome workers' fear.

It was in this realm—the anxiety of Southern workers that had been nurtured by generations of poverty and defeat on the land—that the ultimate contest between the CIO and Southern management was waged. And it was in this realm that elements of the Southern past could effectively be harnessed to defeat the prospect of a unionized present. To overcome fear, workers had to gain from their association with the CIO *some* sense of security. Anything that made the CIO appear weak undermined this possibility. Harassment by local sheriffs or company police, organized beatings, varied tactics of public ridicule—all served to emphasize the CIO's relative powerlessness. It thus heightened rank-and-file apprehensions that there was no real prospect for any kind of relationship with the company other than the one they had always known.

Another method of undermining the CIO's cultural credibility involved efforts to portray organizers as aliens in the region. The importance of this tactic was evidenced by the amount of time and resources invested by Southern management in painting the CIO as a conspiracy of "outsiders." Perhaps no participants in Operation Dixie were more aware of the impact of this anti-union tactic than Southern-born members of the CIO's organizing team. Among potential management weapons, the "outsider" label was, Mississippi organizers felt, "the biggest thing they had."[47] It was "played to the hilt" in Alabama.[48] And it was used "constantly" in the Carolinas.[49] Mill owners made much of the "foreign" names of CIO leaders—Baldanzi and Bittner in Atlanta, and Rieve of the Textile Workers. In Mississippi, a photograph of Jacob Potofsky, president of the Amalgamated Clothing Workers, was tacked on a bulletin board inside

the plant and illuminated with a floodlight. Next to it was a
sign: "Does this man look like he's interested in your welfare?" Though an organizer characterized the tactic as "pa-
thetic," the more relevant fact was that the plant remained
unorganized.[50]

More provocative tactics could also serve as effective
means of winning the cultural battle over the CIO's legiti-
macy. Few company maneuvers could be as shocking and
as effective as a sudden lockout or its extension—outright firing of the work force. In Jasper, Alabama, an effective CIO organizing drive in a small company had signed up a
majority of the thirty employees. The company promptly
fired all the active CIO supporters. As a result the workers
struck on August 30, 1946, and the strike continued until September 6, when the company shut the plant down and
ceased operations entirely. The CIO filed charges with the
NLRB, both on the discharge of particular individuals and
on the lockout, but the union was still awaiting a hearing
as Operation Dixie ground slowly to a halt at the end of
the year. As organizers themselves saw it, the message
sent to all Alabama workers in the vicinity was that the
CIO was helpless against corporate power.[51] Such events became so commonplace that organizers learned to anticipate
them. "I don't believe we should go on with the election at
present. If Korn [Company] should have a lockout it would
be just that much more Hell on our hands. It is bad
enough with Sumter Casket Company."[52] Attempts to organize furniture plants around Sumter, South Carolina, met
with similar opposition that proved so effective that the internal correspondence of the CIO was filled with complaints.
The tone of this correspondence revealed clearly enough
the extent to which CIO leadership had to fight against a
sense of helplessness. One despairing CIO staff director summarized the situation in one embattled textile town in his
state: "They have discharged several of our leading people;
they have closed up one mill and undoubtedly will close another mill if I file a petition. There have been threats of violence and Earp finds it extremely difficult to carry on any
normal work."[53] Such events led the South Carolina state di-

rector to a conclusion in July that many other CIO people would reach before the end of 1946: "I think [organizers'] efforts will be better spent in other situations until the excitement and hysteria die down in Sumter."[54]

During a campaign at the large Milliken Mills in South Carolina, company management found the threat of a complete shutdown to be their ultimate weapon, one that went beyond identifying and firing individual workers to a strategy that threatened the entire labor force. During the course of the CIO's campaign, the plant's owner, Roger Milliken, arrived at the plant to deliver a speech to the employees, with the local press in attendance. Later, the press reported that Milliken had advised his employees: "If you people want your job you'd better not vote for a union, because I've already closed two plants down where they voted the union in. And they were not put back to work."[55]

Sometimes, selected heavy layoffs could send the same signal as would a threat to fire the entire work force. The United Packinghouse Workers lost an election in Kansas City, where "there was a very small vote due to the tremendous lay-offs."[56] In Black Mountain, North Carolina, the Grove Stone and Sand Company laid off the entire second shift, and also fired a truck driver on its first shift who had been active in the organizing campaign.[57]

In such a climate of hostility, it is understandable that the oral tradition surrounding Operation Dixie goes beyond the J. P. Mooney legend and similar stores of individual courage to include literally scores of stories of unexpected confrontations with mobs organized by management. In Florence, South Carolina, an organizer opened his door one Friday night to find a mob of over twenty "second-hands and bosses," who informed him that if he was not out of town by Saturday night, he would be "'tarred and feathered and taken back to Georgia."[58] In Brucetin, Tennessee, two women organizers who were renting a room from a Methodist minister and his wife awoke one morning to a mob of 150 men approaching, one of whom yelled to the minister, "You better git them women outta there!" So confident of the outcome were the mob leaders that they had

called some newspapermen from Memphis the night before
to alert them to a story of CIO organizers being run out of
town. The newspapermen duly arrived and asked the organizers if they intended to leave, to which one replied, "No,
we don't run." One of the newspapermen persisted, however, and asked the women for a picture of them with their
suitcases. The CIO organizers declined to cooperate in this
bit of anti-union journalism and the newspapermen remained until they were later able to get a photograph of
the two women coming out of a restaurant where they had
just eaten breakfast. The photo duly appeared in the next
edition.[59]

Aside from scores of incidents that like these two, ended
peacefully, the labor press reported that some seventeen organizers and union members had been severely assaulted
in the South during the first five months of Operation
Dixie, including at least one case in which a law enforcement officer had been directly responsible for the assault.[60]
When not involved directly in assaults, police often looked
the other way when mobs harassed organizers or drove
them out of town.[61] Bittner expressed labor's outrage at
such treatment: "One of the worst things about this situation is that the law enforcement officers in some towns are
working in close collusion with employers or have become
suddenly blind to the beating of organizers and union members."[62] A labor attorney summarized: "We had towns
where organizers were beaten up, primarily by the textile
companies or by the local police at the insistence of the textile companies. We couldn't get any help from the police."[63]

It is not surprising, then, that many of the organizers'
early meetings turned into strategy sessions that revolved
around what kind of trouble to anticipate and what to do
in certain situations. Here was a stark test of the CIO's internal cohesiveness, the caliber of its organizers, and the
range of their inventiveness. Organizers discussed ways in
which they should attempt to protect themselves—both
physically and also from "the mental things that happened."[64] The importance of "the mental things" cannot be
underestimated; a certain level of morale had to be main-

tained in order for organizers to keep going in the presence of intense and often brutal opposition. This was not easily done. A Tennessee organizer summarized the dynamics with remarkable understatement: "Employers limit your appeal, once they know you're coming."[65] However described, whether with understatement or anger, the product of effective employer opposition was to stir an aura of resignation among organizers.

"Paternalism," then, was a word that described an entire range of elaborate and specific methods of social control, from artful conciliation to unrelenting pressure. The degrees of pressure, in turn, ranged from threats of dismissal to mob violence. Whatever its sundry guises, Southern paternalism was grounded in the employer's ready access to the formal instruments of social authority—the courts, the police, the state legislatures, the churches, and the media. Southern industrialists possessed such access. The CIO did not. In this sense, Southern paternalism was as much a product of past struggles as it was an instrument of winning the particular struggle of 1946.

The CIO was forced to accept a contest on grossly unequal grounds. It never found a way to redress the balance.

VII
Southern Religion

The cultural reach of Southern industry, grounded in economic power and extending to judicial and political influence, embraced matters of religion as well. The cause and effect of cultural and economic influences were sufficiently intertwined as to make for a kind of social integration that was deeply rooted in the historical experience of Southern people. But the extent of this integration is not easily specified. Generations of agricultural life, originally structured upon and subsequently sustained through segregation, produced social circumstances that easily distinguished the region from the rest of the nation.[1] Widespread poverty contributed to a thin material infrastructure, including, for example, a minimal network of roads that in turn heightened the isolation of rural life. In such a setting, the crossroads chapels of the South served many functions beyond matters of faith, including their existence as an essential component of social life. Southern churches were the week-in, week-out magnet of social interaction. The preacher was expected to be entertaining, and when he was not, his constituents tended to look elsewhere.

In stirring the emotions and in generating guilt, the role of the South's fire and brimstone ministers created a social specimen that has been subjected to much scholarly examination.[2] But while such mutations of conventional religion clearly deserve the attention they have received, it is equally important to note the central role of the Southern church as an ongoing social institution.

A Southern minister, musing about the reasons his largely working-class parishioners attended church, concluded there were four: "because they have been hurt and need comforting; because they are lonely and need company; because they are often reminded in their work that they are relatively low on the social totem pole, and they want to enjoy a different status somewhere; and because almost anyone can participate in the control of the church."[3]

Faced with such motivations on the part of a congregation, the Southern minister who attempted to focus upon serious analyses of the Bible—and especially those ministers so determined to systematize the educational functions of Christianity that they organized "Bible study" classes— soon encountered strong resistance among the working poor. As one Southern minister summarized his parishioners' negative response to classes on the Bible, they "simply did not come to church to go to school again."[4]

The ambiguity surrounding the churchgoing impulses of Southerners suggests that a certain degree of caution must accompany any characterization of the precise impact of religion on Operation Dixie. But however qualified the conclusion, there can be no doubt that there was some influence.[5] Indeed, the heritage of Southern religion intruded time and again upon the organizing efforts of the CIO. The thrust of much anti-union propaganda emanating from religious sources can be summarized in a single phrase: belonging to a labor union was an un-Christian thing to do. As a mill village preacher in South Carolina phrased the options posed by Operation Dixie: "It's either Christ or the CIO."[6]

Motive is, of course, very difficult for the historian to assess. Many ministers opposed the CIO as a logical extension of their own world view.[7] But sometimes they were moved by more practical reasons. Ministers trying to raise funds for building campaigns occasionally injected local labor disputes into their sermons in ways calculated to win the admiration and, perhaps, the gratitude of local industrialists. For example, on the eve of a textile election in Georgia, a minister in the mill village of Clarksdale took time out from his fund-raising campaign to go on the radio with a unique blend of religious and secular messages. As later characterized before a Senate committee, the minister "quoted liberally from the Bible, thus inducing a religious attitude among his listeners" and then swung into a "vicious attack" on CIO leaders whom he characterized as "intruders," "Communists," "a bunch of humbugs," and "parasites living off the common laboring people." Said the minister in his prepared radio address: "I am against it because it isn't Bible. Luke 3:14 says be content with your wages."[8]

However, the level of invective emanating from individual ministers was modest compared with the virulent anti-union "Christian" message of *Militant Truth*. Author John Roy Carleson characterized this remarkable "newspaper" as "a combination of . . . Bible-belt fundamentalist, Flag-waving, and Red-and-labor-baiting" that made it "an irresistible potion for impressionable southerners."[9]

Militant Truth featured a masthead with illustrations of the Holy Bible superimposed on a cross and an adjoining American flag. The editor of the newspaper, Sherman Patterson, stalked the Southern countryside in search of labor disputes into which he might intervene, although he assured one inquiring reporter that his purpose was "not to fight unions"; rather, he said, *Militant Truth* was to "promote fundamental Christianity and constitutional Americanism."[10] *Militant Truth* added to its monthly attack on unions with an undated "Special Labor Edition," first put out in 1945 and distributed throughout the course of Operation Dixie.[11] Such editions would "appear mysteriously" in workers' mailboxes right before an NLRB election. Although the paper listed a price of thirty-five cents for an annual subscription, the paper came to most recipients free, "compliments of a friend."[12] To one reporter who posed as a Southern manufacturer, Patterson said that he had a circulation of 45,000. He added that he could not make a profit at less than the 50,000 level, but that he had been receiving adequate contributions from various businessmen in the meantime to take

care of the deficit.[13] In addition, Patterson had plans to
produce at least 100,000 copies of another "Special Labor
Edition" early in 1946.[14]

Militant Truth's ultimate weapon went beyond the por-
trayal of unionism as an un-Christian activity. Helpful as
this was, it did not quite have the shock power of one
other available weapon: the Red issue. It appeared in stark relief in Patterson's "Special Labor Edition." In articles such
as the one entitled "CIO Communists Agitate Racial
Strife," traditional attitudes about race were mobilized to
present the CIO as a deceptive and alien force driven by un-
Southern motives: "Absolute social and racial equality is
one of the major points in the Communist program in
America . . . to organize the Negro labor in the South."
The inevitable result of CIO activity would be "discontent,
unrest, discord resulting in strikes, class-hatred, and terror-
ism in many of our southern industries." CIO organizers
were not people; they were the "master-minds of the red,
revolutionary program" and Operation Dixie was "the best
weapon yet devised for the purpose of deliberately agitat-
ing race against race and class against class."[15] As presented by the editors of *Militant Truth*, the CIO was not, in
fact, seeking to organize unions. That was a "guise." Its primary objective was "to arouse class-hatred and race-hatred
for the purpose of creating strikes, riots, bloodshed, anarchy and revolution."[16]

In a Southern mill village, hostile ministers or an inflam-
matory anti-union newspaper could have a pronounced negative impact. Yet even well-documented evidence from
selected villages and rural areas cannot provide more than
an impressionistic sense of the role the Southern ministry
played in labor's defeat there. The timing of the CIO's response to religious opposition merits a careful review, however. At the outset of Operation Dixie, potential ministerial
opposition was not seen by the CIO leadership as a high priority challenge. The Atlanta office, logically enough, focused its attention most persistently on employer tactics.
But as the summer wore on, and especially after the succes-

sion of textile defeats in August, the attention of CIO leadership was increasingly directed to the anti-union activities of organized religion. This emphasis first appeared in the early summer in CIO staff reports in which local organizers, attempting to account for unanticipated defeats, cited the opposition of local preachers. There was a self-serving quality to such finger-pointing, of course: it directed attention away from possible failures by the organizers themselves. Nevertheless, grass roots interpretations can be accurate as well as self-serving, so the validity of conclusions reached by organizers cannot be faulted on these grounds alone. What appears to be especially significant is the timing of these interpretations and what that timing revealed about the advance preparation made for Operation Dixie by the CIO's top leadership.

Labor's institutional response to the appearance of *Militant Truth* and to the activities of local ministers in scores of communities across the South took the form of a public relations drive, using the services of a prominent Southern reformer, Lucy Randolph Mason. She was aided in her effort by two other CIO staffers, Ruth Gettinger and John Ramsay. The three were designated "Community Relations Representatives." The efforts of Mason, Gettinger, and Ramsay, loosely coordinated by Bittner out of Atlanta, also fed into an overall public relations effort controlled by Allan Swim, the CIO's national public relations director.[17] Mason was employed by the CIO even before Operation Dixie, as a kind of roving ambassador-at-large. During the Southern drive, she went into Southern towns and cities and contacted ministers, editors, law enforcement officials, and local political leaders. Where possible, she visited these dignitaries prior to the arrival of CIO organizers in those cities.[18] Mason's reports to the Atlanta office and to various state directors, notably those in textile states, offer instructive insights into the patterns of local opposition throughout textile country.

But perhaps more relevant than the substance of her reports was their timing—from early autumn through the winter of 1946. The employment of Mason and her colleagues

Gettinger and Ramsay was a reactive stratagem, one that was enlisted on an ad hoc basis after much of the damage had already been done to the CIO's drive in textiles. All the major drives were well underway before Mason was able to make a local appearance. The decision to expend limited CIO funds in such an effort appears as a direct response to organizers' field reports specifying anti-union activity by religious publications and individual ministers. Both events—the specifying of religious opposition and the launching of a "P.R. campaign" in response to such opposition—came well after the CIO drive in textiles had begun to enter a crisis stage.

Mason's projected role in Operation Dixie was outlined for her by SOC director Bittner at the beginning of September. As late as the first week in September, she was relaying this projected role to subsidiary state directors. "Mr. Bittner says he wants me to go into a number of communities ahead of organizing," she wrote to North Carolina state director Smith on September 6th. By that date, of course, Smith was reeling from a succession of defeats in textile elections.[19]

Mason made what might be described as a "discovery" trip through South Carolina late in August, sounding out the general attitudes of local political, educational, religious, and law enforcement officials. Her reports from a half dozen mill villages and from larger towns impressed the CIO's South Carolina state director, Franz Daniel, and led to the larger role outlined for her by the Atlanta office in September. Informed by her experiences in South Carolina, Mason moved into the heart of the textile industry in North Carolina in September. Together with Ramsay, Mason provided publicity director Swim with materials including favorable quotes from an occasional prolabor clergyman. Ramsay suggested that an organization of ministers and labor leaders be established as a "Religion and Labor Fellowship," a model he had created in other parts of the country. It was an idea, thought Ramsay, "out of which could develop moral stamina for a collective effort."[20]

While such decent but vaguely focused plans were being

suggested, the CIO was daily being assaulted by well-financed and well-coordinated attacks from a phalanx of fundamentalist editors and ministers. The contest was hardly a balanced one.

Nevertheless, the largely extemporaneous efforts of Mason, Ramsay, and Gettinger yielded a measure of tangible results. Wherever they appeared, their presence heightened the morale of organizing staffs in the South. The South Carolina state director wrote to Mason that "the boys in Greenville" had been "very much encouraged" as a result of her work. "Their morale was at a pretty low end due to the furious nature of the attack" they had been undergoing.[21]

And Ramsay, too, stirred admiration. "I don't know how he covered so much territory," said one organizer. "He was always trying to find a, a minister in an area that would stand up for the union. Just one. Just enough to give the workers a reason to say, 'Unions can't be bad, because this preacher's for 'em.' That's what Ramsay tried to do."[22]

However, the CIO's triumvirate of community relations representatives can best be understood as ill-provisioned infiltrators, judiciously picking their way through hostile territory in quest of friendly faces. Back in Atlanta, Swim searched for a more substantive plan of attack. He confided to Ramsay that he was "working out a scheme" by which he hoped "to combat the bad effects of *The Militant Truth*, *The Trumpet* and other vicious anti-labor newspapers which charge that the CIO is un-Christian and communistic."[23] He foresaw a committee "composed entirely of persons who are not connected with the CIO to help combat these publications." Emphasis would be placed on the idea "that Southern laboring people are good, solid, religious citizens imbued with no strange 'isms.' " The committee would alert the public to the fact that the strident religious publications were "interfering with cooperation and understanding between management and labor because they are playing on religious and racial prejudice." He needed Ramsay's help in getting past "square one," however, in that his "contact with such ministers in the South" was so limited that he did "not know where to begin."[24] Unfortunately, by mid-summer, 1946, time no longer remained for the CIO to perform such preliminary organizing tasks. The litany of textile defeats was only weeks away.

What emerges, then, in the realm of tactics is a pattern of organized anti-labor propaganda subsidized by businessmen and emanating from religious sources, and a belated, almost hip-pocket counter-campaign pieced together by the Atlanta office of the CIO. While the details of many of these skirmishes can be traced readily enough through available historical sources, the skirmishes themselves took place within a larger context that is by no means easy to describe precisely. There seems no question that Southern society projected a religious aura more demonstrably than other regions of the nation. But the extent to which the people of the South possessed a genuine "religious sensibility" is a question that has been subjected to much debate among clergymen and historians. And the extent to which religious beliefs worked to undermine the CIO campaign has also been a matter of debate, not least among CIO organizers who were in the field at the time. Where the union prevailed, or lost purely as a result of company tactics other than the use of religion, CIO organizers tended to minimize the adverse impact of church-centered, anti-union propaganda. But in the many locales where company officials made use of *Militant Truth* or mobilized the local ministerial association, CIO organizers tended to emphasize the destructive impact of Southern "religiosity."[25]

A contemporary journalistic view of the anti-labor activities of Southern religious groups was provided by Stetson Kennedy, who published his findings in a book-length study entitled *Southern Exposure*. Kennedy tracked the work of an organization known as the "Christian-American Association," which focused much of its attention upon generating anti-union legislation in Southern states. According to its secretary-treasurer, Vance Muse, the association's "anti-violence bill would implement the power of our peace officers to quell disturbances and keep the color line drawn in

our social affairs." According to the *Houston Post*, Muse announced that he had uncovered the existence across the
South of "Eleanor Clubs," which he described as a "RED
RADICAL scheme to organize negro maids, cooks, and
nurses in order to have a Community informer in every
Southern home." Mrs. Muse, chief clerk of the association,
further confided—as reported by Victor Bernstein in the *Antioch Review*—"that she was worried about the 'Eleanor
Clubs' because they stood for '$15 a week salary for all nig-
ger house help, Sundays off, no washing, and no cleaning
upstairs.' " Letting herself go still further, she said: "Christian Americans can't afford to be anti-Semitic, but we know
where we stand on the Jews, all right. It doesn't pay us to
work with Winrod, Smith, Coughlin, and those others up
North; they're too outspoken and would get us into trouble."[26]

Christian American fought against women's suffrage,
against the child-labor amendment, helped collect $250,000
from the railroads for the cause of striking down the eight-
hour-day bill, fought for a 25 percent limit on federal inheritance and income taxes, and "for 'Americanization of the
Supreme Court' (Austrian-born Frankfurter's decisions in
labor cases having been distasteful to employers)."[27]

The postwar proliferation of organizations like Christian
American across the South demonstrated the enormous
range of the anti-union activities that confronted CIO strate-
gists. But Christian American was not as widespread, nor
its blows as telling, as the carefully aimed editions of *Militant Truth*, sent more often to textile workers than to any others. "In Georgia alone, mass distribution of *Militant Truth*
was made to workers at the following mills: Exposition Cotton Mills, Piedmont Cotton Mill, Gate City Cotton Mills,
Rushton Cotton Mill, Thomaston Cotton Mill, Lowell
Bleachery, Inc., Crompton-Highland Mill, Dundee Mills,
Athens Manufacturing Company, A. D. Julliard, Anchor
Duck Mill, Mandeville Mills, Carolina Mills, Dallas Mill,
and Douglas Mill."[28]

The sudden appearance of violently anti-union material
in people's mailboxes generated a variety of responses.

Often, the response was chilling. As a textile organizer recalled:

> When these people would get them, they had never seen them before. "Why am I getting this, all of a sudden?" Well, the people you had persuaded, that believed in the union or were convinced, or were union sympathizers, you could explain to *them* what it was. But for many others, I think it put that doubt [there]. Sometimes a person will be for you, and not move because there's a nagging doubt in the back of their mind that maybe they're wrong. I think there's people who believe they're going to vote for the union until they get in the booth. Then they think, "Am I making the right choice?" I really believe that. The *Militant Truth* wouldn't be as effective now, but I would say it was effective then, to the extent it gives them ammunition to hide behind, people who were afraid.[29]

The speed with which *Militant Truth* seemed to shadow the CIO organizing staff was impressive. "If we started organizing a plant today, well, within two weeks the people were getting *Militant Truth* in their homes."[30] Even the organizers sometimes got a copy. "Every motel I'd check into, somebody would send me a copy," reported James Jackson from Mississippi. "I got it for years! I could be at a place a couple of weeks and the thing would start showing up."[31] As another Mississippi organizer recalled it, the paper "showed up where we showed up."[32]

Yet the impact of *Militant Truth*, like that of the work of Christian American, could not be described as pervasive. Not all employers felt that such primitive roundhouse blows as those favored by *Militant Truth* and Christian American were the most effective means of fighting Operation Dixie. A Tennessee textile executive, noting *Militant Truth*'s characterization of Sidney Hillman of the Amalgamated Clothing and Textile Workers of America (ACWA) as "an alien-born communist," informed the paper's editors that "we are fighting the Amalgamated [Clothing Workers] and

fighting Hillman as strenuously as we can, but we don't
care to use poisoned weapons."[33]

It is important to specify, then, that as widespread as the
use of *Militant Truth* was, many companies selected other
means, including other uses of religious representatives, to
combat the CIO campaign. *Militant Truth* represented the
most visible evidence of a coordinated regional effort that distributed centrally produced propaganda material to scores
of local communities. But at least as often, Southern employers mobilized only local ministerial allies.

CIO organizers dispatched to every section of the South
testified to the varieties of local employer-ministerial cooperation. What impressed many CIO organizers—so starkly that
they remember rich details forty years later—was the in-
stant notoriety they found they had acquired by the mere
act of arriving in a mill village and identifying themselves
as members of the CIO.

> The company would not only make radio announce-
> ments, they'd get a preacher on Sunday: "We have a
> labor organizer in town who is nothing but an agitator
> and will tell nothing but lies to get you to join and
> sign a union card and have an election!" The com-
> pany would put it out in leaflets! And then the
> preacher would take that leaflet and read it at the pul-
> pit![34]

Among the targeted giants of the textile industry, anti-
CIO campaigns by local ministers were sometimes augmented by the sudden appearance in town of traveling
tent-show revivalists. When, against heavy opposition, the
CIO organizing staff at the huge Avondale Mills chain in Alabama began to make some progress in the summer in 1946,
there abruptly appeared "long-haired preachers" who "set
up tents" and began to "preach about God and the Sav-
ior." "But," remembered an Avondale organizer, "the first
thing you know, they were preaching that the union is the
'mark of the beast.' "[35]

Though opinion was not unanimous, organizers were in
general agreement that fundamentalist preachers were most

responsive to offers of various sorts from mill owners. But among the giants of the textile industry, as distinct from the small mills, ministerial support for mill owners seemed broader. "The management made sure in most Southern cities, especially textile towns like Kannapolis, that they went all the way from the Fundamentalists up through the Baptists, Methodists and Presbyterians."[36]

The linkage of mill-owner money and ministerial cooperation is one conjectural feature of the politics surrounding Operation Dixie that seems beyond precise documentation. There can be no doubt that CIO organizers—and friendly outside associates such as Lucy Randolph Mason—*believed* that financial considerations were a key component of ministerial opposition to the CIO. But since prudence dictated that payments, if any, be made in cash, and subsequent acknowledgment of such disbursements clearly constituted injudicious politics on the part of mill owners as well as ministers, verifying historical evidence is all but impossible to discover, beyond the fact that mill owners routinely contributed to Southern churches.

Occasionally, an isolated incident verified direct "gifts" of a kind that seemed to go beyond the boundaries of routine contributions. One young female textile worker sheepishly confided to a CIO organizer her "bad manners" when confronted with evidence of employer largesse to the local minister. The minister appeared in a country store proudly showing off the new suit he had received from the mill owner. The young worker responded, "You know, if I didn't work so cheap, he couldn't afford to give them suits away. I feel like I helped give you that suit." The young woman added, in terms that dramatized the mixture of assertion and deference that made up Southern working-class life, "I just couldn't help but say it."[37]

But such evidence, however vivid, must be used cautiously in attempting an overall assessment of the impact of organized religion on Operation Dixie. What is clear is the overwhelming nature of public ministerial opposition to the CIO as compared with public ministerial support. The latter was so rare that when it did occur, CIO personnel were ecstatic. A long-time organizer in textiles attributed his success in organizing a plant outside Hickory, North Carolina, to the presence of "a liberal preacher there." "We got him, and that did it. That's an organizer's dream, but it doesn't happen very often."[38] Another organizer referred to a minister of "one of the more affluent Presbyterian churches," a man who had come from Canada and was "very pro-labor." Unfortunately, his usefulness was limited, because "he probably didn't have a single worker, a blue-collar person, as a member of his church."[39] In a similar manner, Lucy Mason encountered in the editor of a Baptist newspaper in Greenville, South Carolina a "liberal old gentleman" with whom she had had a "good talk." Unfortunately, the old gentleman was intimidated: "He can't tackle these mill village men," she said.[40]

What comes to the surface, through such bits and pieces of scattered written and oral evidence, is a central fact about the political and social climate that surrounded Operation Dixie: The CIO was being quietly and profoundly overwhelmed by the totality of the cultural opposition it encountered during Operation Dixie. In one sense, this conclusion is ultimately verified by the halting, well-intentioned, but hopelessly inadequate efforts by the CIO itself to establish the basics of a labor-religious coalition.

The national, regional, and local efforts of the CIO in the South illustrate this fact quite clearly. At first glance, the CIO seemed to have some imposing religious allies on whom to draw. The CIO enjoyed the support, for example, of the Federated Council of the Churches of Christ in America, which had created an Industrial Relations Division under the chairmanship of Yale sociologist Liston Pope and church leaders James Meyers and Cameron Hall. The CIO could also count on Willard Uphaus, executive director of the National Religion and Labor Foundation, which in turn had ties within Southern Baptist churches through a Southern affiliate, the Fellowship of Southern Churchmen. The latter published a well-informed and authoritative journal,

Economic Justice, under the committed editorship of Nelle Morton.

The CIO could also count on individual Southern ministers previously recruited by Mason, Ramsay, and Gettinger during the organizing months of 1946. Logistical support, after a fashion, existed in the form of pamphlets generated by Allan Swim in the CIO's Atlanta office. Such materials as "The CIO and the Churches," "The Church and the Labor Unions," and "The Church's Answer to Labor's Critics" could be supplied from Atlanta to all cooperating ministers and CIO organizers for local distribution across the South.

Beyond this, different internationals tried varying strategies to cope with the problem. The Packinghouse Workers, for example, tried to harness the language of the Bible and used a UPWA staff newsletter to provide appropriate biblical quotations to organizers for ammunition throughout the region.[41] Similarly, Operation Dixie's assistant public relations director in Atlanta, E. Paul Harding, notified all state directors that the CIO had been opposed in many areas by the Holiness Church, but without approval from those in charge of the denomination. He suggested that staff members circulate a notice to that effect, adding that "The Pentecostal Holiness book of Discipline says that a paragraph against joining oathbound secret societies, is not intended to prevent Holiness members from joining labor unions."[42] The CIO also published a full-color, full-length comic book entitled "The Bible and the Working Man," which began: "The Truth about workers and their struggles to better their lives by group action is an old story."[43]

At the tenth annual convention of the Texas State Industrial Union Council, Operation Dixie's director in that state gave those in attendance some very clear examples of "new ways to talk."

We are going to win. And we don't say in our program that we are going to win because God is on our

side—we know we are going to win because we are
on God's side. CIO to me is the practical application
of Christian principles. This program . . . is as Christian as anything that has ever been offered to the American people. That is practical Christianity.[44]

Some sections of the CIO went so far as to try to alter
those elements of an aggressively male working-class culture that—experience in Operation Dixie had begun to
suggest—might be counterproductive. Textile organizers
were admonished to drink soft drinks rather than beer, and
to consider wearing ties when approaching workers. Some
organizers were told to give up "cussing" and others were
advised to open union meetings with prayers.[45]

However, such tactical suggestions as to how to alter cultural habits were not as strong as the culture itself. One organizer, fully in sympathy with these new tactics, said, "I
tried to get the real religious people to be my in-plant leaders." He then added, in a tone of deprecation that cast a
shadow over the depth to which CIO organizers took such
suggestions to heart: "Get them sob sisters first. Then it's
OK."[46]

Similarly, it was easier for organizers to consider, and in-
tellectually accept, the utility of "not cussing" than it was
to erase a lifetime habit. And previous beliefs about "accepta-
ble" male behavior could not be easily put into cold stor-
age, even temporarily. Though the Packinghouse Union
could generate an internal staff newsletter offering useful biblical quotations, the union's radical and somewhat secular
leadership felt it necessary to spell out to the newsletter's recipients that "some areas may respond well to Biblical quotations."[47] Such remarks probably reveal more about the
psychological distance between the union and Southern culture than they do about trade unionists' flexibility. In such
ways, the very "progressiveness" of the CIO sometimes
proved unhelpful.

But there were even more ominous signs pointing to the
ineffectiveness of labor's reactive campaign against organ-

ized Southern religious opposition. The Northern affiliates of religious groups that cooperated actively with the CIO had observable goodwill, but they also had very few Southern connections. The bulletin of the National Religion and Labor Foundation, *Economic Justice* was, under Nelle Morton's leadership, well informed and quite relevant to the Southern scene. But it also was easily dismissable in a cultural sense. "Progressives" in the South read *Economic Justice*; mayors and police chiefs did not.

In this sense, much of labor's religious effort traveled a rather small and circular path—from the committed few to the committed few. Labor leaders quoted friendly ministers and vice versa; a kind of "inter-quote" developed that left out most Southern leaders.

A striking earnestness nevertheless characterized the ethical, church-oriented literature generated by the CIO. Among the biblical quotations the CIO thought appropriate was Ecclesiastes 4:9–10: "Two are better than one because they have good reward for their labor. For if they fall, the one will lift up his fellow: But woe to him that is alone." The Packinghouse Workers also suggested Job 31:13–14 as "one for the boss." "If I did despise the cause of my servants when they contended with me, what then shall I do when God riseth up?"[48]

Yet at the level of individual decision making by workers— at the level where the CIO succeeded or failed in NLRB elections—labor's counter-campaign had a distant, almost abstract quality that utterly failed to translate into organizational breakthroughs during local organizing campaigns.

While the CIO attempted to use the Bible in a different way and to suggest "woe to him that is alone," labor's corporate opponents were harnessing other biblical quotations to reinforce themes about communism and race mixing. By the summer of 1946, a political affinity had been reached between corporations on the one hand, and law enforcement officers and state and local officials on the other; the corporate use of the Bible could be far more effectively distributed throughout Southern society than anything that could reasonably be expected from the small platoon of "Community Relations Representatives" led by Lucy Randolph Mason.

In this sense, it was not so much the Bible itself as the uses to which the Bible could be put by a well-financed coalition of business and religious leaders that caused the CIO so much difficulty.

Corporate power, not Southern religion by itself, defeated the CIO during Operation Dixie. But the ability of corporations to exploit the complex heritage of Southern religion was one of the ingredients of their successful war against the CIO.

This unsigned postcard with its threatening anti-union message was mailed in Winston-Salem, N.C., to organizer Ed McCrea on March 4, 1948. (Photo by David Haberstich. Courtesy of Ed and Bea McCrea.)

An undated photo of the employees of the Carolina Wood Turning Company in Bryson City, N.C. They are celebrating the results of an NLRB election just held there, which saw the CIO win over the AFL by 81 votes to 1. (George Meany Memorial Archives.)

An office of the Textile Workers Union of America (TWUA), probably in Tennessee. (Photo by Paul Christopher. AFL-CIO Region VIII Collection, SLA.)

The Southern Organizing Committee's sound truck used during Operation Dixie. (CIO Publicity Department, North Carolina Papers, ODA.)

Members of the United Packinghouse Workers of America on strike at the Jones-Chambliss packing plant in Jacksonville, Fla., on March 25, 1949. While the company had been paying workers a minimum hourly wage of 40 cents, strikebreakers were paid a minimum wage of 65 cents. (United Packinghouse Workers Collection, SLA.)

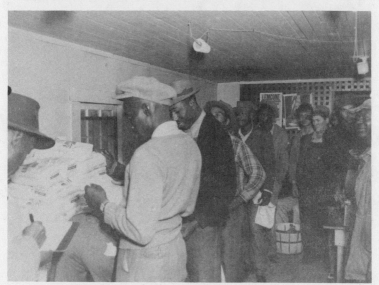

Distribution of goods at the CIO commissary set up for striking workers at the Greene Brothers Lumber Co. in Elizabethtown, N.C. (CIO Organizing Committee, North Carolina Papers, ODA.)

Workers outside the office of Greene Brothers Lumber Company in Elizabethtown, N.C., target of a prolonged organizing campaign by the International Woodworkers of America during Operation Dixie, and a strike in 1948. (CIO Organizing Committee, North Carolina Papers, ODA.)

CIO-sponsored Christmas party for families of striking workers at Greene Brothers Lumber Co., Elizabethtown, N.C. (CIO Organizing Committee, North Carolina Papers, ODA.)

Poster distributed by the International Woodworkers of America, quoting Franklin D. Roosevelt on union membership. (CIO Printed Material. ODA.)

A group of unidentified CIO workers in Tennessee in 1949. (Photo by Paul Christopher. AFL-CIO Region VIII Collection, SLA.)

A CIO field representative conducts a meeting of furniture workers in Lenoir, N.C., in 1952. (CIO Publicity Department, North Carolina Papers, ODA.)

CIO President Philip Murray addressing a Labor Day rally in Birmingham, Alabama, in 1950. Steel works can be seen in background. (AFL-CIO Region VIII Collection, SLA.)

This flyer was sent to many organizers across the South during
Operation Dixie in hopes of shaking their resolve. (Photo by David
Haberstich. Courtesy of Donald McKee.)

DO YOU WANT THE C. I. O.

AFTER SEEING THIS?

Do You Know the "Distinguished Gentleman" Shown Above?

——HE IS——

GEORGE BENJAMIN

Fourth Vice-President

TOBACCO WORKERS INTERNATIONAL UNION

And that isn't all about this "distinguished gentleman." He was recently placed in charge of organizing the tobacco plant employees — INCLUDING

THE WHITE EMPLOYEES — in the State of North Carolina!!

The C. I. O. Believes in This .... Do YOU?

(Turn the Page If You Want to See More)

This flyer was an effort to mobilize racial prejudice against the CIO. The irony here is that the Tobacco Workers International Union under criticism was an AFL, not CIO, affiliate, one which did not share the CIO's progressive position on inter-racial organizing. (Photo by David Haberstich. Courtesy of Donald McKee.)

A sign outside one of the CIO Organizing Committee's offices in North Carolina during Operation Dixie. (Photo by Herman R. Parrott. George Meany Memorial Archives.)

Members of the United Packinghouse Workers of America, Local 309, on strike against the W. W. Pickle Company in Montgomery, Alabama, on December 17, 1951. (Photo by Lasse-Film Center. UPWA Collection, SLA.)

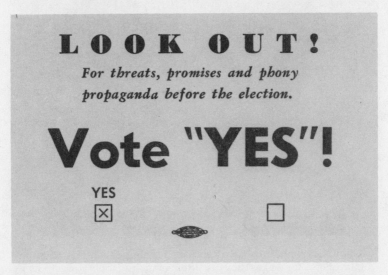

Handbill distributed by the CIO prior to union elections. (CIO Organizing Committee, North Carolina Papers, ODA.)

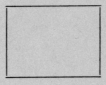

Compliments of the

TEXTILE WORKERS UNION of AMERICA
C. I. O.

By marking your X in the left-hand square you can get lighter work loads, more pay and security through a strong union.

TWUA-CIO X		

A handbill distributed by the CIO's Textile Workers Union of America. (CIO Organizing Committee, North Carolina Papers, ODA.)

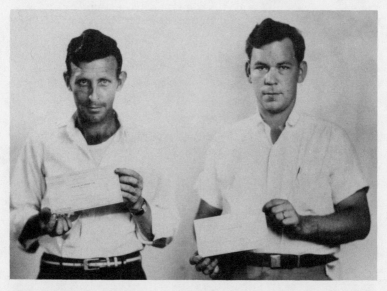

CIO publicity photo of two workers holding checks for back pay totaling $850. for wages they lost after being fired for union activity by the Lenoir Mirror Co. in Lenoir, N.C. (CIO Publicity Department, North Carolina Papers, ODA.)

Red, white, and blue badge distributed by the CIO prior to union elections. (CIO Organizing Committee, North Carolina Papers, ODA.)

Handbill distributed by the CIO prior to union elections. (CIO Organizing Committee, North Carolina Papers, ODA.)

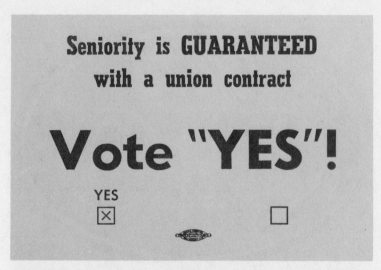

Handbill distributed by the CIO prior to union elections. (CIO Organizing Committee, North Carolina Papers, ODA.)

Meeting of an International Woodworkers of America local, most probably the local at Greene Brothers Lumber Co. in Elizabethtown, N.C. (CIO Organizing Committee. North Carolina Papers, ODA.)

Anti-CIO flyer circulated during Operation Dixie, connecting union activity with Communism and the familiar image of exploitive Northerners. (Photo by David Haberstich. Courtesy of Donald McKee.)

PLEASE READ THIS—

The National Committee of the Communist Party, meeting in New York on July 16-18, 1946, revealed the true nature and purpose of the CIO drive when it reported:

"As we all know, the Southern organizing drive of the CIO ranks in importance with the establishment of the CIO itself and with the organization of CIO-PAC. A successful organizing drive in the South will not merely mean the addition of hundreds of thousands of new members. It will bring about a basic shift in the relation of forces in the country in favor of the labor-progressive coalition. It will mean a **higher form of unity of Negro and white on the basis of a great advance in the economic, SOCIAL and POLITICAL position of the NEGRO people.** It will be the most decisive step in the direction of transforming the South from a politically backward section of the country into one of the most advanced and progressive, since the Negro-labor-poor farmer coalition will become the political backbone of the new South."

The Matter is Entirely in Your Hands!

VOTE AGAINST C.I.O.
FRIDAY, JANUARY 24

If you want to vote AGAINST the C. I. O. being your bargaining agent, write an "X" in the box which says NO at the bottom right corner of ballot.

This Pamphlet Prepared and Paid For
by the
ANTI-C. I. O. COMMITTEE

Anti-CIO flyer distributed prior to a union election, playing upon Southerners' fears of blacks, communists, and unions. (Photo by David Haberstich. Courtesy of Donald McKee.)

VIII

Ideological Schism
The View from Within

Industrial unionism was a tactical goal grounded in ideology: the belief that workers in America could protect themselves from systematic exploitation only by organizing themselves into a strong national institution. The CIO was not, however, "one big union." It was a coalition of a number of large industrial unions, such as the United Mine Workers, United Auto Workers, United Steelworkers, United Electrical Workers, and a number of smaller unions such as Fur and Leather, Longshoremen, National Maritime Union, and Food and Tobacco. In 1946, the CIO Executive Board included representatives of forty-one internationals.

Ideological conflict within this coalition eventually culminated in the purge of the federation's left-wing unions in 1949-1950. Throughout the first year of Operation Dixie, there were neither obvious purges of the left nor overt witch-hunts staged by the CIO leadership. However, the absence of dramatic ideological explosions did not mean that tensions were not operating, even in 1946, and even in the CIO's Southern sector. By the time Operation Dixie was officially launched in May 1946, hairline cracks and fissures in the CIO's foundation had already become visible.

The ideological divisions that became deadly and ravaged the organization by the end of the decade can be seen by 1946—germinating on a national level and within the context of organized labor's relationship to the Democratic Party, generally, and to the Truman administration, specifically. To understand what happened at the grass roots level in the South, it is necessary to review the rapidly changing climate of national politics, and the impact of these shifting conditions upon the CIO's national leadership. Inevitably, the analysis comes to focus on the shifting stance of the CIO's national president, Philip Murray, who served as the real and symbolic spokesman of the center-left coalition that had originally created the CIO out of the AFL. It was the breakup of this coalition, under the pressure of national and international events, that gave definition to the postwar ideological crisis that shattered the CIO and shackled the future course of industrial unionism in America. To trace Philip Murray's passage from cooperation with the CIO's left to hostility and thence to implacable opposition is to trace, first, these national and international pressures, second, their impact on the CIO, and, finally, the local ramifications in the South that brought Operation Dixie to a formal end in 1953.

These relationships are sufficiently complicated that it is prudent to see them as a sequence: the coming of the cold war between the United States and the Soviet Union; the resulting divisions in the CIO over foreign policy; the impact of these tensions on organizing in the face of an aggressive postwar business community out to domesticate the entire labor movement; and, finally, the disastrous spectacle of CIO unions raiding one another as rival factions fought for survival in a completely altered postwar environment. The proclamations of Philip Murray also serve as instructive signposts to the battle. The onset of 1946 found Murray firmly planted in the center, attempting to shape the mood of the federation as well as to be responsive to it. The world of industrial unionism was, of course, inherently "progressive" in traditional political terms; the CIO's political spectrum arrayed liberals on the right, Socialists in the center, and "fellow travelers" and Communists on the left. It may be seen that Murray represented a political coalition that was far to the left of the AFL (and to the left of the American mainstream as well).[1] However, in the early days of 1946, the CIO's successes of the 1930s still fresh in the minds of many people. And, many of those who had benefited from the CIO's successes were not terribly worried about the political coloration of others in the CIO's rank-and-file.

In a climate in which the cold war had not yet taken firm root in the minds of most Americans, CIO regulars had grown accustomed to the presence of political radicals in the organization. Clearly, the left had played a major role in the CIO's successes in the 1930s, and their contributions were well understood. Historian Nelson Lichtenstein has gone so far as to conclude that the ten years after 1935 made for a period in which the behavior of Communist unionists was often difficult to distinguish from that of other CIO members. "As vocal supporters of the New Deal and the war effort, the Communists moved easily within the social democratic current of the late 1930s and the social patriotic enthusiasm of the wartime mobilization."[2]

The "ease" of this association can be exaggerated, however. Communists, Socialists, and liberals all sought to have the CIO reflect their own basic orientation. The seeds of conflict were always present, as were doubts about the reliability and integrity of ideological rivals. Nevertheless, the wartime experience, as Lichtenstein points out, helped create an environment where cooperation seemed conceivable. Accordingly, the CIO entered the postwar period with its left, center, and right in seemingly sturdy coalition. New Deal liberals, Socialists, and Communists—industrial unionists all—served on the same CIO committees, worked together on local CIO joint boards, industrial union councils, and political action committees, and in general displayed a noticeable degree of solidarity. It was a period when "there was some unrest and a little picking here and there, but a lot of joint effort."[3] Such cooperation was quite visible at the local level. An organizer for the left-wing, racially integrated Food, Tobacco, Agricultural, and Allied Workers recalled a rally in Memphis in 1946 to save wartime Office of Price Administration. FTA organizers demonstrated alongside" young white veterans who were members of right-wing CIO unions, on the streets handing out leaflets, getting petitions, in front of the post office." This local labor unity extended to politics.

We had a big campaign and for the first time, every poll was watched in Memphis. And they were all watched by young white veterans. Now, by ten o'clock that morning, they'd locked them all up on the grounds that they were disrupting. Each one of the poll judges called the police and said, "This guy's disrupting." So, they were all in jail. They kept them there until the polls were closed and then released them without any charges. There was a joint effort in '46; there was a tremendous feeling there, still, of rank-and-file unity, because we were all commonly being attacked.[4]

This cooperation was due in part to a legacy of unity forged in the fight with the AFL that led to the CIO's formation, and from the sense of common purpose that had been rewarded during World War II.

However, this unity concealed tensions that had generated intense arguments inside the CIO as the war had neared its end. Aggressive industrial unionists found themselves stymied by a coalition of CIO conservatives, Communists, and much of the national leadership. The division had appeared as early as 1944 when several left-wing leaders, including Harry Bridges, Joseph Curran, and Julius Emspak, publicly endorsed national service legislation to draft strikers "at the same time that CIO policy called for its denunciation in the strongest terms." Moreover, the intransigence of Southern textile mill owners in flaunting National War Labor Board orders had driven Emil Rieve to resign from the board and had led TWUA to call a series of strike ballots throughout textile country. Only when news of overwhelming strike votes by the rank-and-file reached Washington did the NWLB (heretofore responsive to Southern congressional influence on labor issues affecting textiles) grant a long overdue pay raise.[5] Similar pressures in other mass production industries caused Reuther and Rieve to lead a fight in March 1945 to withdraw formally all CIO representatives from the NWLB. Backed by the votes of union leaders from conservative and Communist-influenced internationals, Murray blocked the effort and reaffirmed labor's no-strike pledge.[6]

The coming of the cold war, coupled with the postwar business offensive against organized labor, sharply intensified the external pressure on the CIO coalition. As foreign policy issues came to dominate national life, the opposition of left-led unions to the Marshall Plan "threatened to turn a section of the CIO into the core of an opposition political movement that would be strong enough to spread disquiet in Washington but weak enough to invite massive retaliation by a government armed with extensive formal and informal power over the labor movement."[7]

Wartime labor unity under Roosevelt broke under Truman's cold war policies. Some labor radicals, such as Len DeCaux, editor of the *CIO News* in Washington, saw Murray's actions as predictably reactionary:

When it gradually became clear that Truman was embarking on the opposite course, Murray at first tried to soft-pedal things in CIO, to avoid dissension in the midst of brewing strike struggles, and possibly because of some lingering uncertainly. In the spring of 1946, after the Churchill-Truman declaration of Cold War at Fulton, Missouri, Murray began trying more openly to swing CIO into line. What Hillman might have done, who knows? He died July 10, 1946, still on record for Big Three and world-labor unity, and against the growing American-Century imperialism. But the lines were not yet sharply drawn [in July 1946]. About Murray there was little doubt. At first cautious about antagonizing the CIO's still influential left wing, he was soon privately—even in my unsympathetic presence—referring to "those people" in disparaging, sometimes caustic terms. Long before the 1946 CIO convention, which officially registered CIO's switch, Murray could hardly hide his feelings. They were evident at Steel's May convention in Atlantic City. They burst out emotionally at the September Conference of Progressives in Chicago.[8]

Other leftists saw Murray's politics as reflecting an inner agony. Frank Emspak, the historian and son of the UE's influential Julius Emspak, emphasized the political dilemma facing the CIO president: "If a union allows non-member communists to influence its policies it ceases to that extent to be a union, and becomes a revolutionary agency. If it forbids communists to join or hold office it sets up control over private opinion." To Emspak,

> The Steel Workers feared isolation from the American public because of attacks on their patriotism. Although Murray said he had only contempt for those who would impugn the patriotism of the USW, he in effect did their bidding when he attacked the left. The Steel Workers and Murray were afraid of losing what they thought they had won during the war—the good will and trust of the American people and perhaps some of the politicians. During the war, Murray was respected as a trade union leader and statesman; he did not want to lose that respect because of the Communists."[9]

Labor's internal debate took place in a national climate that underscored the high stakes involved. In June, the Republican National Committee chairman, B. Carroll Reece, had characterized the upcoming election as "a stark choice between 'Communism and Republicanism'" and had presented the CIO-PAC's support for the Democratic Party as damaging evidence to that effect.[10] A California congressional candidate announced that "a vote for Richard Nixon is a vote against the Communist-dominated PAC with its gigantic slush-fund," and expanded the list of reprehensible associations by accusing his opponent, Helen Gahagan Douglas, a prominent New Deal liberal, of "consistently voting the 'Moscow-Pac-Henry Wallace line.'"[11]

Inside labor, Murray may have had qualms about launching an all-out anti-Communist campaign, but his subordinates in the Steelworkers did not. Nor, as Emspak has pointed out, did Murray do anything to stop them. In August, David McDonald blasted the Communist Party at a district meeting of the Steelworkers in Cleveland. In October, New England steel locals condemned Communist activity in their organizations and James Carey, the CIO's national secretary and close associate of Murray, attacked the leadership of the Electrical Workers. AFL president William Green meanwhile seized the opportunity to assault his considerable body of enemies in the CIO by warning American workers against the danger of an "'insurrection inspired by Communist leaders' within and 'the forces of fascism in America' without."[12]

What followed within three months of Labor Day in 1946 was instrumental in deepening the antagonisms between left and right, both in organized labor and in the country as a whole. Six months after Operation Dixie had officially begun, its embattled short-term prospects suddenly were further burdened by the intrusion of the emerging cold war.

One month before the national election of November 1946, the Electrical Workers held its national convention. One of the most militant CIO unions, it served as a lightning rod for conservative reaction within and outside the CIO. At that convention, a militant slate was reelected by a five-to-one margin over a slate calling itself "UE Members for Democratic Action."[13] The sinners characterized the dissidents as "wreckers who urge us to substitute for the principle of unity and democracy within our ranks, divisions, witch-hunts and purges."[14]

The congressional elections in November 1946 constituted a landslide for the Republicans and delivered a strong message to organized labor about its future. The results implied that the "national mood" would likely be quite different from the New Deal years. The Republicans won 246 seats in the House to the Democrats' 188, and 51 seats in the Senate to the Democrats' 45. Only three-eights of the eligible voters had cast ballots, and the Democratic vote dropped from 25,000,000 to 15,000,000. In addition, only 75 of the 318 candidates supported by the CIO-PAC won their races.[15]

In effect the election results, as one historian has put it, "reinforced the efficacy of red-baiting" and led Truman to take more drastic steps: The loyalty program "became a shuttlecock in party politics." As an attempt to slow the Republicans' momentum, Truman signed Executive Order 9835, "which launched a purge of the federal civil service and inspired imitative purges at every level of American working life."[16] As the fast-disintegrating wartime popular front disappeared from politics, the Americans for Democratic Action came to represent "the vital center of mainline liberalism," having as members Eleanor Roosevelt, "a galaxy of the big names of the New Deal era," "major anti-Communist labor leaders and the spokesmen of the NAACP."[17]

The eighth annual CIO convention in November 1946 brought into full view the dilemma in which the CIO leadership found itself. Everyone was aware of the stakes involved, and of how much rode on labor's ability to remain unified. Prior to the convention, Murray had insisted on assembling an ideologically balanced committee of six people from the executive board to draft a compromise resolution. He intended to then present it to the convention as part of his opening speech, without asking for debate. The compromise resolution denounced meddling by political parties in the internal affairs of the CIO. This bow to the right was accompanied by a bow to the left with the inclusion of "other political parties" along with reference to the Communists. This phrase at once reduced the extent to which the resolution might have calmed the right. Thus the Association of Catholic Trade Unionists thought the resolution, "with its implication that Democratic Party interference was as culpable as that of the communists, was much too weak." The *New York Times* interpreted the right's response as a decision to yield only to Murray's call for the appearance of unity.[18] This they were willing to do purportedly because "the price of their refusal to yield might have been Mr. Murray's refusal to accept the presidency again. They did not want to risk the consequences at this time." In his speech Murray added that "This organization is not and must not be Communist-controlled and inspired." He then made a gesture to reassure the moderates and persuade the pro-

Communists to support the resolution. The statement, he said, was "designed to chart a course for the overall conduct of our International unions. It should not be misconstrued to be a repressive measure. I am definitely opposed to any form of repression in this movement of ours."[19] Only two delegates refused to endorse the resolution, both Communists and officers in the National Maritime Union. They were immediately "harangued openly by their comrades," whereupon they rushed to the platform to inform Murray that they would change their votes.[20] One unamused observer described the incident as yet one more "unedifying spectacle of Communists voting to denounce themselves." "Like overpowered captains who hoped to trade servility for time, they turned the other cheek."[21]

Yet the CIO's constitution and administrative structure gave Murray little more than the power to remove certain individuals from his own CIO staff. Intervention on a large scale was constitutionally impossible because the CIO, recalling its own expulsion from the AFL, originally created for itself an organization with limited powers in the national headquarters. Nevertheless, the events of the year showed Murray's evolution in 1946. Early on, he sounded a call for calm and a continuation of the CIO's democratic heritage at the Steelworkers' convention in May 1946.[22] While his inner circle of advisers urged him to take a strong stand against the Communists, Murray was torn. He warned against "the intrusion of ideological ideas or beliefs into trade union matters," and was careful to add: "We ask no man his national origin, his color, his religion, or his beliefs."[23] However, in his speech to the Conference of progressives in the fall of that year, Murray burst out, to the consternation of the popular frontists, that organized labor "wants no damn Communists meddling in our affairs."[24]

It was at this time that the CIO leadership made an effort to influence public opinion by preparing a pamphlet entitled "Americans! 7,000,000 of them," aimed at answering the charge of communism, largely in the context of the Southern drive. If there were Communists in the CIO, labor's leaders said, it was only because employers had hired them first—"generally when their industries were operating non-union."[25]

This was a pretty thin reed, given the whipping winds of anticommunism coursing through the CIO and the society as a whole. But the defensiveness of the left at the end of 1946 cast in bold relief the changes that had occurred within labor during the year. The CIO's radical wing had decided that a conciliatory course in 1946 would give them a chance to reorganize their forces within the CIO so that a center-left coalition could retake the offensive in 1947. Participation in Operation Dixie was consistent with this aim, as the Highlander conclave of left-led unions concluded early in 1946. A participant recalled the options:

> What shall be our role in Operation Dixie? We know the rules of the game. We know that if we go in and organize, that we're organizing in the name of the CIO and that they can give jurisdiction to whoever they want. A number of positions developed. One was distrust. A group of people said, "We're being fooled into this thing. If we do it, we'll do a lot of organizing and they'll just take over the locals and we won't get them." Well, [FTA President] Henderson's answer to that was, "Look, if we go in and do the organizing, we have ten of our people in there and they have ten of their people, and we're working in tobacco and our people are going to be tobacco workers—we're the ones who are going to win the support of these people. We're going to organize them and we'll win their support."[26]

Henderson prevailed, primarily because his position made sense in light of the FTA's impression of organizers employed directly by the CIO; the FTA people were confident they could develop deeper and more lasting ties with the rank-and-file workers in the Southern tobacco industry.

> Our people would be there day and night. They wouldn't sleep. They wouldn't be drinking coffee. They were workers out of the factories. "Not only are

we going to work, we're going to outwork them. In our field, Food and Tobacco, we're going to make arrangements for rank-and-file workers to get out of our factories, go in with their people, and really organize."[27]

The FTA's fears of the CIO's use of jurisdictional assignment as a weapon for defeating left-wing unions were well founded, however. By 1947, the CIO was assigning tobacco workers to the United Transport Service Employees' Association.[28]

Such events constituted a form of "raiding" by administrative action. Actual raiding followed soon afterward—and in a manner that put to rest any possibility that Operation Dixie could somehow rescue itself from the setbacks of 1946. The Republican congress, elected on a platform that promised to restrain labor, had passed the Taft-Hartley Act. Its provisions for non-Communist affidavits for officials of unions wishing to appear on NLRB election ballots brought politics to the very center of the organizing process. In March 1947, the U.S. secretary of labor demanded publicly that the Communist Party be outlawed, and the U.S. commissioner of education went on an anti-Communist speaking tour.[29] The Truman Doctrine was unveiled in the same month and precipitated a great deal of pressure on labor's left wing, tightening the requirements for proof of loyalty and patriotism as well. Alongside the Marshall Plan and the Taft-Hartley Act, it represented three levels of pressure that collectively split the CIO's center-left coalition irreparably. The primary reverberations of the Truman Doctrine and the Marshall Plan were felt by the CIO as support for both came to be used as the litmus test for patriotism.

The strategy was effective. During 1947, major upheavals hit three CIO unions with the largest Communist membership—the United Electrical, Radio and Machine Workers (UE), the National Maritime Union (NMU), and the International Union of Mine, Mill and Smelter Workers (IUMMSW). An official anti-Communist caucus was set up within UE. The Communist slate was defeated in the Maritime Union and a secessionist movement was begun in Mine, Mill after left-wing Reid Robinson was reelected to the presidency in January 1947. By midyear, Murray was instructing the CIO executive board:

> If Communism is an issue in any of your unions, throw it to hell out . . . and throw its advocates out along with it. When a man accepts . . . paid office in a union . . . to render service to workers, and then delivers service to outside interests, that man is nothing but a damned traitor.[30]

The center-left coalition was dead and the isolation of the left was complete.

The impact of these dynamics upon what was left of Operation Dixie soon became clear. The CIO had many goals in the South: to organize textiles, to overcome racial segregation both in the workplace and in Southern society as a whole, and to end the political hegemony of race-baiting "Dixiecrat" conservatives. All were components that were necessary to complete the structural requirements for a truly national movement of industrial unionism, one that could be strong enough to lead postwar American society toward the egalitarian "new day" that progressives had long envisioned.

Perhaps no other local union in the South symbolized—in its black and white membership—these ambitious goals more fully then the 10,000-member Local 22 of the Food and Tobacco Workers Union at the R.J. Reynolds Plant in Winston-Salem, North Carolina. The foundation of the union was made up of black women workers in the "stemmeries," who had played a militant and decisive role in the union's original struggle for recognition. In the increasingly conservative climate of cold war politics, Reynolds moved in 1947 to break the union when the contract then in force expired, by refusing to go along with demands for a wage increase. The resulting strike earned the sympathy of the progressive Southern religious group, the Fellowship of Southern Churchmen. But the Communist leanings of the FTA also generated anxiety among those Southerners. In a re-

vealing exchange of letters, Nelle Morton of the fellowship
wrote for advice from a close friend, South Carolina's state director for Operation Dixie, Franz Daniel:

> We are in a dilemma as we face the FTA-CIO Local 22
> strike at Reynolds Tobacco in Winston-Salem. When
> we see a clear-cut issue of injustice the Fellowship has
> not been timid to act. . . . The issues of the strike are
> entirely justified in every way. While we have no
> proof, we believe that the union is pretty well commu-
> nist controlled. The company has a paternalistic atti-
> tude toward the workers and is determined to break
> the union. So they are seeking every weapon to use in
> the breaking. . . . Suppose the strike is won and the
> *Party* becomes more powerful than ever through the
> union locals. What will that do to labor and ultimately
> to the strikers in the plant?[31]

The CIO state director's response provided an indication
of the fence CIO leaders were trying to straddle:

> In my opinion, the Fellowship should issue an appeal
> on behalf of the strikers . . . prefaced by a brief state-
> ment calling attention to the current charge of Commu-
> nist domination. Nothing would be gained by
> ignoring or denying the charge—but so what? You are
> not asking for relief for the leaders of the union. You
> are asking for relief of strikers whose cause is a just
> one. If the strike is won, there is a chance to clean up
> the union. If it is lost, there will be no chance to elimi-
> nate the C.P. . . . I personally believe the charges of
> C.P. domination are well grounded. I want that
> changed. And I believe it can be changed if the strike
> is won.[32]

Nelle Morton found this response to be "clear-cut and fine"
and "just the assurance we needed."[33]

Local 22's representatives, though supported by the Fel-
lowship of Southern Churchmen, were ostracized by New
York unionists when they attempted to raise strike funds.
"*Now* we were isolated," said Local 22's Karl Korstad. "The

right-wing unions, on the whole, would not attend joint meetings. The Electrical Workers helped us, but it was pretty much our group." National politics, as distinct from internal CIO politics, also intruded. In the middle of the strike, the House Un-American Activities Committee called in three leaders of FTA to testify on Communist affiliations.[34] Not only had the spirit of cooperation vanished, it had been accompanied by a change in attitude among the CIO leadership as to the purpose and function of labor organization. The left-wing unions had clearly become a liability to labor's cause as as whole.

John Russell, the Fur and Leather Workers' Southern district director assessed the situation as one of the CIO becoming preoccupied with "respectability."

> They wanted to buy respectability, of course. No question about this. They just ached for it. I remember Baldanzi making a speech at the 1947 convention in Boston. And he flayed the living hell out of those people who talked, as he said, "with a forked tongue, lied about things, didn't say who they were," and these things. And I forget exactly how he phrased it, but anyway, it was to the effect that these people "who wouldn't sign the [Taft-Hartley] non-Communist oath didn't deserve any protection, because obviously they are Communists," and words along these lines.[35]

A deep bitterness lingers in the memories of Southern radicals caught in the clutches of labor's internal cold war of 1946-1950. Russell, for example, remembered George Baldanzi as "a fancy speaker," but "empty as hell, of course." Russell also saw him as one of the leaders in the move to "buy respectability," people whose motivations he described in the following way: "They probably wanted any members they could get, because they were the kind of guys who thought in terms of: If you could pick up a group of workers, even if it means making a deal that puts chains around those workers, that's fine."[36]

Such rancor was rooted in the raiding—as early as 1947—to which left-led unions in the South were subjected.

The attempts to reduce the membership of FTA, for example, were challenges to which they could not fully respond at first, because of the leadership's initial refusal to sign the non-Communist affidavits demanded by the Taft-Hartley Act. The CIO's big opportunity came with an election at R.J. Reynolds in Winston-Salem in 1950. The 1947 strike ended without Reynolds' full recognition of workers' demands, and agitation and calls for a new contract and a union election had flared intermittently ever since. So determined was the CIO to break FTA that it sent in organizers from unions that could not even remotely claim jurisdiction over tobacco workers. They were under instructions to recruit workers for the United Transport Service Employees-CIO (UTSE), and away from the Tobacco Workers International Union-AFL, and, of course, Local 22. Such "draftees" in union-busting look back on the events with a regret that, at times, exudes its own kind of bitterness.

> Now this is, as far as I'm concerned, one of the black marks in our history of the CIO. Even though they [the FTA] were expelled, they were a trade union. They were a good local union in that plant. True enough they were communist-dominated, but hell, John L. Lewis used the communists to organize workers. And they were a good union. And in order not to let the [AFL] Tobacco Workers have it, the CIO goes in there. And I went in there on it. I was sent in there. And we had a fairly good-sized staff. And we were organizing them for the United Transport Service Employees Union. A very vicious strike it was. And it was a race strike, really. Blacks were striking and the whites were scabbing. And of course, then, this was when the [AFL] Tobacco Workers Union moved in and then we [in the CIO] moved in.[37]

An election was finally held on March 8, 1950. Although it was possibly the largest union election ever held in the South, the results were "inconclusive." "No Union" received 3,426 votes; Local 22 won 3,323 votes; the TWIU-AFL received 1,514, and UTSE-CIO 541. A runoff election

was then scheduled for March 23, between Local 22 and
"No Union." Local 22 received 4,428 votes, "No Union,"
4,383, with 133 votes challenged. After the NLRB rules on
the challenged votes, Local 22 lost the election by 66 votes.

> The outcome hinged on the challenged ballots, and of
> course, again, the Labor Board ruled on the chal-
> lenged ballots in favor of management. And, as a re-
> sult, there is not a union in R. J. Reynolds to this day.
> Now, if we'd all stayed out of there, and helped Local
> 22 to win that thing, they'd be in the labor movement
> today. And they'd be in the AFL-CIO today.[38]

By this process, black workers in the South became inad-
vertent casualties of the cold war in labor. But the CIO itself was also a casualty, for struggles such as the one over
Local 22 ate away the morale of the CIO's organizers.

> You know, we were supposed to be bitter anti-
> communists. This is the time prior to when UE, Mine,
> Mill and Smelter—there was ten unions that were ex-
> pelled. And Murray was really bitterly opposed to
> them. So, when it came to the second round between
> the FTA and "no union" at that Reynolds plant, we
> did nothing. Nor did the [AFL] Tobacco Workers; in
> fact, they even told their people to vote "no union."
> That's a black page in our history. I really think, to
> me, that's one of the worst things that we've done in
> all the years we were in the South. The amount of en-
> ergy, over months, all these organizers, both from
> UTW, from the CIO, and MONEY!! All kinds of
> money! Workin' people's money! Poured in here, try-
> ing to take people who are *already* in a union, to *an-
> other* union! There's no God-given sense to it, you
> know. Maybe it isn't the ideal union. I don't think it
> is to this day, but it also *could* be! But, my God, all
> this energy and all this money is being used that
> should have been out here being used to organize some-
> thing else. It did about as much to prevent us from suc-
> ceeding in the South as anything management did.[39]

Unfortunately for the CIO, the Winston-Salem story was not an isolated one. A struggle inside the Packinghouse Workers affected the entire local labor movement in Fort Worth, Texas, so that organizers for other unions wanted to "cringe." One CWA organizer recalled,

I really got involved, where I could see it, when we put our little one-room organizing office in Fort Worth, me and another representative, in the Packinghouse Workers' hall. And the internal fight in the United Packinghouse Workers Union was just bloody! I mean bloody! Some people at CIO were trying to expel them. They didn't want to be expelled. Two huge locals, Armour's and Swift's, two of the largest locals in the union, were out there in that one hall, and two or three smaller ones.

He remembered officers coming in often from Packinghouse headquarters in order to help the regional director try to restore order, since he was unable to do so on his own.

The communists didn't like him and the anti-communists didn't like him, so he was very ineffective. Things were in a constant turmoil, and you'd sit there and you'd cringe! You'd lock your door when things were going on, because you didn't even want to talk to anybody about it. Or you'd go out on a leaflet run. You'd go home! You'd do anything to keep away from it, but you were constantly drawn into it because these people were fighting for the minds of nearly 10,000 people—right there in Fort Worth, right where we had our office! Bad. Disruptive. People who were terrific people were calling other terrific people all kinds of names. And going out and putting out leaflets, leaflets at the plant, tearing the plant up.[40]

Here was the major impact the purge had on the later stages of Operation Dixie—the loss of committed organizers and the dissipation of energy, money, and morale. But it was an impact that occurred after, not before, the basic defeat in textiles in 1946. From the standpoint of the left-led un-

ions, the CIO "raided and counter-raided till those workers
didn't know where the hell they were. If they'd spent all
the money organizing that those bastards used to destroy unions, they would have organized the textile industry in the
South."[41] This sweeping conclusion, spoken in bitterness
and exasperation, is clearly excessive. Defeat in textiles had
already occurred. But one of the complaints of Fur and Leather's John Russell has a more enduring resonance:

> Cannibalism is what it is. You eat yourselves up. You
> eat your people up. If you've got a company union, or
> a union that's completely bought and sold to the em-
> ployers, that's a different thing. But that wasn't the [sit-
> uation] in these cases. These were honest trade
> unions, basically. You may disagree with them, but
> they're honest in that sense: that they did get some
> raises, get some money, and did benefit the workers
> and things like this. It wasn't necessary.[42]

The agonies imposed on the CIO by the cold war—and
the agonies that CIO imposed on itself—had their counterpart in that segment of the nation's progressive political community that stood outside the labor movement. The
red-baiting political climate of 1946, engendered by the business community, aggressively exploited by the Republican
Party, and defensively manipulated by the Truman administration and its loyalty program, had culminated in a smash-
ing GOP victory in the 1946 congressional elections. These
events convinced many liberals that the progressive cause—
so dependent at critical moments on the rhetoric and personal prestige of Franklin Roosevelt—had never really
achieved the ability to stand by itself. Some liberals felt that
this defeat flowed from the failure to create an organized progressive constituency; others saw it as a failure of image,
traceable to the ease with which liberalism could be tarred
with the brush of communism. Accordingly, some progressives aligned with the American Civil Liberties Union focused on "an atmosphere increasingly hostile to the
liberties of organized labor, the political left and many minorities," and called attention to an "excitement bordering on

hysteria" that characterized "the public approach to any issue related to Communism."[43]

While a number of such progressives fought as best they could against the Truman loyalty oath—a campaign waged in a steadily deteriorating climate of free discussion—other liberals saw the problem as "moral and ideological." For them, it centered upon "the refusal of so many progressives to disassociate themselves strongly from Communists and pro-Communists." From this perspective, the paramount urgency was the reestablishment of American liberalism as a movement in the native progressive tradition. This they hoped to accomplish by creating a new institution, called the Americans for Democratic Action. "By mid-1946, these two lines of thought and action were already struggling for dominance; by 1947, they formed two poles, with most progressives being drawn toward one or the other."[44]

The politics of the postwar years produced no such dilemmas for one other organized group–the American Federation of Labor. The AFL had made substantial gains in the 1937–1941 period by offering itself as a cooperative alternative to employers threatened by the CIO. Such tactics constituted an old AFL tradition that reached all the way back to the time of the Knights of Labor in the late nineteenth century. Indeed, in 1936 the president of the International Association of Machinists-AFL, A. O. Wharton, had written that the Supreme Court's decision to uphold the Wagner Act had led many employers to accept the unavoidable and come to some kind of agreement with organized labor. However, he noted that "These employers have expressed preference to deal with A.F. of L. organizations rather than Lewis, Hillman, Dubinsky, Howard and their gang of sluggers, communists, radicals and soapbox artists, professional bums, expelled members of labor unions, outright scabs and the Jewish organizations with all their red affiliates."[45]

This machinists' union made substantial gains by approaching employers with the "backdoor pact." Union officials would negotiate a "soft agreement" with the employer and prepare to collect dues, without having consulted any of the workers. Once the deal had been closed, the em-

ployer would then present the workers with their new
union, or merely post a notice on the bulletin board to that effect. "Organizing the employer rather than the employee became a widespread practice," a tactic that many AFL
officials considered "a major strategy in their fight with the
CIO."[46]

Ultimately, events over the next two generations were to
reveal the hollowness of a political stance based not on
what the AFL advocated, but rather on the negative principle of what it did not avocate. For its part, the Americans
for Democratic Action did not materialize as "a vital center," but rather as an ineffective forum for the opinions of a
small group of politically interested intellectuals. The CIO,
shackled with Taft-Hartley and after another round of defeats in the 1950s with article 14B of the Landrum-Griffin
Bill, gradually subsided into a quiescent business unionism.
Not only workers in the South but large sectors of the Northern working population were left unorganized and isolated
from any kind of "labor education."

The practical results were quite real. But the ideological implications are less easily sorted out. One radical veteran of
the postwar organizing campaign offered this general assessment of the long-term meaning of the labor politics that
swirled around Operation Dixie:

> I think that by '48—that was the [CIO] convention
> that finally told the story. You accept the Marshall
> Plan, you tie American labor to American foreign pol-
> icy. Now it's a different thing when you strike. You're
> striking against your country. And now it's a different
> thing when you ask for wage increases. I think the com-
> promise was that you would tie wage increases to two
> things: cost of living and productivity. You got a wage
> increase to make up for the cost of living. This, in a
> way, takes the struggle out of the trade unions, be-
> cause when labor agrees to this—that your wages are
> going to be tied to productivity—you make the assump-
> tion that productivity is a function of labor only, and
> not a function of management.[47]

He added, by way of a general summation, "Historically, it seems to me that whenever a trade union gets tied to a nation's foreign policy, they tie their hands. They no longer have freedom."[48]

As a comment on the crippling limitations that cold war politics imposed on the CIO, the judgment stands the test of time. However, the identical comment, ironically enough, can be made about the effect of the foreign policy pronouncements of the CIO's left wing. Indeed, it is important to remember that the vulnerability of the CIO's left wing to a purge was not solely a product of external cold war politics. The frequent shifts in Soviet foreign policy—and the slavish parroting of these shifts by American Communists, including those in the CIO—provided abundant evidence that the CIO's left was not an autonomous institutional vehicle for expressing the aspirations of the American working class. Indeed, to many liberals and Socialists in the CIO's right and center, the left's defense against the purge, focusing as it did on repeated calls for "rank-and-file democracy," was totally unconvincing. How could CIO leftists picture themselves as the defenders of trade union democracy when the same people had, since the Nazi-Soviet pact of 1939, followed every twist and turn of Soviet foreign policy? It was a question that the CIO's national leadership increasingly put to the movement's militants as the cold war deepened and as the American labor movement as a whole found itself on the defensive.

The Communist Party's official response was to explore loftiness in the name of avoiding the issue:

> Just as the advocates of Christianity could not be thrown out by the Roman Emperors, and just as the roar of the Inquisition commanding that Galileo stop proclaiming the earth round could not stop the advance of science, so today the trade union movement cannot turn back the clock of history.[49]

Unfortunately, the CIO's left did not believe the evidence that Stalin's regime represented the gulag more than it did "the clock of history."

As 1947 drew to a close, the anti-Communist forces within the CIO and in the nation as a whole were evolving into a powerful and solid opposition, against which the left was becoming ever less capable of fighting. The Wallace campaign also added fuel to the red-baiting issue. Once several CIO unions had demonstrated official support for his campaign, the CIO executive council met in January 1948 and came out, 33 to 13, in support of the Marshall Plan and in opposition to Wallace. The CIO-PAC then spent some $513,000 that year on Truman's race.[50] There is no doubt but that Wallace's resounding defeat "strengthened the resolve and the nerve of the anti-Communists within the CIO."[51] It also strengthened the resolve of Catholic trade unionists in the anti-red movement, to the extent that "the convention hall and the hotel lobbies were swarming with priests."[52]

By the time of the CIO's national convention in 1948, Murray was referring to Communists as "ideological dive-bombers, pouting people, small cliques, degraded thinkers, dry rot leaders,[and] afflictions on mankind."[53] One year later, Murray addressed the 1949 delegates with references to the "sulking cowards, apostles of hate, lying out of the pits of their dirty bellies."[54]

In such a manner, the CIO fought its way back into the mainstream of the Democratic Party. Unfortunately for labor, that mainstream represented an accommodation to corporate America that severely circumscribed labor's influence on national policy. The price of respectability was high.

IX

Aftermath

In the end, calm and quiet closed over Operation Dixie, leaving the South, to all appearances, pretty much as it had been before. Business domination of politics and the economy continued unabated. Racial segregation remained the way of life. In soft Southern accents, "Dixiecrat" politicians still demonstrated their legendary parliamentary skill in the U.S. Senate and on key House committees. Their long association with Republicans in the majority conservative coalition in Congress continued to shape the limits of policy debate in twentieth-century America. A chastened CIO, finding itself in increasing agreement with AFL conservatives, completed its evolution from industrial unionism to business unionism by merging with the craft unions in a reunited AFL-CIO in 1956. The South's premier industry, textiles, remained overwhelmingly nonunion and the region's workers maintained their status as the nation's lowest paid employees.

As a large-scale organizing campaign Operation Dixie died in December 1946 when the organizing staff was cut in half. Organizers for left-wing unions, under attack in the CIO, pulled out of the Southern drive by degrees in 1947–1948. The UAW, whose funds and technical advice had been a significant force, left in 1948. The same year, the Southern Organizing Committee ceased functioning in Texas, Louisiana, and Mississippi. Alabama was abandoned in 1949. A desultory effort continued in the rest of the South until Operation Dixie was officially closed in 1953. In the course of these efforts, the CIO made a summary conclu-

161

sion on the subject of hiring Southern organizers to combat
the charge of "outside agitators." In the staff retrenchment
that came at the end of 1946, the CIO completely deempha-
sized the hiring of Southern staff. Experience, not regional af-
filiation, became the sole criterion.[1]

In 1949, Southern membership in the CIO was no
greater than the 400,000 total that had existed on the day
when George Baldanzi opened the Atlanta office of Operation Dixie in 1946. To the prewar Southern membership in
textiles of 27,750, another 42,450 were added during the
war. Thus at the outset of Operation Dixie, TWUA counted
70,200 in a work force of approximately 580,000. Four years
later, TWUA workers covered under Southern contracts to-
taled 81,095. The Southern drive had added a mere 10,805.
In 1949, Emil Rieve, president of the TWUA, forthrightly conceded that "we are worse off today in the South than we
have been" and added that the TWUA's influence in the textile industry "is probably less today than it was a few years
ago."[2]

The failure of Operation Dixie raised the most central questions about workers, about the CIO, and about the American labor movement in general. In the spring of 1946,
hopes had been high; in the autumn, all was doubt and confusion. Had the union encountered a part of America that
was organically resistant to it? Had Southern working people, so shortly removed from the heritage of land tenantry
and sharecropping, silently absorbed a tradition of submission and defeat, of resignation and apathy? Had evangelical
religion somehow undermined people's capacity for self-
help, even as it consoled them and uplifted the spirit? Was
race somehow an insuperable barrier? Was something
called "the Southern heritage" in all of its manifestations—
religious, racial, and individualistic—a force so powerful it
overwhelmed the small groups of organizers the CIO dispatched throughout the region? Had a hierarchy of caste
and class, nurtured by an aggressive corporate environment, simply proven too strong?

Or was the fault within the labor movement itself? Was

it too traditional and bureaucratic? Or perhaps too ideological and radical? Was it cynical, innocent, or otherwise, as
the saying goes, incapable of meeting the demands of history? Hovering over Operation Dixie from beginning to end
was the enormous political, cultural, and economic power
mobilized by Southern corporations. And giving an especially sharp definition to the struggle was the ruthless intransigence of the Southern mill owners. Their contempt for
the CIO was an expression of their contempt for the "white
trash" who worked for them.

In addition, it must be remembered that the specific
shape of the events of 1946 was not the product of that
year alone. Many generations of life in the South had gone
into the creation of the arrogance of the mill owner. The social values and habits of the Southern elite had been crafted
over many generations during which a rigid hierarchy had
been fashioned by a few, presided over by a few, and enforced with privately controlled police power. In conduct,
as in allegiance, the "patty rollers" who protected against
runaway slaves were brothers under the skin to the mill village sheriffs who protected the textile company against the
restless "lint-heads." The naked mechanisms of social control that enforced inherited class and caste relations in Southern mill villages were of a kind and type that went beyond
the imagination of most Americans. As a genteel Southern
lawyer, sobered over time by the cold fury of mill village justice and law enforcement, remembered forty years after
Operation Dixie, "Those fellows from Michigan and
Pennsylvania who came down here were astounded at
what we were running into. And I guess they still are."[3] A
student of the textile industry, similarly sobered by the implications of his own research, settled upon the words "hostility," "absolute rule," "total control," and "intransigence"
as the most appropriate descriptions of the conduct of textile management with respect to trade unions.[4] A black organizer in lumbering reflected on other patterns: "There was
a meanness about these policemen. A special meanness. It
came from a long way back, you know."[5] In overt and in sub-

tle ways, Operation Dixie encountered a kind of resistance that "came from a long way back."

Yet factors within the CIO itself also helped defeat the drive, although to give them too much of the responsibility would imply that had a slightly different path been taken, Operation Dixie would have had a radically different result. The evidence does not support such a conclusion. Had the South been organizable through sheer will and effort, the CIO staff of 1946 possessed enough of these qualities to have succeeded. One comes away from a prolonged study of the people and events that formed the day-to-day life of Operation Dixie with the settled feeling that the men and women of the CIO cared enough, and tried hard enough. But more than will was required.

At the institutional core of the Southern drive was the Textile Workers Union of America. The TWUA invested the most time and resources of all the CIO internationals and it was the organizing teams in textiles that were buffeted most disastrously by the hurricane of opposition that became the decisive force in Operation Dixie. Fashioning a judicious appraisal of the TWUA is necessarily a complex process, for the union lived in an industrial environment that was different from that of most CIO internationals. The single most influential difference was the structure of the textile industry itself. Made up of thousands of relatively small production units (even "giants" such as Cannon with its 25,000 workers could not be compared to U.S. Steel or General Motors), the textile industry was authentically competitive in ways that the oligopolistic industries of steel, auto, and rubber were not. For both management and labor, the acceptance of the administrative apparatus of collective bargaining was an historic compromise that was much more practically achieved in industries dominated by three or four giant producers than was the case in textiles. Textile producers lived closer to the margin, were perennially short of capital and, thus, incorporated a number of competitive dynamics that encouraged an intransigent anti-labor attitude.

Prior to the coming of the CIO, the United Textile Work-

ers (AFL) under Frank Gorman never developed effective organizing momentum, and the great uprising from below in
the South of 1934 caught the leadership by surprise. The
most successful organizers in textiles were Emil Rieve and
George Baldanzi, and they quickly rose to leadership after
Sidney Hillman put together the Textile Workers Organizing Committee under the CIO in 1937. The union contracts
subsequently won in the North came after hard struggles
and yielded contracts at levels below those obtained in the
nation's other major industries. After many defeats, the
union developed a methodical approach that struck its
friends as prudent and its critics as cautious. However characterized, the day-to-day organizing life in textiles did not encourage union activists to have stars in their eyes.

When the union first systematically began to turn its attention to the South during World War II, it encountered a
world even more resistant than that presided over by the
mill barons of New England. The hierarchical nature of
Southern society, grounded in an authoritarian racial caste
system and protected by docile religious and journalistic institutions ready to provide serviceable apologetics on demand, assisted in fortifying across the region a deep
hostility to the TWUA. Demagogic attacks, grounded in provincial attitudes, could always be effectively mounted
against "outsiders" with names like Baldanzi, Rieve, and
Bittner.

Faced with such an implacable and elaborately armed industrial opposition, the TWUA had difficulty fashioning a
clear organizing strategy in the South. It had difficulty assess-
ing the Southern working class as well. "The Southern Textile Worker is a small-town, suspicious individual, who is
extremely provincial, petty, gossip-mongering, who is completely isolated and knows only his mill." In the late 1930s,
such was the settled conclusion of a highly placed textile
union official, Solomon Barkin, research director of the
TWUA in New York. Southerners were "easy prey to explosive situations" and therefore too much should not be read
into those occasions when they mounted strikes in mill villages. Such incidents needed to be understood as a mo-

ment of "novelty" in the dull life of the mill town. "For the most part," Barkin believed at the time, Southern mill hands were "mute and undisciplined."[6]

While Barkin was committing his thoughts to paper in 1939, a Southern journalist was giving even more elaborate expression to the same ideas in a manuscript that would be published the following year. W. J. Cash's *The Mind of the South* was a sustained attempt to explain the peculiarities of the region and its people. Cash, too, wrestled with the apparent paradox of working-class deference on the one hand and, on the other, abundant evidence of assertion, sometimes violent assertion, by the same people. As observers, both Barkin and Cash noted the oral traditions of Southern society and the generally low level of education that yielded very little in the way of written evidence about popular belief. In Barkin's phrase, Southern mill workers were in that sense "mute."

A different kind of "distancing" from Southern workers was visible in the views of others who defended mill workers by romanticizing them. George Baldanzi found in the South "a much greater appreciation of human values than is found in the North." Southerners, he believed, were "by nature kindly," were "strongly religious," and tended to "react to human tragedy with a sort of calm fatalism." In a judgment he otherwise did not elaborate upon, Baldanzi saw Southern textile workers, provincial though they were, as representing "the best of what remains of truly American folklore."[7]

Aside from such excursions into remote theorizing, the textile leadership came under criticism for being physically remote from the daily struggles of Operation Dixie. Bittner, Baldanzi, and the Atlanta office in its entirety were criticized for being an elite "palace guard," out of touch with grass roots realities. Bittner "didn't have the contacts and experience" to analyze the South with sophistication. The initial fanfare surrounding the launching of the campaign was, in retrospect, also seen as an error "that instantly put people on their guard, and made the South as a whole defensive." Such propaganda produced by the CIO leadership was seen as "talking to their own people rather than to the public, and the newspapers really dressed it up, calling it an 'invasion.' "[8] The problem, many believed, began with the name itself. "Operation Dixie" almost seemed to beg the opposition to employ the "invasion" metaphor.[9] Southern organizers agreed: The CIO leadership "advertised" too much, and in the wrong way. "Here comes Sherman's army again! Be ready!"[10] The effect was to "immediately put people on the defensive."[11] The result was a "damn tragic error."[12]

Internal dialogue in labor's ranks about such tactical matters was fundamentally unbalanced. Northern organizers had, in effect, scalps on their belts, and could turn aside unwanted advice from Southern staffers with an incontrovertible fact: "Look, I organized 30,000 workers in Pittsburgh (or Detroit, or Akron) and what have you people done down here?" As a Southern organizer explained years later, "There was no answer for that, because what they said was true."[13]

Clearly, the entire issue surrounding the proper initial "positioning" of the Southern campaign, one that might be summarized as a debate over a "high-profile" or "low-profile" approach, sheds significant light on the condition of the American labor movement in the immediate aftermath of World War II. Baldanzi was right on two counts. The campaign needed Southern organizers who understood the local culture; it also needed programmatically experienced Northern organizers to bring coherence to the organizing process. But the debate that took place over what to call the campaign, and how to present it to the American and Southern public, also revealed that Southern CIO staff members were to have little prestige and thus little decision-making power within the campaign itself. If the Northern model of "transforming" victories did not quite fit the realities at work in the Southern textile industry, there was no Southern dissenter with enough internal clout in the CIO to prevail at the level of policy.

What overall final appraisal can be made of these internal disputes? Northern organizers did have more experience; they did "know more." The inexperience of Southern organizers was a constantly recurring problem. At the height of the organizing drive in the heart of textile country in 1946, the North Carolina state director, William Smith, felt it necessary to remind his predominantly Southern-born staff of the most basic rules of organizing. He complained that the Kannapolis staff was carrying on a recruitment campaign "without any method or purpose other than [to] sign up as many workers as possible." He insisted that this technique left the CIO with only "an unorganized crowd of card-signers." Smith's instructions to the Kannapolis staff concentrated on the most elementary truths: "You should, right at the outset of any organizing drive, concentrate on setting up committees in every department and on every shift. Make this your *number one job* in beginning any organizing drive. Don't try to do it all alone. Do it through and with the committees, and it will be done better and much sooner. Don't be a LONE RANGER. Organize your work and your work will be organized."[14]

Smith wrote at a pivotal moment in the textile campaign, which was, itself, the critical center of Operation Dixie. It is important to assess precisely what had gone wrong by the time he wrote these exasperated instructions on August 5, 1946. It is also vital to isolate precisely what Smith's textile organizing staff was failing to achieve that, as the CIO's experience taught, needed to be achieved. In short, organizing doctrine (the CIO's institutional memory) and operational conduct (running the Southern campaign) merged at Kannapolis in August in ways that revealed the strategic and tactical trauma of the American labor movement in 1946.

It is necessary to pull together a number of threads imbedded both in the history of Operation Dixie and in the formative years of the CIO in order to detect the unraveling of the labor movement and the dissipation of its energy that began in 1946. The CIO's own contributions to the failure of Operation Dixie arose from hazards found within every organization. In military terms, "doctrine" can be defined as that strategy that has worked most effectively before and has, as a result, become the conventional wisdom. Thus do military organizations prepare to fight the last war. The CIO was hamstrung by the same dynamic, facing new conditions but armed with the tactics that had proven most successful in the last "war." Unfortunately, these tactics were the legacy of a Northern encounter, a society not matched by what the CIO found in the South. Nor was the surrounding climate of 1946 the same one in which the CIO's conventional wisdom had developed in the Depression. As a group possessing an institutional memory, the CIO was really quite young in 1946. Its essential organizing experience had been packed into the eventful five-year period between 1936 and 1941. In that brief period, the CIO had organized much of America's industrial work force that was concentrated in the steel, auto, rubber, and electrical industries. The only major American industry that remained unorganized was textiles.

Yet broad as it must have seemed, this sweeping organizing experience was really quite narrow in terms of the tactics it employed. The sit-down strikes of the 1930s—often conducted by a small and militant sector of the work force—brought major companies to a standstill. After a tense period of confrontation, the new unions were recognized. Even where the sit-downs were massive and involved large numbers of workers, participants were incorporated quickly, as part of the euphoria of the "sit-down era."

It is important to specify that it was not the sit-downs per se that constituted the essence of the "Northern model" that the CIO followed; rather, it was the transforming impact on the potential for organizing that was achieved by unionizing a bellwether company in a bellwether industry. This achievement, whether it was through a sit-down or not, sent a transforming message of possibility to every unorganized worker in every smaller plant in the affected industry. Such a circumstance could, in a moment, rally thousands of workers to the union cause. It could, in short, overcome worker deference and "fear." In the late 1930s, the industrial rank and file was not so much *recruited* to the CIO as it was *mobilized* for a particularly dramatic kind of job action. This mobilization was in part an emotional response to a particular time, the Depression, and to a particular place, highly centralized mass production industry with choke points that could be shut down to cripple the entire operation. The infancy of Southern industry made such action impossible. Thus, twentieth-century tactics that had produced dazzling Northern successes could not bridge the gap to a region languishing, in many respects, in the nineteenth century.

Had the CIO been able to effect a "transforming" breakthrough in any of the region's textile giants, perhaps Southern workers by the hundreds of thousands could have been mobilized to join the CIO. To have been "transforming" in this sense, the breakthrough victory would have had to be a decisive one over a powerful and widely known company. Anything less could not be expected to change rapidly the calculus of power between Southern industry and labor. The "Northern model" of attacking the bellwether textile plants, then, was one that fired the imagination and determination of both organizers and workers.

In the absence of such a galvanizing experience, the difference between temporary mobilization and permanent recruitment became quite clear. Instead of rapidly pulling enthusiastic masses of previously unorganized workers to the cause, as it did in the Northern sit-downs, the CIO in the South would be forced slowly, painfully to recruit skeptical workers—one union card at a time. Many of those Southern workers the CIO tried to organize were in the most secure positions they and their families had ever known. Most of them constituted the first generation to look to factory work as a way out of the mountains or off the farm. Without a clear demonstration of the advantages of union membership—one that did not exist in the South—workers proved reluctant to risk the present for the unknown benefits of an uncertain future. Lacking a striking Southern success to which it could point in trying to convince Southern workers that a union was an attainable goal, the CIO's only recourse lay in the long-term education of unorganized workers to the benefits of union membership. In the end, the

CIO could neither mobilize nor recruit Southern workers who were seemingly impervious to its educational campaign.

Simply put, the CIO faced the central organizing dilemma: one cannot want for people what circumstances do not encourage them to want for themselves. As a result, in case after case across the South, it became evident that the CIO's inability to get off the ground by forming in-plant committees forced CIO staffers into trying to organize Southern workers' unions *for* them—a tactic that most organizers agreed could never really be expected to produce a high rate of success. In August 1946, North Carolina's embattled state director lectured the Kannapolis staff on the need to avoid behaving like "lone rangers" and to proceed with the organization of in-plant committees. But if one fact was clear from the reports of the previous nine weeks of effort (however elliptical those reports might have been in terms of numbers of signed union cards), it was that the Kannapolis staff could not fashion reliable in-plant committees. Staff organizers therefore functioned as "lone rangers" out of necessity, rather than choice. In the absence, then, of a transforming breakthrough, the CIO had to recruit rather than mobilize. And to recruit they had first to educate the workers. Unfortunately, the CIO had neither the time nor resources for such a necessarily lengthy "educational" campaign. "Education" involved many ingredients—a knowledge of what other American workers under CIO leadership had done for themselves, the management tactics that had to be overcome, the worker solidarity that had to be built, specific steps toward building it, and all the other components of American labor's collective experience that bore directly on the task at hand in the South. In essence, "education" could be summarized as a believable blueprint for action—one that sustained hope among powerless people.

But unable to do what *would* work, the CIO's effort consisted of an amalgam of techniques that *might* work: an educational effort wherever workers were ready to listen; continued attempts to achieve a "transforming" breakthrough in places like Kannapolis or Avondale that might mobilize large numbers; and the quiet, methodical signing of workers in smaller plants.

The great days of the 1930s had been days of mobilization; in the South, the more pedestrian future turned on steady numerical recruitment. The time would come—by 1946 for some, and by the late 1940s for almost everyone— when CIO leaders would "read" organizers' reports with an eye to what the reports meant in terms of permanent recruitment. They would look for and demand that reports reflected the completion of sequential organizing tasks and that results would focus on numbers rather than on description. The presence or absence of signed CIO cards and accompanying initiation fees verified whether recruitment was taking place in a given organizing campaign. Hundreds of organizers' reports during the decisive first six months of Operation Dixie in 1946 are filled with narrative rather than numbers. The CIO leadership's demands for numbers had not yet become an institutional cornerstone of CIO practice. In any event, as Operation Dixie proceeded in the South, the numbers were not there to report.

It may be noted in passing that judgments as to whether a given organizer's report represented "creative rhetoric" or a serious narrative about organizing in-plant committees depended on the specific tactical and strategic situation at the time a report was written. In mid-July 1946, in Kannapolis, after weeks of sustained organizing efforts by the largest staff in the South, it was ominous to discover the local lead organizer explaining the absence of signed cards as a function of the staff's preoccupation with (still) trying to set up in-plant committees. The same report, written in the first week of June, would have been far more understandable. The essential point, applicable throughout the crucial summer of 1946, was that the fundamental organizational distinctions between "recruitment" on the one hand and "mobilization" based on a transforming victory on the other were not clearly understood by most organizers at most levels of either the CIO or textile union hierarchy.

No quick fix can be suggested that might have changed

the outcome of Operation Dixie. Economic power in the South was too closely interwoven with local governments, newspapers, police forces, and religious leaders; together, they were able to mobilize a level of opposition that the CIO did not have the cultural credibility to defeat. Moreover, even had the CIO somehow been able to withstand the coordinated corporate assault, it still had the internal problem—the massively debilitating internal problem—that grew out of deeply embedded Southern traditions on race. At its best the CIO stood for a restructuring of race relations that would not gain ground anywhere in America until the civil rights movement some twenty years later.

Beyond these problems, sobering as they were, was an ideological dilemma that generated the most dismaying kinds of political problems. The CIO's origins and its goal of organizing all industrial workers necessitated some kind of approach that could transcend ethnic and racial barriers and ideological divisions. This reality set in motion a certain leftward dynamic that harmonized badly with the conservative postwar national political climate. Taking all these factors into account, it cannot be regarded as a surprise that the CIO's Southern drive failed.

Once established and with a collective self-image, organizations become increasingly invested in preserving their place in society. As a result, voices from the far corners of the organization are seen as troublesome, and therefore as ever less legitimate; and bad news that runs counter to the collective self-image is less and less welcome. An antidemocratic dynamic evolves as less diversity of opinion is permitted at the top levels of leadership. The lower the level of internal democracy, the less likely that organization is to entertain conflicting reports from the field. To remain successful in democratic terms, an organization needs to be self-regenerating, creating an institutional climate that allows for change from "the bottom" and encourages creativity at "the top." Such an institutional climate is conceivable, though rarely attained in history to date, in or out of labor movements.

Organizations whose members see themselves as "progressive" are in no sense immunized against this evolving dynamic of institutional rigidity. Even revolutions, once deemed "successful" by those in charge, are institutionalized in order to preserve their gains and secure the new order. This dynamic is clearly at work in the CIO's purge of its own left wing in the late 1940s, and earlier when locals of left-wing unions were raided by internationals to their right on the political spectrum. True, in the late 1940s the national political climate was such that the threat to the CIO's respectability was great, and the pressure to purge those internationals was intense. And clearly, many committed labor activists saw the purge as the only chance to salvage any position at all for the CIO in the increasingly constricted national political and economic order. However, during this process the organizing energy of those left-wing internationals was lost; ironically, it was those same unions, racially innovative as they were, that had done the most to begin chipping away at the intricate hierarchical structure of Southern economic and social relations. There was, of course, a countervailing irony; the left-led unions, dutifully tracking Soviet foreign policy without consulting the local membership, were caught in their own hierarchical assumptions.

If anything, the ideological struggle in the CIO eventually encouraged each faction to turn inward, to become more secular and—a by-product—more righteous about its own past policies. Worse, ideology provided an institutional way not to hear criticism. The TWUA habitually turned away criticism of its own ponderous approach by viewing such criticism as reflecting merely the "biased" or "doctrinaire" opinion of "radicals." Transparently, left-led unions did regard the Baldanzis of the TWUA with contempt. But awkwardly for the TWUA's self-image, so did Southern-born liberals such as Jim Pierce of the CWA, who regarded the union as structurally and operationally "weak." Said Pierce:

> The Textile Workers could never decide to do anything, or how to do it, and still can't. Back and forth, back and forth. They get militant for a few days; then

somebody hits them and they slump back down. That has its effect on people. Union representatives can only be really good if they've got good strong unions to back them up. And they didn't have it in textiles.[15]

There is an irony here that seldom is a feature of internal debates within the world of trade unionism. The steel and autoworkers who came South to convey the Northern model of organizing to Operation Dixie's Southern cadres, as well as Southerners like Pierce from mass-based industries, possessed a view of organizational possibility that was simply not a part of the heritage of textile organizing. This sense of possibility was part of the strength of unions like the UAW, but it was derived from grandly successful experiences that had no real counterpart in the history of the TWUA. Veteran textile organizers had learned to roll with the punches; those who could not simply left. The style that eventually came to characterize the union reflected these dynamics. Such modes of procedure made men like Jim Pierce impatient and induced in radicals like John Russell and Karl Korstad something approaching a state of controlled rage.

But the old hands of the TWUA had learned, in bitter defeats in New England as well as in the South, that mill owners were different from other "captains of industry." Less secure than most, they were, in the words of a black organizer, "meaner" than most. Whether one like the style of the TWUA or not, that style was a product of experiences that had been internalized over two generations of disappointing organizing campaigns.

What can be said about the TWUA and about the participants in every other union in Operation Dixie is that they brought a certain kind of dignified hope for a better life into the corners of the South that no one else had ever visited. Granted, this hope was not encased in a perfect institutional vehicle. Granted, the people in Operation Dixie did not always perform unerringly. Nevertheless, it is possible to agree with a summary judgment of Alabama's Frank Parker who said: "I lived through the whole thing. I was in the movement before it started. And I was in the movement after it was over. And I'm happy they came. I'm happy they helped. But it could have been better."[16]

In the modern era of global markets and multinational corporations, the old militants in America's mass production industries have been thrown on the defensive. Hard-won wage levels have been taken away, job security destroyed, and hopes for a new kind of "economic democracy" shattered. It has all been very sobering—rather like a textile organizer's experience, one might say.

Forty years after the fact, it seems clear that the high tide of American labor came in the 1935–1945 decade, when labor's long-held dream of a new day for industrial workers seemed to be in sight. Beyond matters of wages and working conditions, the conceptions of society embedded in that dream were generous, egalitarian, and democratic. In the highly stratified corporate world of the 1980s, critical components of the dream, as well as the relationship of organized labor to the dream itself, have become quite problematic.

Operation Dixie happened at the moment of labor's apogee when hopes were still lofty but when resources had begun to shrink and the corporate opposition had armed itself for a massive counterattack. All the tensions implicit in such a pivotal historical turning point surfaced in Operation Dixie. The legacy has been a bitter one, for within the ranks of the trade union movement, there were no winners, only losers. For American labor, Operation Dixie was, quite simply, a moment of high tragedy from which it has yet to fully recover.

Notes

CHAPTER I

1. Robert Christie, *Empire in Wood: A History of the Carpenters' Union* (Ithaca, N.Y.: New York State School of Industrial Relations, 1956), pp.19–45; Stuart Bruce Kaufman, *Samuel Gompers and the Origins of the American Federation of Labor, 1848–1896*, (Westport, Conn.: Greenwood Press, 1973), pp. 38–39; Daniel Rogers, *The Work Ethic in Industrial America, 1850–1920* (Chicago: University of Chicago Press, 1978); Herbert G. Gutman, *Work, Culture, and Society in Industrializing America: Essays in American Working-Class and Social History* (New York: Vintage Books, 1966).

2. Michael Rogin, "Voluntarism: The Political Functions of an Anti-Political Doctrine," *Industrial and Labor Relations Review* 5 (July 1952): 521–535; Joyce Kornbluh, *Rebel Voices: An IWW Anthology* (Ann Arbor: University of Michigan Press, 1968).

3. Ronald L. Filippelli, *Labor in the U.S.A.: A History* (New York: Knopf, 1984), p. 168. Nelson Lichtenstein places AFL membership at 4,078,000 in 1920, 3,600,000 in 1924, and 2,150,000 in 1932 (*Labor's War at Home: The CIO in World War II* [Cambridge, Eng.: Cambridge University Press, 1982], pp. 279, 296, 315).

4. Milton Cantor, *The Divided Left: American Radicalism, 1900–1975* (New York: Hill and Wang, 1978); Sidney Howard, *The Labor Story: A Survey of Industrial Espionage, 1619–1973* (New York: Praeger, 1974); Richard Edwards, *Contested Terrain: The Transformation of the Workplace in the Twentieth Century* (New York: Basic Books, 1979); David Montgomery, *Workers' Control in America: Studies in the History of Work, Technology, and Labor Struggles* (Cambridge, Eng.: Cambridge University Press, 1979); William Preston, Jr., *Aliens and Dissenters: Federal Suppression of Radicals, 1903–1933* (New York: Harper and Row, 1966).

5. Robert H. Zieger, *American Workers, American Unions,*

1920–1985 (Baltimore: Johns Hopkins University Press, 1986), on pp. 32–34, provides a succinct discussion of federal unions.

6. David Brody, "The Emergence of Mass Production Unionism," in Brody, *Workers in Industrial America: Essays on the Twentieth Century Struggle* (New York: Oxford University Press, 1980), pp. 82–94; Lichtenstein, *Labor's War at Home*, pp. 9–11.

7. The historic debate within the AFL is effectively summarized in James O. Morris, *Conflict Within the AFL: A Study of Craft versus Industrial Unionism, 1901–1938* (Ithaca, N.Y.: Cornell University Press, 1958). However, an in-depth study of the struggles involved in the creation of the CIO and the AFL's response at all points along the way is presented by Walter Galenson, *The CIO Challenge to the AFL: A History of the American Labor Movement, 1935–1941* (Cambridge, Mass.: Harvard University Press, 1960), pp. 3–74. Galenson also provides individual chapters that chronicle the beginnings of industrial unionism in seventeen industries.

8. Sidney Fine, *Sit-Down: The General Motors Strike of 1936–1937* (Ann Arbor: University of Michigan Press, 1969); Irving Bernstein, *Turbulent Years: A History of the American Worker, 1933–1941* (Boston: Houghton Mifflin, 1971), pp. 572–634; Galenson, *The CIO Challenge to the AFL*, especially pp. 75–192, 239–282. J. Raymond Walsh provides a more contemporary view of events, especially pp. 48–138, and also an examination of the CIO's early tactics, pp. 165–195, in *CIO: Industrial Unionism in Action* (New York: Norton, 1937). Benjamin Stolberg, *The Story of the CIO* (New York: Viking, 1938), captures the spirit of the time as well. Peter Friedlander presents a case study in *The Emergence of a UAW Local, 1936–1939: A Study in Class and Culture* (Pittsburgh: University of Pittsburgh Press, 1975). Although Friedlander notes at the outset that he disagrees with some of Fine's assumptions and analysis (p. xv), he presents a clear picture of the impact of the Flint sit-down on nearby workers, and on the recruitment of those workers into the UAW (pp. 10–21). Daniel Nelson provides a view of the sit-downs in the rubber industry in "Origins of the Sit-Down Era: Worker Militancy and Innovation in the Rubber Industry, 1934–1938," *Labor History* 23 (spring 1982): 198–225. See also Zieger, *American Workers, American Unions*, pp. 46–48.

9. David Brody, "The Expansion of the American Labor Movement: Institutional Sources of Stimulus and Restraint," in *Institutions in Modern America*, ed. Stephen E. Ambrose (Baltimore: Johns Hopkins University Press, 1967); P. K. Edwards, *Strikes in the United States, 1881–1974* (New York: St. Martin's, 1981), pp. 12–51,

134–172; Thomas R. Brooks, *Picket Lines and Bargaining Tables: Organized Labor Comes of Age, 1935–1955* (New York: Grossett and Dunlap, 1968); Leo Huberman, *The Labor Spy Racket* (New York: Modern Age Books, 1937).

10. None of the Flint strike leaders could be credited with originality in forging the sit-down weapon. It had been tried unsuccessfully in the Midwest in 1935 and again in the auto industry in Atlanta in 1936. The tactic of the occupational strike had its origins in Europe, where it was popularly known as "the Polish strike." What made Flint special was that the sit-down had worked against the nation's largest corporation. See Wyndham Mortimer, *Organize! My Life as a Union Man* (Boston: Beacon, 1971); Fine, *Sit-Down*; Michigan Labor History Society, *Sit-Down* (Detroit: The Society, 1979).

11. Lichtenstein, *Labor's War at Home*, pp. 19–20; Filipelli, *Labor in the U.S.A.*, p. 185; Edwards, *Strikes in the United States*, pp. 142–143; Vernon H. Jensen, *Nonferrous Metals Industry Unionism, 1932–1954: A Story of Leadership Controversy* (Ithaca, N.Y.: Cornell University Press, 1954), pp. 10–13.

12. Lichtenstein, *Labor's War at Home*, pp. 17–19.

CHAPTER II

1. Nelson Lichtenstein, *Labor's War at Home: The CIO in World War II* (Cambridge, Eng.: Cambridge University Press, 1982), pp. 110–117; Paul A. C. Koistinen, "Warfare and Power Relations in America: Mobilizing the World War II Economy," in *The Home Front and War in the Twentieth Century: The American Experience in Comparative Perspective*, ed. James Titus (Proceedings of the Tenth Military History Symposium, Oct. 20–22, 1982; Washington, D.C.: U.S. Air Force Academy and Office of Air Force History, 1984), pp. 91–110.

2. David Montgomery, *Workers' Control in America Studies in The History of Work, Technology, and Labor Struggles* (Cambridge, Eng.: Cambridge University Press, 1979), pp. 153–175; Bert Cochran, ed., *American Labor in Midpassage* (New York: Monthly Review, 1979), pp. 46, 150; Joshua Freeman, "Delivering the Goods: Industrial Unionism During World War II," in *The Labor History Reader*, ed. Daniel J. Leab (Urbana and Chicago: University of Illinois Press, 1985), pp.383–406.

3. Paul David Richards, "The History of the Textile Workers

Union of America, CIO, in the South, 1937–1945," unpublished Ph.D. dissertation, University of Wisconsin, 1978, p. 184 (hereinafter cited as "History of Textiles").

4. John Wesley Kennedy, "A History of the Textile Workers Union of America, CIO," unpublished Ph.D. dissertation, University of North Carolina, 1950, pp. 23–33 (hereinafter cited as "A Textile History)"; Richards, "History of Textiles," p. 150.

5. Art Preis, *Labor's Giant Step: Twenty Years of the CIO* (New York: Pioneer, 1964), pp. 257–283.

6. A sense of desperation prevailed among many workers in wartime mass production factories who were laid off in 1945. "They've closed up Willow Run," exclaimed a representative of the CIO. "Nobody wants Willow Run. Nobody wants the 51,950 pieces of machinery. And nobody wants the more than 20,000 human beings who go with the plant" (quoted in William Tuttle, "Cold War Politics, 1945–1961," in *A People and a Nation*, vol. 2, ed. Mary Beth Norton et al. [Boston: Houghton Mifflin, 1982], p. 843).

7. Sidney Lens, *Left, Right, and Center: Conflicting Forces in American Labor* (Hinsdale, Ill.: Regnery, 1949), pp. 363–364; Bruce Morris, "Industrial Relations in the Automobile Industry," in *Labor in Postwar America*, ed. Colston E. Warne et al. (Brooklyn, N.Y.: Remsen, 1949), pp. 399–417; Lichtenstein, *Labor's War at Home*, pp. 221–232.

8. Richards, "History of Textiles," p. 95.

9. Roger Ransom and Richard Sutch, *One Kind of Freedom: The Economic Consequences of Emancipation* (New York: Oxford University Press, 1977); Lawrence C. Goodwyn, *Democratic Promise: The Populist Moment in America* (New York: Oxford University Press, 1976); David E. Conrad, *The Forgotten Farmers: The Story of Sharecroppers in the New Deal* (Urbana: University of Illinois Press, 1965); Glenn Gilman, *Human Relations in the Industrial Southeast: A Study of the Textile Industry* (Chapel Hill: University of North Carolina Press, 1956); Margaret J. Hagood, *Mothers of the South: Portraiture of the White Tenant Farm Woman* (Chapel Hill: University of North Carolina Press, 1939); Jennings J. Rhyne, *Some Cotton Mill Workers and Their Villages* (Chapel Hill: University of North Carolina Press, 1930).

10. Benjamin Stolberg, *Nation*, Dec. 1929, p. 43.

11. Ibid., pp. 38, 40, 57. "Runaway" textile companies had, by 1935, left "ghost towns across New England where textile mills had thrived" (Jacquelyn Dowd Hall, Robert Korstad, and James Leloudis, "Cotton Mill People: Work, Community, and Protest in

the Textile South, 1880–1940," *American Historical Review* 91 [April 1986]: 278).

12. Richards, "History of Textiles," pp. 58–59. The bitterness of the 1934 strike, during which no fewer than 11,000 troops were called out by various state governments, left long and angry memories.

13. Kennedy, "A Textile History," pp. 84–94.

14. Richards, "History of Textiles," pp. 99–103.

15. By 1945, the comparative regional employment figures were North, 629,000; South, 579,000 (Richards, "History of Textiles," p. 152).

16. Textile Workers Union of America, Proceedings, Constitutional Convention, Philadelphia, May 15–19, 1939, p. 131.

CHAPTER III

1. CIO News Release, Atlanta, June 4, 1946. See George Baldanzi to Van Bittner, July 1, 1946, CIO Organizing Committee, North Carolina Papers, ODA); Robert Oliver, Texas state director, to "All Local Unions," June (n.d.) 1946, Texas Labor Archives, Special Collections Division of The University of Texas at Arlington Libraries; Arlington, Texas, 51-18-11 (hereinafter referred to as UTA).

The South Carolina director, Franz Daniel, seemed to resist this centralization. As late as August 21, and again on August 29, long after this policy had become accepted elsewhere, Bittner was forced to express his anger at unilateral filings for NLRB elections coming out of South Carolina (Van Bittner to Franz Daniel, Aug. 21 and 29, 1946, CIO Organizing Committee, South Carolina Papers, ODA; Van Bittner to William Smith, North Carolina state director, Aug. 21, 1946, CIO Organizing Committee, North Carolina Papers, ODA). Even when officers were willing to accept such rules and regulations, there was no insurance that the organizers under their direction would comply (Boyd E. Payton, regional director, TWUA, form letter to eight TWUA organizers working in Virginia, Sept. 10, 1946, CIO Organizing Committee, Virginia Papers, ODA; also Boyd E. Payton, personal interview, Charlotte, N.C., June 27, 1984). One example of CIO staff members who did try to comply is found in Robert Oliver to A. J. Pittman, director, District 8, United Packinghouse Workers of America, dated as "1946," UTA, 51-13-8.

On the PAC issue, Bittner wrote Daniel: "I think the PAC in

South Carolina is about as useful as Bill Green as a CIO organizer.
. . . If I had my way about it, as vice chairman of PAC, I would simply dissolve PAC in South Carolina and I expect to work toward
that end" (Van Bittner to Franz Daniel, July 3, 1946, CIO Organizing Committee, South Carolina Papers, ODA).

2. Bittner was described variously by some who knew him as
"phlegmatic," "pompous," or "dull," by Packinghouse Workers'
President Ralph Helstein as "essentially immobile," and by histo-
rian Irving Bernstein as a man "whose supply of vitriol was inex-
haustible" (Irving Bernstein, *Turbulent Years: A History of the
American Worker, 1933–1941* [Boston: Houghton Mifflin, 1971];
p. 544). Relevant are: Ralph Helstein, personal interview, Chicago,
Oct. 13, 1984; Karl Korstad, personal interview, Greensboro, N.C.,
March 29, 1982; Jim Pierce, personal interview, Charlotte, N.C.,
June 26, 1982; John Russell, personal interview, Arden, N.C.,
March 12, 1983; Raymond J. Schnell, personal interview, Surf
City, N.C., June 27, 1982; Daniel Starnes, personal interview, Okla-
homa City, Aug. 10, 1984.

3. Jane and Joel Leighton, personal interview, Annapolis, Dec.
9, 1986.

4. These portraits are assembled from the correspondence written by these men (to be found in the Operation Dixie Archives),
by an interview with one state director, Charles Gillman
(Riverdale, Ga., July 17 and 21, 1984), and the following interviews with other retired CIO staff members: Lida Hurtt, personal interview, Charlotte, N.C., June 27, 1984; James Jackson, personal
interview, East Point, Ga., July 19, 1984; B. T. Judd, personal interview, Knoxville, Tenn., Feb. 28, 1983; Melville Kress, personal interview, Piney Flats, Tenn., Feb. 26, 1983; Nicholas Kurko, personal
interview, Fort Worth, Aug. 4, 1984; Frank Parker, personal interview, Birmingham, Ala., July 23, 1984; Pierce interview; Lillian
Roehl, personal interview, Silver Spring, Md., March 16, 1984.

5. F. Ray Marshall, *Labor in the South* (Cambridge, Mass.: Harvard University Press, 1967), p. 247.

6. Ibid.

7. See Chapter VIII on ideological warfare within the labor
movement.

8. *CIO News*, May 6, 1946; "Labor Drives South," *Fortune*, Nov.
1946, p. 138. As late as September 1946, CIO officials were still having difficulties in keeping organizers focused on the big plants
and away from the small ones—a tendency that must have been unavoidable on occasion, in order to achieve *some* results and main-

tain morale. However, according to the North Carolina state director, the CIO had "had some very sad experiences with these small plants," and he insisted that organizers follow the CIO's strategy (William Smith to "All Staff Members," Sept. 12, 1946, CIO Organizing Committee, North Carolina Papers, ODA).

9. Sidney Fine, *Sit-Down: The General Motors Strike of 1936–1937* Ann Arbor: University of Michigan Press, 1969).

10. Marshall, *Labor in the South*, p. 256; Frank T. De Vyver, "The Present Status of Labor Unions in the South, 1948," *Southern Economic Journal* 16 (July 1949): 1–22.

A number of veteran CIO organizers had obviously understood the need to target "bellwether plants," in the sense that the industry wage would not be changed significantly until the big plants were organized (Schnell interview; John Thomas, personal interview, Oak Ridge, Tenn., Aug. 14, 1984; James Touchstone, personal interview, Meridian, Miss., July 27, 1984).

11. However, the *CIO News* reported that seventy-eight organizers were working in North and South Carolina as of July 29, 1946, an increase due perhaps to a decision to concentrate more of the CIO's personnel on textile states, or an exaggeration by the labor press.

12. Details of the conclave of FTA organizers at Highlander Folk School were provided by Karl Korstad (Korstad interview). Under the general heading of "problems of setting up an ad-hoc committee" such as Operation Dixie, one notes that the drive in Mississippi operated more or less out of the hip pocket of the Mississippi state director, Robert Starnes, throughout the summer of 1946. It was not until August 20 that Starnes found permanent office space in Jackson (Starnes to Eugene Albert Roper, Jr., quoted in Roper, "The CIO Organizing Committee in Mississippi, June 1946–January 1949," unpublished M.A. thesis, University of Mississippi, 1949, pp. 1–2.

13. Parker and Starnes interviews; Geneva Sneed, personal interview, Knoxville, Tenn., Aug. 14, 1984. A sophisticated discussion of the benefits that accrue from assigning organizers to their "home" industries is offered in a letter from Toby Mendes to George Baldanzi, June 21, 1946, in the course of resisting Baldanzi's decision to transfer him elsewhere (CIO Organizing Committee, North Carolina, ODA).

14. Van Bittner to "All State Directors," June 3, 1946, and S. H. Dalrymple, secretary-treasurer, CIO Organizing Committee, to "All State Directors," June 3, 1946, CIO Organizing Committee,

South Carolina Papers, ODA. For examples of the controversy between state directors and field staff, see Glenn Earp, Gene Day, and Bill Hopps, Sumter, S.C., to Franz Daniel, July 9, 1946, CIO Organizing Committee, South Carolina Papers, ODA; Franz Daniel to Glenn Earp, July 12 and July 17, 1946, CIO Organizing Committee, South Carolina Papers, ODA.

At the close of June, the initiation fee was still not being collected. In Georgia, the CIO's state director, Charles Gillman, was "very much disturbed" as a result of the "organizing efforts in Athens, Georgia, and the failure to charge the initiation fee of $1.00" (George Baldanzi to John McCoy, second vice president, American Federation of Hosiery Workers, June 26, 1941, CIO Organizing Committee, Tennessee Papers, ODA).

Perhaps as an effort to compete with the CIO, the AFL was not attempting to collect initiation fees under the Southern campaign it had begun at the same time, although there *was* some confusion over the exact nature of official policy on this matter, as was also the case in the CIO (Anthony Valente, international president, UTWA-AFL, to Paul Smith, regional director, AFL, Richmond, Va., Sept. 27, 1946, Joseph Jacobs Collection, SLA/GSU 1039-208. See also Ward B. Melody, Texas District Council, American Newspaper Guild, to Franz Daniel, Sept. 27, 1946, CIO Organizing Committee, South Carolina Papers, ODA.)

15. Nancy Blaine, Report of Activities, July 21–26, 1946, CIO Organizing Committee, North Carolina Papers, ODA.

16. Sumter, South Carolina, was but one of many towns in which police harassment made it extremely difficult for the local organizer to do his job. "Late yesterday afternoon the Chief of Police picked him up and paraded him all over town in the police car. No charges were filed and Earp was released immediately" (Franz Daniel to Van Bittner, July 30, 1946, CIO Organizing Committee, South Carolina Papers, ODA).

17. For details of anti-union newspapers published by religious fundamentalists, see *CIO News*, June 3, 1946. Also see Stetson Kennedy, *Southern Exposure* (Garden City, N.Y.: Doubleday, 1946). "The activities of mill village preachers in Liberty and Easley are distinctly bad" (Lucy Randolph Mason, Atlanta, to Franz Daniel, Sept. 14, 1946, CIO Organizing Committee, South Carolina Papers, ODA).

18. In an effort to cope with the hostility of local police and elected officials, the CIO hired Mason to be its Southern public relations representative. She would visit communities in advance of

an organizing campaign in order to persuade unfriendly officials over to the CIO's side or, at least, to urge them to enforce the law and protect the rights of the organizers. For further information about Mason's experiences with the CIO, see Lucy Randolph Mason, *To Win These Rights: A Personal Story of the CIO in the South* (New York: Harper and Brothers, 1952). The matter is treated in greater detail in Chapter VII.

19. Edmund F. Ryan, Alabama state director, Textile Workers Union of America, to George Baldanzi, Oct. 25, 1946, CIO Organizing Committee, Tennessee Papers, ODA.

20. "In the Handleman Mills, Incorporated, of 208 eligible voters, 154 had signed up with us on a $1.00 basis. The organizer there did a good job and worked hard. The workers at the outset had several issues which bothered them. They, therefore, wanted the union. However, the employer granted them their requests and there was no longer any interest in the Union. Two or three days prior to the election our organizers were sure we would win this one, but despite the fact that we had 154 paid up, we only got 38 votes" (William Smith to Van Bittner, Oct. 10, 1946, CIO Organizing Committee, North Carolina Papers, ODA).

21. "Comer is fighting the union with two weapons—on the one hand a very paternalistic system as regards wages, insurance, health, home and safety conditions; and on the other hand a very vicious system of outright firing, discrimination and every conceivable way to terrorize workers whom he finds belong to the Union" (Edmund F. Ryan to Emil Rieve, general-president, TWUA, Oct. 25, 1946, CIO Organizing Committee, Tennessee Papers, ODA).

22. Edwin E. Pieper, Report of Preliminary Plant Survey, Ecusta Paper Corporation, July 19, 1946, CIO Organizing Committee, Tennessee Papers, ODA.

23. Van Bittner to state directors, July 1, 1946, CIO Organizing Committee, South Carolina Papers, ODA.

24. D. D. Wood to Dean Culver, Concord, N.C., July 9, 1946, CIO Organizing Committee, North Carolina Papers, ODA; Van Bittner to Franz Daniel, Spartanburg, S.C., Aug. 27, 1946, CIO Organizing Committee, South Carolina Papers, ODA; Texas State Nineteenth Industrial Union Council, CIO, Proceedings, Nineteenth Annual Convention, Austin, Tex., Oct. 19–20, 1946, p. 22; Frank Ellis, vice president, United Packinghouse Workers of America, to A. J. Pittman, director, District 8, Sept. 5, 1946, UTA, 15-17-1.

25. Harry Stroud, Activity Report, July 1–7 and 8–14, 1946,

CIO Organizing Committee, North Carolina Papers, ODA; R. C. Thomas to William Smith, July 17, 1946; CIO Organizing Committee, North Carolina Papers, ODA.

26. Donald Swazey to Ernest Pugh, Virginia state director, July 30, 1946, CIO Organizing Committee, Virginia Papers, ODA; Joe Kirk to Draper Wood, July 1, 1946, CIO Organizing Committee, North Carolina Papers, ODA.

27. Edmund F. Ryan to Emil Rieve, Oct. 26, 1946, CIO Organizing Committee, Tennessee Papers, ODA; Edmund F. Ryan to George Baldanzi, Oct. 25, 1946, CIO Organizing Committee, Virginia Papers, ODA.

28. Dean Culver to D. D. Wood, July 19, 1946, CIO Organizing Committee, North Carolina Papers, ODA. The intent here is to describe the remarkable ingenuity of organizers under the pressure of intense opposition and defeat; it is not in any way intended to denigrate their efforts or to call into question their honesty. One of the greatest challenges in organizing is the ability to keep going each day, especially when previous efforts have not been very successful. The euphemisms in these field reports can be understood as organizers' efforts to convince *themselves* to keep going, as well as attempts to calm the fears of their supervisors. However understandable, such reports did not do much to help the cause. As one veteran organizer, who had had extensive supervisory experience and routinely received field reports from local organizers, said, "The experienced director didn't look at rhetoric on reports; they just looked at numbers." Going one step further, if an organizer sent in a lengthy "narrative report, you could bet it was just crap" (Pierce interview). For a more detailed analysis of this important component in the interior life of Operation Dixie, see Chapter IX.

29. CIO Executive Board Minutes, CIO Headquarters, Washington, D.C., July 22, 1946; *CIO News*, July 22 and 29, 1946.

30. The AP wire report on the CIO meeting was picked up by a number of the nation's metropolitan dailies; *Newsweek*, July 8, 1946, also carried an optimistic report on the CIO's Southern drive.

31. A detailed case study of the protracted struggle against one of the bellwethers—the Cannon chain—is presented in the next chapter. The CIO had been making even less headway in another textile-dominated state: South Carolina. By August 29, 1946, the CIO had held only one election in the state during the drive, and that election did not even involve textiles (Bittner to Daniel, Aug.

27, 1946). Perhaps it was from such difficulties that at least one CIO organizer said that everyone knew that being sent to South Carolina was "like being sent to Siberia" (Lloyd Gossett, personal interview, East Point, Ga., July 21, 1984).

32. "To all Caramount Workers," Aug. 6, 1946, CIO Organizing Committee, North Carolina Papers, ODA.

33. "Elections Won," undated CIO compilation, CIO Organizing Committee, Virginia Papers, ODA.

34. William Smith to Frank Bartholomew, July 17, 1946; George Baldanzi to Hannah Pickett Mills Company, July 24, 1946; D. D. Wood to William Smith, July 29, 1946; D. D. Wood to Frank Bartholomew, Aug. 9 and 12, 1946—all CIO Organizing Committee, North Carolina Papers, ODA.

35. "Elections Won," undated CIO compilation.

36. William Smith to R. C. Thomas, Aug. 10, 1946, CIO Organizing Committee, North Carolina Papers, ODA. Smith was even more direct to his Western area director, Wade Lynch: "You have been calling me quite often and telling me how much you are doing in the Western area. However, I fail to see any initiations or membership cards coming in. What are you doing—holding them back to make a big showing at one time—or are you just not getting any?" (William Smith to Wade Lynch, Aug. 14, 1946, CIO Organizing Committee, North Carolina Papers, ODA).

37. By October, CIO staff anxiety over the situation in textiles was being expressed openly in letters to one another. "I am terribly anxious to get going in the textile industry" (Van Bittner to Franz Daniel, Oct. 11, 1946, CIO Organizing Committee, South Carolina Papers, ODA); "May I suggest that you begin to transfer most of the staff not engaged in the textile industry" (Van Bittner to Charles Gillman, Georgia state director, Oct. 11, 1946, CIO Organizing Committee, Tennessee Papers, ODA). Also see Van Bittner to Ernest Pugh, Virginia state director, Oct. 11, 1946, CIO Organizing Committee, Virginia Papers, ODA; Van Bittner to William Smith, Oct. 11, 1946, CIO Organizing Committee, North Carolina Papers, ODA; George Baldanzi to Van Bittner, "re: Peerless Woolen Company," July 27, 1946, CIO Organizing Committee, North Carolina Papers, ODA; Paul Christopher, Tennessee state director, to Franz Daniel, Nov. 23, 1946, CIO Organizing Committee, Tennessee Papers, ODA.

38. Ryan to Rieve, Oct. 25, 1946; *CIO News*, Sept. 30, 1946; "Labor Drives South," *Fortune*, Nov. 1946, p. 139.

39. *Fortune* delineated quite clearly the intimate relationship be-

tween the CIO's overall chances of success in the South and its performance in textiles ("Labor Drives South," p. 138).

40. Walter Orrell, personal interview, Linwood, N.C., May 12, 1982.

41. Jerome Cooper, personal interview, Birmingham, Ala., July 24, 1984

42. Palmer Weber, personal interview, Charlottesville, Va., April 15, 1984.

43. Ibid.

44. "When I first got into the CIO [in 1946], there was a fire and a verve, a crusading fervor in the movement" (Kress interview).

45. "The Southern drive failed because we followed a Northern strategy" (Tom Knight, personal interview, Jackson, Miss., July 28, 1984).

46. "Our situation in Charleston is largely dominated by extreme left wing elements. As a result, we are losing our wide membership" (Franz Daniel to Van Bittner, Sept. 10, 1946, CIO Organizing Committee, South Carolina Papers, ODA). This interpretation must be assessed against countervailing evidence offered by Daniel when he was not under the pressure of explaining to Bittner, his superior, the reasons for the textile organizing failure in South Carolina. For example, three weeks later, when writing to a competing colleague, Tennessee State Director Paul Christopher, Daniel managed a different overall assessment: "Progress is slow, but very healthy" (Franz Daniel to Paul Christopher, Oct. 3, 1946, CIO Organizing Committee, South Carolina Papers, ODA).

47. "This [organizing defeat] does not make me feel too happy. . . . The company embarked on a purely Communistic campaign in the last few days prior to the election" (Frank Ellis to A. J. Pittman, United Packinghouse Workers of America, Sept. 8, 1946, CIO Organizing Committee, Tennessee Papers, ODA).

48. "We had a lot of organizers who talked over the heads of the workers. Educated fools. We had a meeting where a rep was talking about trying to get some key contacts in the plant. Said he would go to town to see if he could 'ascertain' what kind of guy this fellow was. I said, 'Ascertain' hell! Just go out there and see if he lives there! *Talk* to him!' That guy used that word all the time. 'Ascertain!' " (Judd interview).

49. Van Bittner to Anthony Lucio, July 3, 1946, CIO Organizing Committee, South Carolina Papers, ODA; Chris Dixie, personal interview, Houston, July 31, 1984; Charles Wilson, personal interview, Fairfield, Ala., July 25, 1984; Jackson interview.

50. *CIO News*, Sept. 23, 1946; Nov. 11, 1946; Jan. 27, 1947; Feb. 3, 10, 17, and 24, 1947; March 3, 10, 17, and 24, 1947; April 14 and 21, 1947. It should be recorded that a great many organizers— probably a clear majority, based on the available evidence— handled the question of "blame" with considerable poise, and could later recount vivid details, without any pejorative overtones, of tension between organizers and workers. Even a wry humor could be achieved, as demonstrated by Ray Schnell, a steelworker sent south by his International to work in Operation Dixie: "In house-to-house work, you could almost tell when a worker is really shooting you a curve. He might be telling you what he thinks you want to hear, or he might just tell you right out. I've had them pull guns on me and tell me to get the hell off their porch and everything else. And you're pretty sure, then, that they don't want the union" (Schnell interview).

51. Smith to Bittner, Oct. 10, 1946.

52. These issues form the bases of Chapters IV–VIII.

53. Report on CIO Organizing Staff Meeting, Chattanooga, Tenn., Dec. 2, 1946, CIO Organizing Committee, Tennessee Papers, ODA.

54. "CIO's 'holy crusade' to organize a million southern workers moved off to a flying start in May in Atlanta, Ga." (*CIO News*, May 13, 1946).

55. See James E. Fickle, *The New South and the "New Competition": Trade Association Development in the Southern Pine Industry* (Urbana: University of Illinois Press, 1980). Also see Jerry Lembcke and William M. Tattam, *One Union in Wood: A Political History of the International Woodworkers of America* (New York: International Publishers, 1984).

56. Marshall, *Labor in the South*, pp. 256–259; De Vyver, "Present Status of Labor Unions in the South," pp. 10–14; Roper, "The CIO Organizing Committee in Mississippi," pp. 17–33; United Furniture Workers of America, "Resume of Minutes of the General Executive Board Meeting," New York, Dec. 7–8, 1946, p. 9.

57. F. Ray Marshall, "Some Factors Influencing the Growth of Unions in the South," in Industrial Relations Research Association, *Proceedings of the Thirteenth Annual Meeting*, ed. Gerald G. Somers (St. Louis: The Association, 1960), pp. 166–182.

58. William Smith to "Dear Sir and Brother," sent to twenty-three staff members, Dec. 2, 1946, CIO Organizing Committee, North Carolina Papers, ODA.

59. George Baldanzi to William Smith, Dec. 13, 1946, CIO Organ-

izing Committee, North Carolina Papers, ODA; Paul Christopher to Melville Kress, Nov. 13, 1946, CIO Organizing Committee, Tennessee Papers, ODA.

60. Jesse Smith to Baldanzi, Dec. 11, 1946, CIO Organizing Committee, North Carolina Papers, ODA; Baldanzi to Smith, Dec. 13, 1946.

61. See Chapter IV.

CHAPTER IV

1. This is not to imply, however, that textiles were the only "runaway" shops. To name several others, managers of industries engaged in furniture, wood and wood products, and tanneries that required tree bark as part of the production process all saw the advantage in moving operations closer to the Southern forests.

2. A detailed historical overview of textile workers and the dynamics of life in mill villages from 1880 to 1980 are among the subjects of an extensive work in progress entitled, "Like a Family: An Oral History of the Textile South," a project of the Southern Oral History Program at the University of North Carolina at Chapel Hill. See Jacquelyn Dowd Hall, Robert Korstad, and James Leloudis, "Cotton Mill People: Work, Community, and Protest in the Textile South, 1880–1940," *American Historical Review* 91 (April 1986): 245–286; Jacquelyn Dowd Hall, "Disorderly Women: Gender and Labor Militancy in the Appalachian South," *Journal of American History* 73 (Sept. 1986): 354–382. John G. Selby provides a relevant case study of life in High Point, North Carolina, in "Industrial Growth and Worker Protest in a New South City: High Point, North Carolina, 1859–1959," unpublished Ph.D. dissertation, Duke⅗ University, 1984.

John Shelton Reed explores some of the differences between Northern and Southern labor, in part by examining that which has so often been referred to as "different regional characteristics" (John Shelton Reed, *One South: An Ethnic Approach to Regional Culture* [Baton Rouge: Louisiana State University Press, 1982]).

3. Cannon's Amazon mill at Thomasville had technically been organized during World War II, but the result could not be considered an indication of successes still to come. "Management hostility [at Amazon] was so intense the NWLB contract remained virtually unobserved" (Paul David Richards, "The History of the

Textile Workers Union of America, CIO, in the South, 1937–1945," unpublished Ph.D. dissertation, University of Wisconsin, 1978, p. 167, hereinafter cited as "History of Textiles").

4. The twenty-first mill was at York, South Carolina. This summary of the Cannon complex was compiled by the CIO team there. See William Smith to Van Bittner, Atlanta, Aug. 9, 1946, CIO Organizing Committee, North Carolina Papers, ODA.

5. The strongest argument against the small plant approach was experiential: the TWUA had tried it once before—in 1938–1941. "Success, coming slowly, painfully, was measured in terms of footholds rather than membership or dues" (Richards, "History of Textiles," pp. 92–93).

6. Walter Orrell, personal interview, Linwood, N.C., May 12, 1982; Robert Freeman, personal interview, Kannapolis, N.C., Nov. 6, 1964. Freeman was born and raised in Kannapolis and joined the CIO staff there in the early summer of 1946.

7. As one staff member put it, "You couldn't *get* an office in Kannapolis, I'll guarantee you that, 'cause Cannon owned every nail in the buildings down there" (Orrell interview).

8. "Initial Report on the Kannapolis Situation," July 9, 1946, CIO Organizing Committee, North Carolina Papers, ODA.

9. Freeman interview.

10. Ibid.

11. When organizers used the word "emotional," it often had the effect of glossing over something they could not fathom. While a perfectly understandable response to a frustrating situation, it was not a term of sufficient precision that it would help them find out and isolate what the *concrete* problems, in fact, *were*. The form and style of this unsigned report indicate that it was probably not written by Culver, but, rather, by his most gifted subordinate, Harry St. Clair Stroud ("Initial Report on the Kannapolis Situation").

12. Harry Stroud, "Weekly Report, 7/8–7/14," 1946, CIO Organizing Committee, North Carolina Papers, ODA.

13. Nancy Blaine, "Report of Activities, 7/14–7/20," 1946, CIO Organizing Committee, North Carolina Papers, ODA.

14. Harry Stroud, "Weekly Report, June 24–June 30," 1946, CIO Organizing Committee, North Carolina Papers, ODA. Also Joe Kirk, Jr., "Report of Week's Work, Monday June 24th," 1946, CIO Organizing Committee, North Carolina Papers, ODA.

15. Marcelle Malamas, "Report of Activities for 6/23–6/29, 1946," CIO Organizing Committee, North Carolina Papers, ODA;

Stroud, June 24–30, 1946, CIO Organizing Committee, North Carolina Papers, ODA.

16. Marcelle Malamas, "Report of Activities for 6/9–6/15, 1946," CIO Organizing Committee, North Carolina Papers, ODA.

17. Ibid.

18. Fred Wingard to D. D. Wood, CIO area director, "Weekly Report," June 24–29, 1946, CIO Organizing Committee, North Carolina Papers, ODA.

19. Draper Wood to Bruno Rantane, June 25, 1946, Textile Workers Union of America, Greensboro-Burlington, (N.C.) Joint Board Papers, ODA. The CIO staff did try, however, to use workers' previous contact with organized labor to their advantage, with one organizer reporting that she had spent the "entire day" in the office, working on a "draft of letter to Cannon workers who signed pledge card two years ago" (Malamas, "Report of Activities for 6/23–6/29, 1946"). The Malamas report referred to workers signed up during the wartime campaign at the Amazon plant in Thomasville, North Carolina. (See note 3, Chapter IV.)

20. Ibid. For additional examples of organizers' work with veterans, see Stroud, "Weekly Report, June 24–June 30," 1946, and Kirk "Report of Week's Work, Monday, June 24th," 1946.

21. "Initial Report on the Kannapolis Situation."

22. Ibid.

23. Associated Press dispatch, "Rules of Conduct Given to CIO Men," Concord, N.C. June 28, 1946, CIO Publicity Department, North Carolina Papers, ODA.

24. Dean Culver to "Dear Friend," July 10, 1946, CIO Organizing Committee, North Carolina Papers, ODA.

25. Dean Culver to Draper Wood, July 9, 1946, CIO Organizing Committee, North Carolina Papers, ODA.

26. Harry Stroud, "Weekly Report," July 22–28, and Joe Kirk, Jr., "Weekly Report," July 22–28, both from CIO Organizing Committee, North Carolina Papers, ODA.

27. Draper Wood to Dean Culver, July 9, 1946; Draper Wood to Frank Bartholomew, July 9, 1946; and Draper Wood to Clyde Jenkins, July 9, 1946—all from CIO Organizing Committee, North Carolina Papers, ODA.

28. Draper Wood to Ruth Gettinger, July 9, 1946, CIO Organizing Committee, North Carolina Papers, ODA. Gettinger's later report to State Director Smith on the subject of pastors she contacted in the Concord-Kannapolis area may be understood as an attempt to comply with Wood's directives (Ruth Gettinger to Wil-

liam Smith, July 23, 1946, John G. Ramsay Collection, SLA/GSU, 1566-132).

29. Wood to Gettinger, July 9, 1946.

30. In case Culver was unclear about the dimensions of the weekly workload, Wood added: "If you have mass mailing to go out, please arrange it so it can be worked out on Sundays" (Draper Wood to Dean Culver, July 10, 1946, CIO Organizing Committee, North Carolina Papers, ODA).

31. Identical letters from Draper Wood to Dean Culver, Frank Bartholomew, and Clyde Jenkins, July 19, 1946, CIO Organizing Committee, North Carolina Papers, ODA.

32. Dean Culver, "Report of Activity, Concord-Kannapolis Situation, Week of July 21st," 1946, CIO Organizing Committee, North Carolina Papers, ODA.

33. See pages 40–42, Chapter III.

34. William Smith to Van Bittner, Aug. 8, 1946, CIO Organizing Committee, North Carolina Papers, ODA.

35. Dean Culver to Draper Wood, Aug. 5, 1946, CIO Organizing Committee, North Carolina Papers, ODA.

36. Dean Culver to Draper Wood, Aug. 12, 1946, CIO Organizing Committee, North Carolina Papers, ODA.

37. Dean Culver to Draper Wood, Aug. 20, 1946, CIO Organizing Committee, North Carolina Papers, ODA.

38. In actual contributions, as distinct from pledges, CIO internationals other than the TWUA put an average of $90,000 per month into Operation Dixie between the opening of the campaign and the general reappraisal that took place at the National CIO Convention in October 1946. To this sum must be added the $95,000 per month invested by the TWUA itself. These figures may best be described as highly informed estimates rather than an exact accounting. Overall expenditures, according to Marshall, are "impossible to calculate" (Ray Marshall, "Some Factors Influencing the Growth of Unions in the South," in Industrial Relations Research Association, *Proceedings of the Thirteenth Annual Meeting*, ed. Gerald G. Somers (St. Louis: The Association, 1961), p. 166 n.; CIO Executive Board Minutes, Washington, D.C., Jan. 22 and 23, 1948).

39. Dean Culver, "Report of Activity," Oct. 9, 1946, CIO Organizing Committee, North Carolina Papers, ODA.

40. Dean Culver, "Suggestions," ca. Sept. 17, 1946, CIO Organizing Committee, North Carolina Papers, ODA.

41. Concord *Tribune*, Oct. 23, 1946, CIO Organizing Committee, North Carolina Papers, ODA.

42. "I have a feeling in my bones that this coming year is going to be one of great activity for us, and I do not think it will be all bad. I am sure you will be interested to know that this past week has been one of the greatest activity there has been since I have been in here. That does not mean the mills are organized, or even started. But compared to the deadness that has been here, the widely scattered reaction and the few members that have suddenly started signing up, coming to the office, and showing a general interest is most heartening. We may organize something here yet this year" Joel Leighton to Emil Rieve, Jan. 18, 1947, CIO Organizing Committee, North Carolina Papers, ODA).

Certainly, different individuals possessed differing degrees of competence. For a range of scholarly opinion, see Richards, "History of Textiles"; Patricia Hammond Levenstein, "The Failure of Unionization in the Southern Textile Industry: A Case Study," unpublished M.S. thesis, Cornell University, 1964); John Wesley Kennedy, "A History of the Textile Workers Union of America, CIO," unpublished Ph.D. dissertation, University of North Carolina, 1950 (hereinafter cited as "A Textile History"). Also relevant are Joseph A. McDonald, "Textile Workers and Unionization: A Community Study," unpublished Ph.D. dissertation, University of Tennessee, 1981); Barry E. Truchil, "Capital-Labor Relationships in the United States Textile Industry: The Post-World War II Period," unpublished Ph.D. dissertation, State University of New York at Binghamton, 1982; Ralph R. Triplette, Jr., "One-Industry Towns: Their Location, Development, and Economic Character," unpublished Ph.D. dissertation, University of North Carolina, 1974). For particular attention to conflict among TWUA leadership at different points in history, see Daniel Regis Knighton, "A Special Case of Union Influence on Wages: The Textile Workers Union of America," unpublished Ph.D. dissertation, University of North Carolina, 1972; Boyd E. Payton, *Scapegoat: Prejudice/Politics/Prison* (Philadelphia: Whitmore, 1970); Boyd E. Payton, personal interview, Charlotte, N.C., June 20 and 27, 1984.

43. The nine states were North and South Carolina, Georgia, Alabama, Texas, Virginia, Mississippi, Tennessee, and Louisiana.

44. Research Department, Amalgamated Clothing and Textile Workers Union of America, New York, "Textile Workers Union of America: Representation Elections in the South," statistical compilations for 1946 by the author. The "other unions" cited above included one mention of "AFL," presumably the UTWA, the ILGWU, and District 50 (Frank T. De Vyver, "The Present Status

of Labor Unions in the South, 1948," *Southern Economic Journal* 16 [July 1949]: 13).

45. Bessie Shankle, personal interview, Kannapolis, N.C., Nov. 6, 1986.

46. Doris Sloop, personal interview, Kannapolis, N.C., Nov. 6, 1986.

47. Ray Beam, personal interview, Kannapolis, N.C., Nov. 6, 1986.

48. Sloop interview.

49. Chuck Wilson, personal interview, Kannapolis, N.C., Nov. 6, 1986.

50. Ibid.

51. Shankle interview.

52. Ibid.

53. A detailed history of the 1934 general strike by Janet Irons of Duke University is forthcoming.

54. Freeman interview.

55. Shankle interview.

56. Ibid.

CHAPTER V

1. Ralph Helstein, personal interview, Chicago, Oct. 13, 1984. It should be noted that unionization in the telephone industry had a long and complex history, in part a result of the structure of the industry itself. While there was a history of cooperation between them, particularly in the Southwest, the CWA did not join the CIO until 1949. For a detailed discussion, see John N. Schacht, *The Making of Telephone Unionism, 1920–1947* (New Brunswick, N.J.: Rutgers University Press, 1985), especially pp. 100–190.

2. Van Bittner, in an early organizing meeting in Atlanta, *CIO News*, May 13, 1946.

3. *CIO News*, May 13, 1946.

4. *CIO News*, May 6, 1946 and June 10, 1946.

5. *CIO News*, June 24, 1946.

6. *CIO News*, Nov. 25, 1946. One political writer referred to this activity by saying that "dark Mississippi" is "sorely sick with Bilbonic plague" (Walter Davenport, "Headache Down South," *Collier's*, July 13, 1946, p. 14, Carey Haigler Collection, SLA/GSU, 952–16). The Washington, D.C., CIO Council pressed the labor secretary into ending the practice of separate lines at U.S. Employ-

ment Service offices, with separate sets of interviewers and separate sets of files for each race (*CIO News*, Sept. 30, 1946).

7. Ralph Helstein, international president, United Packinghouse Workers of America, Chicago, "To All District Directors, Field Representatives, and Affiliated Local Unions," July 12, 1946, UTA, 51-15-11. According to Helstein, the arrests of these thirty-one blacks, more than half of whom were veterans, had been the result of a "dispute between a white shopkeeper and a Negro customer. They culminated in lynch threats, an armed invasion of the Negro district, wanton destruction of Negro property and wholesale arrests and beatings of Negro citizens." He assured staff members that any financial help they might provide would "pay dividends to coming generations."

8. Donald Henderson, general president, FTA, Philadelphia, "To CIO International Unions, Industrial Union Councils, Regional Directors and Labor Editors, and to FTA International Vice-Presidents, Regional Directors, International Representatives and Organizers, and Local Union Presidents," Aug. 1, 1946, UTA, 36-1-2; *CIO News*, Aug. 26, 1946.

9. *CIO News*, Aug. 5, 1946.

10. James Augustine Gross, "The NAACP, the AFL-CIO, and the Negro Worker," unpublished Ph.D. dissertation, University of Wisconsin, 1962; James S. Olson, "Organized Black Leadership and Industrial Unionism: The Racial Response, 1936–1945," *Labor History* 10 (summer 1969): 475–486; John Streater, "The National Negro Congress, 1936–1947," unpublished Ph.D. dissertation, University of Cincinnati, 1980; Herbert R. Northrup and Richard L. Rowan, *Negro Employment in Southern Industry* (Philadelphia: University Pennsylvania Press, 1970); F. Ray Marshall, *Labor in the South* (Cambridge, Mass.: Harvard University Press, 1967); Dorothy K. Newman et al., *Protest, Politics, and Prosperity: Black Americans and White Institutions, 1940–75* (New York: Pantheon, 1978).

11. *F.A.C.T.*, first quarter, 1946, SLA/GSU.

12. *CIO News*, Nov. 25, 1946.

13. Jim Pierce, personal interview, Charlotte, N.C., June 26, 1982.

14. Karl Korstad, personal interview, Greensboro, N.C., March 29, 1982.

15. B. T. Judd, personal interview, Knoxville, Tenn., Feb. 28, 1983.

16. Helstein interview.

17. Pierce interview.

18. James Jackson, personal interview, East Point, Ga., July 19, 1984.

19. On the internal racial policies of the postwar AFL and CIO, a solid source, in addition to Northrup and Rowan, is N. F. Davis, "Trade Unions' Practices and the Negro Worker: The Establishment and Implementation of AFL-CIO Anti-Discrimination Policy," unpublished Ph.D. dissertation, Indiana University, 1960. As has been noted by many scholars, the CIO's philosophical commitment to industrial unionism, as distinct from the craft orientation of the AFL, encouraged mass recruitment irrespective of race. However, customs developed within such industrial and craft unions could sometimes prove more powerful than the established philosophies of either the CIO or the AFL. In comparing the racial policies of the (relatively few) AFL industrial unions with those of the (relatively few) CIO craft unions, Davis notes that "the industrial AFL unions generally displayed better racial policies than the craft CIO unions" (p. 41).

20. Woody Biggs, personal interview, Jackson, Miss., July 28, 1984; Pierce and Korstad interviews.

21. Frank Parker, personal interview, Birmingham, Ala., July 23, 1984.

22. Biggs interview.

23. Jerome Cooper, personal interview, Birmingham, Ala., July 24, 1984.

24. Parker interview.

25. Biggs interview.

26. Barney Weeks, personal interview, Montgomery, Ala., July 26, 1984. This incident had a certain impact on a number of organizers in Alabama. Frank Parker also referred to this incident.

27. Biggs interview.

28. Ibid.

29. Private interviews with two sources, not for attribution. One black organizer, with a long association with one of the more left-wing unions, replied to telephone inquiries as to his whereabouts that the organizer in question was "deceased." James A. Gross points out that the focus of a great deal of labor history has centered on those workers who were organized, thus leading to the neglect of the majority of black workers who were not organized at all. He suggests the need for studies and autobiographies of "non-policy-making, non-establishment, non-intellectual Black workers" of the sort that would make "exceptionally valuable" oral history projects. The point is well taken. A problem, how-

ever, is the one that has already presented itself in this study: an un-willingness on the part of at least some retired black organizers to resurrect such memories (James Augustine Gross, "Historians and the Literature of the Negro Worker," *Labor History* 10 [summer 1969]: 536–546.

30. Biggs interview. The same general assessment was made by many organizers (Pierce interview; Daniel Starnes, personal interview, Oklahoma City, Aug. 10, 1984; Parker interview; Charles Gillman, personal interview, Riverdale, Ga., July 17 and 21, 1984.

31. Raymond J. Schnell, personal interview, Surf City, N.C., June 27, 1982.

32. Judd interview.

33. Cooper interview.

34. Weeks interview.

35. Walter Orrell, personal interview, Linwood, N.C., May 12, 1982.

36. Parker interview.

37. Pierce interview.

38. Charles Wilson, personal interview, Fairfield, Ala., July 25, 1984.

39. Lloyd Gossett, personal interview, East Point, Ga., July 21, 1984.

40. Pierce interview.

41. William Smith to Frank Green, Oct. 3, 1946, CIO Organizing Committee, North Carolina Papers, ODA.

42. Franz Daniel to Frank Grasso, International Representative, United Paperworkers of America, Sept. 30, 1946, CIO Organizing Committee, South Carolina Papers, ODA.

43. Van A. Bittner to Anthony Lucio, secretary-treasurer, National Maritime Union Hall, July 3, 1946, CIO Organizing Committee, South Carolina Papers, ODA. It should also be noted here that admonitions that "the *prime objective* of CIO is to organize unions and bring about higher wages and better living standards through genuine collective bargaining" were used to castigate and, eventually, expel suspected Communists from the CIO, because they had priorities that orthodox CIO staffers regarded as "higher" than the "simple goal" of unionization. This issue is explored in Chapter VIII on ideology.

44. John Russell, personal interview, Arden, N.C., March 12, 1983.

45. Weeks interview. Also relevant is Donald Dewey, "Negro Employment in Southern Industry," *Journal of Political Economy* 60

(Aug. 1952): 279–293. Bernard Mergen presents a detailed study of the concrete problems presented to one international in "A History of the Industrial Union of Marine and Shipbuilding Workers of America, 1933–1951," unpublished Ph.D. dissertation, University of Pennsylvania, 1968, especially pp. 138–144.

46. Biggs interview.

47. Pierce interview.

48. Parker interview.

49. Biggs interview.

50. Russell interview.

51. Olson, "Organized Black Leadership and Industrial Unionism," p. 481; August Meier and Elliott Rudwick, *Black Detroit and the Rise of the UAW* (New York: Oxford University Press, 1979), especially pp. 9–30.

52. Liston Pope, *Millhands and Preachers: A Study of Gastonia* (New Haven, Conn.: Yale University Press, 1942); Robert Durden, *The Dukes of Durham* (Durham, N.C.: Duke University Press, 1975).

53. Karl Korstad, "An Account of the 'Left-Led' CIO Unions' Efforts to Build Unity Among the Workers in Southern Factories During the 1940's," paper presented at the Southern Labor History Conference, Oct. 1982, Atlanta; Korstad interview.

54. Russell interview. Clearly employers had history on their side in persuading black workers that unions had never treated them equally. Robert C. Weaver provides illuminating conclusions on this subject in *Negro Labor: A National Problem* (New York: Harcourt, Brace, 1946), especially pp. 215–245. See also Herbert Hill, "Labor Unions and the Negro: A Record of Discrimination," *Commentary* 1 (Dec. 1959): 479–488. Raymond Wolters provides background out of an earlier historical period in "Section 7a and the Black Worker," *Labor History* 10 (summer 1969): 459–474.

55. Biggs interview.

56. Chris Dixie, personal interview, Houston, July 31, 1984.

57. Michael S. Homes provides background on the historical roots of racial wage differentials in the South, in "The Blue Eagle as Jim Crow Bird': The NRA and Georgia's Black Workers," *Journal of Negro History* 57 (July 1972): 276–283.

58. Helstein interview; Steve R. Mauser, field representative, UPWA, to A. J. Pittman, director, District 8, Nov. 6, 1946, UTA, 51-17-1. See also Philip Weightman, vice president, UPWA, Chicago, to A. J. Pittman, Dec. 21, 1946, UTA 57-17-1. Northrup and Rowan provide additional background on blacks in the Southern packinghouses, in *Negro Employment in Southern Industry*. For a

study of black packinghouse workers in Fort Worth, see Moses
Adedeji, "The Stormy Past: A History of the United Packinghouse
Workers of America–CIO, Fort Worth, Texas, 1936–1956," unpub-
lished M.A. thesis, University of Texas, 1975.

59. Helstein interview.

CHAPTER VI

1. Lloyd Gossett, personal interview, East Point, Ga., July 21,
1984.

2. John Russell, personal interview, Arden, N.C., March 12,
1983.

3. Jerome Cooper, personal interview, Birmingham, Ala., July
24, 1984.

4. Woody Biggs, personal interview, Jackson, Miss., July 28,
1984.

5. *CIO News*, Oct. 28, 1946.

6. Paul Schuler to George Baldanzi, Atlanta, June 20, 1946, ODA.

7. Eula McGill, personal interview, Birmingham, Ala., July 24,
1984.

8. *CIO News*, May 27, 1946. For evidence of anxiety stirred
among CIO staff organizers by various corporate campaigns, see
Franz Daniel to Van Bittner, July 30, 1946, CIO Organizing Commit-
tee, South Carolina Papers, ODA; Franz Daniel to John J.
Brownlee, July 26, 1946, CIO Organizing Committee, South Caro-
lina Papers, ODA; Steve R. Mauser, field representative, United
Packinghouse Workers of America–CIO, to A. J. Pittman, Nov. 6,
1946, UTA, 51-17-1. Other sources that bear on this issue are E. K.
Bowers, personal interview, Birmingham, Ala., July 24, 1984;
Purnell Maloney, personal interview, Mebane, N.C., July 11, 1984;
Herbert S. Williams, personal interview, Nashville, Tenn., Aug.
13, 1984; interview; Cooper, Nicholas Kurko personal interview,
Fort Worth, Aug. 4, 1984; McGill interview; Boyd E. Payton, per-
sonal interview, Charlotte, N.C., June 20 and 27, 1984.

9. The statement is meant to apply as a generalization, all exceptions being freely conceded. J. Wayne Flynt, for example, is careful to record occasional exceptions to the pattern of ministerial
support for textile management, noting that established Southern
churches "were largely apathetic about economic injustice" and
were "often" allied to the business community (J. Wayne Flynt,

Dixie's Forgotten People: The South's Poor Whites [Bloomington and London: Indiana University Press, 1979], pp. 70–71).

10. For a searing account, based on local studies, of authoritarian police practices in Southern mill villages, see Paul David Richards, "The History of the Textiles Workers Union of America, CIO, in the South," unpublished Ph.D. dissertation, University of Wisconsin, 1978, pp. 1–12 (hereinafter cited as "History of Textiles").

11. James Jackson, personal interview, East Point, Ga., July 19, 1984.

12. Barney Weeks, personal interview, Montgomery, Ala., July 26, 1984.

13. Jackson interview.

14. Geneva Sneed, personal interview, Knoxville, Tenn., Aug. 14, 1984.

15. Gossett interview.

16. Lloyd Davis, personal interview, Birmingham, Ala., July 23, 1984.

17. McGill interview.

18. Davis interview.

19. Walter Orrell, personal interview, Linwood, N.C., May 12, 1982.

20. McGill interview.

21. Davis interview.

22. Gossett interview.

23. Until very recent years, Southern academics have generally characterized these dynamics in terms of results rather than analyzing the process that produced them. Thus, "each succeeding generation saw more Southerners fall into the socially ignorable ranks of white trash. They became the original lazy men; illiterate, worthless, debilitated" (Thomas D. Clark, *The Emerging South* [New York: Oxford University Press, 1961], p. 26). The disdain that "town people" had for "mill persons" is one of the sociological features of the South that comes through quite clearly in the detailed study of a piedmont town published in the 1950s; (John Kenneth Moreland, *Millways of Kent* [Chapel Hill: University of North Carolina Press, 1958], p. 125).

24. "Memorandum by Lucy R. Mason," Greenville, S.C., Aug. 13, 1946, Lucy Randolph Mason Papers, ODA.

25. Cooper interview. Also relevant are Howard Strevel, personal interview, Birmingham, Ala., July 24, 1984; Chris Dixie, personal interview, Houston, July 31, 1984.

26. Carey E. Haigler to John J. Brownlee, Legal Department, CIO Organizing Committee, Atlanta, Oct. 22, 1946, CIO Organizing Committee, Tennessee Papers, ODA.

27. Dean L. Culver, personal interview, Concord, N.C., July 1, 1982.

28. Frank Parker, personal interview, Birmingham, Ala., July 23, 1984. Also relevant among many others are interviews with Cooper and Orrell; Daniel Starnes, personal interview, Oklahoma City, Aug. 10, 1984; Jim Pierce, personal interview, Charlotte, N.C., June 26, 1982; John Thomas, personal interview, Oak Ridge, Tenn., Aug. 14, 1984; James Jackson, personal interview, East Point, Ga., July 19, 1984. See also Edmund F. Ryan to Emil Rieve, Oct. 25, 1946, CIO Organizing Committee, Tennessee Papers, ODA.

29. Cooper interview.

30. M. W. Lynch, western area director, to William Smith, Aug. 4, 1946, CIO Organizing Committee, North Carolina Papers, ODA; William Smith to M. W. Lynch, Aug. 5, 1946, CIO Organizing Committee, North Carolina Papers, ODA; Pierce, Culver, Dixie, and Orrell interviews.

31. Nelson Lichtenstein presents a thorough examination of interaction between the CIO and the federal government during World War II and the legacy of that relationship in *Labor's War at Home: The CIO in World War II* (Cambridge, Eng.: Cambridge University Press, 1982).

32. Raymond J. Schnell, personal interview, Surf City, N.C., June 27, 1982.

33. Schnell and Gossett interviews; James Touchstone, personal interview, Meridian, Miss., July 27, 1984.

34. Gossett and Melville Kress, personal interview, Piney Flats, Tenn., Touchstone interviews; Feb. 26, 1983.

35. Daniel to Bittner, Atlanta, July 30, 1946.

36. Cooper interview.

37. B. T. Judd, personal interview, Knoxville, Tenn., Feb. 28, 1983; Schnell interview; Jerome Cooper to William Smith, Nov. 5, 1946, CIO Organizing Committee, North Carolina Papers, ODA.

38. *CIO News*, Oct. 28, 1946.

39. *CIO News* Nov. 11, 1946.

40. *CIO News*, Nov. 4, 1946.

41. Touchstone interview. Baldanzi even called on the Internal Revenue Service for help on one occasion during the second month of Operation Dixie. His complaint concerned the Farmers'

States' Rights Association of Rock Hill, South Carolina, and several other organizations that had been soliciting contributions to back a "newspaper propaganda campaign against the CIO under the guise of advertising." Contributors had been told that their contributions would be tax deductible (George Baldanzi to Commissioner Joseph D. Nunam, Internal Revenue Service, Washington, D.C., "Night Letter," June 19, 1946, CIO Organizing Committee, North Carolina Papers, ODA.

42. Weeks interview.

43. Gossett interview.

44. Schnell interview.

45. Orrell interview.

46. Palmer Weber, personal interview, Charlottesville, Va., April 15, 1984. For a closer examination of the Mine, Mill and Smelter Workers "tradition" referred to above, see Vernon H. Jensen, *Nonferrous Metal Industry Unionism, 1932–1954: A Story of Leadership Controversy* (Ithaca, N.Y.: Cornell University Press, 1954); Horace Huntley, "Iron Ore Miners and Mine Mill in Alabama, 1933–1952," unpublished Ph.D. dissertation, University of Pittsburgh, 1977.

47. Touchstone interview.

48. Parker interview.

49. Schnell interview.

50. Tom Knight, personal interview, Jackson, Miss., July 28, 1984.

51. Edmund F. Ryan, Jr., Alabama state director, TWUA, to Emil Rieve, general president, TWUA, Oct. 25, 1946, CIO Organizing Committee, Tennessee Papers, ODA.

52. Glenn Earp to Franz Daniel, July 28, 1946, CIO Organizing Committee, South Carolina Papers, ODA.

53. Daniel to Bittner, July 30, 1946.

54. Ibid. For other examples, see "CIO Organizing Staff Meeting," Chattanooga, Tenn., Dec. 2, 1946, CIO Organizing Committee, Tennessee Papers, ODA. Also relevant is Joseph Pedigo, personal interview, Charlotte, N.C., June 20, 1984.

55. In this case, John Ramsay showed the level of ingenuity to which the CIO could rise in fighting such companies and also, perhaps, the level of desperation within CIO ranks. "As a special effort, I went to New York to contact members of the Milliken family. The family opinion is divided, which may prove helpful in settlement. At least the liberal part of this family know of this situa-

tion. The direct management is not liberal" (John Ramsay to Van Bittner, Atlanta, Aug. 8, 1946, John Ramsay Collection, SLA/GSU, 1556-13).

56. Frank Ellis, vice president, United Packinghouse Workers of America, to A. J. Pittman, July 15, 1946, UTA, 51-17-1.

57. Lynch to Smith, Aug. 4, 1946. Though one effect was to provide CIO lawyers with "abundant evidence of extreme coercion and intimidation," the union compiled rather more proof of this kind during Operation Dixie than it wanted, or could effectively exhaust in court appeals (William Smith to Reed Johnson, examiner in charge, NLRB, 5th Regional Sub-Office, Aug. 5, 1946, CIO Organizing Committee, North Carolina Papers, ODA).

58. Gossett interview.

59. McGill interview. Additional accounts of anti-union mobs, beyond those sources already cited, were offered by J. D. Bradford, personal interview, Birmingham, Ala., July 23, 1984; I. R. Gray, personal interview, Arlington, Tex., Aug. 4, 1984; Kurko interview.

60. *CIO News*, Sept. 30, 1946. The article, quoting Van Bittner, noted that "Bennie Bibb, president of a CIO union at Montgomery, Alabama, was beaten by a deputy sheriff."

61. Ryan to Rieve, Oct. 25, 1946.

62. *CIO News*, Sept. 30, 1946.

63. Cooper interview; Dixie interview.

64. Biggs interview.

65. Kress interview.

CHAPTER VII

1. Connections between Southern agricultural conditions and the development of Southern religion, as well as between religion and Southern racial customs, are explored in Cedric Belfrage, *South of God* (New York: Modern Age Books, 1941).

2. See, for example, Donald G. Mathews, *Religion in the Old South* (Chicago: University of Chicago Press, 1977); John Daniel, *Labor, Industry, and the Church* (St. Louis: Concordia, 1957).

3. Donald W. Shriver in John R. Earle, Dean D. Knudson, and Donald W. Shriver, Jr., *Spindles and Spires: A Re-Study of Religion and Social Change in Gastonia* (Atlanta: John Knox, 1976), p. 18.

4. Ibid.

5. F. Ray Marshall, in *Labor in the South*, (Cambridge, Mass.: Harvard University Press, 1967), also stresses the difficulties inherent

in trying to determine the extent and character of organized religion's influence on people's attitudes toward organized labor. He suggests that, while it is "true that many preachers have fought unions," there have been "other examples in which ministers and churches have organized unions and fought for the right of workers to organize." Marshall also highlights those Southerners who had been "induced to promote unionism" precisely *because* of religious convictions, citing Lucy Randolph Mason as a case in point. It is unclear, to this writer at least, whether Mason's well-documented, progressive efforts arose out of religious convictions or out of a world view that was a product of secular ideology, or even from a cosmopolitan perspective that was partly a product of her class background.

6. "You can either be a Christian or a CIO man, but you can't be both," South Carolina preacher, quoted in Isadore Katz, general counsel, TWUA-CIO, "Taft-Hartleyism in Southern Textiles: Feudalism with a New Face," in testimony before the U.S. Senate, October 9, 1950, CIO Political Action Committee, North Carolina Papers, ODA.

7. H. Shelton Smith, *In His Image, but* . . . : *Racism in Southern Religion, 1780–1910* (Durham, N.C.: Duke University Press, 1972); Liston Pope, *Labor's Relation to Church and Community* (New York: Institute for Religious and Social Studies, 1947); Liston Pope, *Millhands and Preachers: A Study of Gastonia* (New Haven, Conn.: Yale University Press, 1942).

8. Katz, "Taft-Hartleyism in Southern Textiles."

9. John Roy Carleson, *The Plotters*, quoted in CIO material, *Militant Truth* file, ODA.

10. *CIO News*, June 3, 1946. Stetson Kennedy, *Southern Exposure* (Garden City, N.Y.: Doubleday, 1946), p. 234.

11. Kennedy, *Southern Exposure*, p. 235.

12. Ibid., p. 232.

13. Stetson Kennedy, "How *Militant Truth* Works," n.d., CIO Organizing Committee, North Carolina Papers, ODA.

14. Ibid.

15. *Militant Truth*, "Special Labor Edition," n.d., CIO Organizing Committee, South Carolina Papers, ODA.

16. Ibid.

17. William Smith to Wade Lynch, Sept. 6, 1946, CIO Organizing Committee, North Carolina Papers, ODA.

18. Lucy Randolph Mason to Franz Daniel, Aug. 6, 1946, CIO Organizing Committee, South Carolina Papers, ODA; Lucy Ran-

dolph Mason to William Smith, Sept. 6, 1946, CIO Organizing Committee, North Carolina Papers, ODA; Lucy Randolph Mason to Franz Daniel, Aug. 31, 1946, CIO Organizing Committee, South Carolina Papers, ODA.

19. Mason to Smith, Sept. 6, 1946.

20. John Ramsay to Van Bittner, August 8, 1946, John G. Ramsay Collection, SLA/GSU, 1556-13.

21. Franz Daniel to Van Bittner, Aug. 10, 1946, CIO Organizing Committee, South Carolina Papers, ODA; Franz Daniel to Lucy Randolph Mason, Sept. 16, 1946, CIO Organizing Committee, South Carolina Papers, ODA.

22. Jim Pierce, personal interview, Charlotte, N.C., June 26, 1982. For another example of the cordial response to the Mason-Ramsay-Gettinger effort, see Glenn Earp to Franz Daniel, July 28, 1946, CIO Organizing Committee, South Carolina Papers, ODA.

23. Allen Swim to John Ramsay, July 22, 1946, John G. Ramsay Collection, SLA/GSU, 1556-8; Lucy Randolph Mason to Earl Taylor, Sept. 14, 1946, CIO Organizing Committee, South Carolina Papers, ODA; Ramsay to Bittner, Aug. 8, 1946; John Ramsay to Reverend R. Bryce Herbert, pastor, Trinity Methodist Church, Sumter, S.C., Nov. 1, 1946, John G. Ramsay Collection, SLA/GSU, 1568-151.

24. Swim to Ramsay, July 22, 1946.

25. Among sources emphasizing the adverse impact of religion in particular states were Walter Orrell in North Carolina, Eula McGill in Alabama, Woody Biggs, Jim Touchstone, and Daniel Starnes in Mississippi, and B. T. Judd in Tennessee and Georgia. All had spent a good portion of their time organizing in textiles. Among organizers who placed less stress on the hostility of the clergy were James Jackson in Mississippi and Dean Culver in North Carolina. Both also worked in textiles. Interestingly, some organizers made due note of church hostility to the CIO but argued that it could be overcome. This attitude was most noticeable among organizers for left-wing unions, such as John Russell with Fur and Leather, Karl Korstad of Food and Tobacco, and Ralph Helstein, the international president of the Packinghouse Workers.

26. Kennedy, *Southern Exposure*, pp. 250–251.

27. Ibid.

28. Ibid., p. 233.

29. Eula McGill, personal interview, Birmingham, Ala., July 24, 1984.

30. Pierce interview.

31. James Jackson, personal interview, East Point, Ga., July 19, 1984.

32. Woody Biggs, personal interview, Jackson, Miss., July 28, 1984.

33. Kennedy, *Southern Exposure*, p. 235.

34. Lloyd Gossett, personal interview, East Point, Ga., July 21, 1984.

35. Ibid.

36. Pierce interview. J. Wayne Flynt, in *Dixie's Forgotten People: The South's Poor Whites* (Bloomington and London: Indiana University Press, 1979), discusses other more historical aspects of the development of Southern religion that led to the "natural" affinity one would eventually find between Southern corporations and Southern ministers: "As Baptist, Methodist, and Presbyterian laymen entered the middle class, they discarded the concerns that had made many of the reformers in the Populist and Progressive eras. Ministers became better educated, and fewer of them were bivocational, earning a living by farming, in mill or mine, while also pastoring a church. The deacons, stewards, and elders who governed congregations were drawn from the most successful parishioners and dampened the enthusiasm of the occasional minister whose social consciousness challenged the economic order" (p. 99).

It is not meant to imply, here, that religious opposition to the CIO was a monopoly of the Protestant churches, however narrowly or broadly defined. For Catholic opposition, see Neil Betten, *Catholic Activism and the Industrial Worker* (Gainesville: University of Florida Press, 1976), especially pp. 119–121; Douglas P. Seaton, *Catholics and Radicals: The Association of Catholic Trade Unionists and the American Labor Movement, from Depression to Cold War* (London and Toronto: Associated University Presses, 1981). The emphasis herein is upon Protestant churches because the Catholic sector of the Southern working class was, except in isolated pockets of the region, quite small.

37. McGill interview.

38. Dean L. Culver, personal interview, Concord, N.C., July 1, 1982.

39. Barney Weeks, personal interview, Montgomery, Ala., July 26, 1984.

40. Lucy Randolph Mason to Franz Daniel, Sept. 14, 1946, CIO Organizing Committee, South Carolina Papers, ODA

41. Frank Ellis, director, UPWA Organizing Department, "Staff News Letter," Oct. 26, 1946, UTA, 51-17-6.

42. E. Paul Harding, assistant public relations director, to "All State Directors, CIO Organizing Committee," Oct. 31, 1946, CIO Organizing Committee, South Carolina Papers, ODA.

43. "The Bible and the Working Man," n.d., c. 1946, ODA.

44. "Transcript of Proceedings, Tenth Annual Convention of Texas State Industrial Union Council, CIO, Austin, Texas, October 19 and 20, 1946," UTA (no box or file number).

45. Walter Orrell, personal interview, Linwood, N.C., May 12, 1982.

46. B. T. Judd, personal interview, Knoxville, Tenn., Feb. 28, 1983.

47. Ellis, "Staff News Letter," Oct. 26, 1946. (2nd ref).

48. Ibid.; see also Daniel, *Labor, Industry and the Church*, especially chap. 4, "What Does the Bible Say About Labor," for other examples of usable "pro-labor" biblical quotations.

CHAPTER VIII

1. For a most illuminating discussion of the idea of "fellow travelers," see David Caute, *The Fellow Travellers: A Postscript to the Enlightenment* (New York: Macmillan, 1973), especially his treatment of the popular front era, pp. 132–184.

2. Nelson Lichtenstein suggests that "by 1943 the Communists were a powerful force in unions representing between a quarter and a third of all CIO union members." *Labor's War at Home: The CIO in World War II* (Cambridge, Eng.: Cambridge University Press, 1982), p. 142.

3. Karl Korstad, personal interview, Greensboro, N.C., March 29, 1982.

4. Ibid.

5. In average hourly wages textiles ranked 132nd out of 135 industries surveyed in 1944—$25 per week at a time when the Bureau of Labor Standards estimated that $35.75 was necessary in Southern mill villages to sustain "an emergency level budget," ("Statement of Textile Workers Union of America in the Matter of Southern Cotton Textile Mills," U.S. Senate, Hearings, Jan. 9, 1945, pp. 12,881–12,898, quoted in Lichtenstein, *Labor's War at Home*, pp. 210–216).

6. Lichtenstein, *Labor's War at Home*, pp. 215–216.

7. Ibid., p. 235.

8. Len DeCaux, *Labor Radical: From the Wobblies to the CIO, a Per-*

sonal History (Boston: Beacon, 1970), p. 454.

9. Frank Emspak, "The Break-Up of the Congress of Industrial Organizations (CIO), 1945–1950" unpublished Ph.D. dissertation, University of Wisconsin, 1972, p. 83 (hereinafter referred to as "The Break-Up of the CIO").

10. David Caute, *The Great Fear: The Anti-Communist Purge Under Truman and Eisenhower* (New York: Simon and Schuster, 1978), p. 26.

11. Ibid., p. 27.

12. "Labor Hears Challenge for Record Production," *Journal*, Winston-Salem, N. C., Sept. 3, 1946.

13. Art Preis, *Labor's Giant Step: Twenty Years of the CIO* (New York: Pioneer, 1964), p. 337.

14. *CIO News*, Sept. 16, 1946.

15. Caute, *The Great Fear*, p. 27.

16. Ibid.; Bert Cochran, *Labor and Communism: The Conflict that Shaped American Unions* (Princeton, N.J.: Princeton University Press, 1977), pp. 248–271.

17. Cochran, *Labor and Communism*, p. 262.

18. Douglas P. Seaton, *Catholics and Radicals, The Association of Catholic Trade Unionists and the American Labor Movement, from Depression to Cold War* (London and Toronto: Associated University Presses, 1981), pp. 201–202.

19. Cochran, *Labor and Communism*, p. 267. One author claims that, in fact, the CIO's executive board in November 1946 had authorized Murray "to take over the funds and property of any local or state council that refused to conform" (Caute, *The Great Fear*, p. 352; Max M. Kampelman, *The Communist Party vs. the CIO: A Study in Power Politics* [New York: Praeger, 1957], pp. 47, 49, 55, 58).

20. Cochran, *Labor and Communism*, p. 267.

21. Ibid.

22. Philip S. Foner, *The Fur and Leather Workers Union: A Story of Dramatic Struggles and Achievements* (Newark, N.J.: Norden, 1950), p. 675.

23. Emspak, "The Break-Up of the CIO," p. 81.

24. Cochran, *Labor and Communism*, p. 266.

25. Pamphlet, Box 158, File 272, ODA.

26. Korstad interview.

27. Ibid.

28. Ibid.

29. Caute, *The Great Fear*, p. 28.

30. Kampelman, *The Communist Party vs. the CIO*, p. 110.

31. Nelle Morton to Franz Daniel, June 3, 1947, The Fellowship of Southern Churchmen File, ODA.

32. Franz Daniel to Nelle Morton, June 5, 1947, The Fellowship of Southern Churchmen File, ODA.

33. Nelle Morton to Franz Daniel, June 7, 1947, The Fellowship of Southern Churchmen File, ODA.

34. Korstad interview.

35. John Russell, personal interview, Arden, N.C., March 12, 1983.

36. Ibid.

37. Raymond J. Schnell, personal interview, Surf City, N.C., June 27, 1982.

38. Ibid.; Nannie Tilley, *The R. J. Reynolds Tobacco Company* (Chapel Hill: University of North Carolina Press, 1985); Robert Korstad, dissertation in progress, University of North Carolina.

39. Ibid.

40. Jim Pierce, personal interview, Charlotte, N.C., June 26, 1982.

41. Russell interview.

42. Ibid.

43. "Report on 1946–1947, American Civil Liberties Union," as quoted in Caute, *The Great Fear*, p. 28.

44. Alonzo L. Hamby, *Beyond the New Deal: Harry S Truman and American Liberalism* (New York: Columbia University Press, 1973), p. 147.

45. Foner, *The Fur and Leather Workers Union*, p. 500.

46. Sidney Lens, *The Crisis of American Labor* (New York: Sagamore, 1959), p. 93.

47. Korstad interview.

48. Ibid.

49. Kampelman, *The Communist Party vs. the CIO*, p. 110.

50. Caute, *The Great Fear*, p. 352.

51. Ibid., p. 353.

52. Ibid.

53. Kampelman, *The Communist Party vs. the CIO*, p. 157.

54. Caute, *The Great Fear*, p. 353.

CHAPTER IX

1. Paul David Richards, "The Textile Workers and Operation

Dixie, 1946 to 1950," paper presented at the Southern Labor History Conference, Atlanta, Feb. 23, 1976, p. 11.

2. Emil Rieve, Minutes of Southern States Directors Meeting, Textile Workers Union of America, May 5, 1949, Organizing Reports and Summaries, p. 1, TWUA Papers, Wisconsin Historical Society, Madison, quoted in Frank Emspak, "The Break-Up of the Congress of Industrial Organizations (CIO), 1945–1950," unpublished Ph.D. dissertation, University of Wisconsin, 1972, p. 182.

3. Jerome Cooper, personal interview, Birmingham, Ala., July 24, 1984.

4. Paul David Richards, "The History of the Textile Workers Union of America, CIO, in the South, 1937–1945," unpublished Ph.D. dissertation, University of Wisconsin, 1978, pp. 2, 3, 213, passim (hereinafter cited as "History of Textiles").

5. Interview not for attribution. See Chapter V, note 29.

6. Solomon Barkin to Emil Rieve, Oct. 25, 1939, "RE: My Trip South, Oct. 10–24th, 1939," as cited in Richards, "History of Textiles," pp. 132–139.

7. George Baldanzi, "Problems of Organization in the South," memo to Emil Rieve, Isadore Katz, Solomon Barkin, and Payne, April 8, 1942, as cited in Richards "History of Textiles," pp. 176–179.

8. Frank Parker, personal interview, Birmingham, Ala., July 23, 1984; James Touchstone, personal interview, Meridian, Miss., July 27, 1984; Dean L. Culver, personal interview, Concord, N.C., July 1, 1982.

9. Raymond J. Schnell, personal interview, Surf City, N.C., June 27, 1982.

10. Parker interview.

11. Touchstone interview.

12. Kress, Melville personal interview, Piney Flats, Tenn., Feb. 26, 1983.

13. Parker interview.

14. Smith to "All North Carolina Staff," Aug. 5, 1946, CIO Organizing Committee, North Carolina Papers, ODA.

15. Jim Pierce, personal interview, Charlotte, N.C., June 26, 1982.

16. Parker interview.

Bibliography

A major portion of the primary documentation for this study has been collected from The Operation Dixie Archives in the Manuscript Department of Perkins Library at Duke University, in Durham, North Carolina. These written records have been combined with an extensive range of oral interviews with retired CIO organizers across the South. A third component of this project came from other manuscript collections, including the Southern Labor Archives at Georgia State University in Atlanta; the labor collections at the University of Texas-Arlington, and at the Catholic University of America; the Southern History Collection at the University of North Carolina at Chapel Hill; and the library at the AFL-CIO headquarters in Washington, D.C. In addition, invaluable primary materials were provided by Keir Jorgensen, of the Research Department of the Amalgamated Clothing and Textile Workers Union in New York, N.Y.

Primary Sources

Operation Dixie Interviews:

Beam, Ray. Kannapolis, N.C., Nov. 6, 1986.
Biggs, Woody. Jackson, Miss., July 28, 1984.
Boartfield, C. D. Memphis, Aug. 12, 1984.
Bowers, E. K. Birmingham, Ala., July 24, 1984.
Bradford, J. D. Birmingham, Ala., July 23, 1984.
Conn, Lewis and Richard. Washington, D.C., Oct. 13, 1986.
Cooper, Jerome. Birmingham, Ala., July 24, 1984.
Cotton, Eugene. and Ralph Helstein, Chicago, Oct. 13, 1984.
Culver, Dean L. Concord, N.C., July 1, 1982.
Davis, Lloyd. Birmingham, Ala., July 23, 1984.
Dickenson, F. M. Memphis, Aug. 12, 1984.
Dixie, Chris. Houston, July 31, 1984.

Doyle, Draper. Soddy, Tenn., July 15, 1984 (AFL).

Frazier, W. B. Chattanooga, Tenn., July 16, 1984.

Freeman, Robert. Kannapolis, N.C., Nov. 6, 1986.

Gillman, Charles. Riverdale, Ga., July 17 and 21, 1984.

Gossett, Lloyd. East Point, Ga., July 21, 1984.

Gray, I. R. Arlington, Tex., Aug. 4, 1984.

Helstein, Ralph, and Eugene Cotton. Chicago, Oct. 13, 1984.

Hobby, Wilbur. Durham, N.C., March 4, 1984 (AFL-CIO).

Horton, Myles. New Market, Tenn., July 13, 1984.

Hurtt, Lida (Peggy). Charlotte, N.C., June 27, 1984.

Jackson, James, East Point, Ga., July 19, 1984.

Judd, B. T. Knoxville, Tenn., Feb. 28, March 1 and 3, 1983.

Knight, Tom. Jackson, Miss., July 28, 1984.

Korstad, Karl. Greensboro, N.C., March 29, 1982.

Kress, Melville. Piney Flats, Tenn., Feb. 26, 1983.

Kurko, Nicholas. Fort Worth, Aug. 4, 1984.

Leighton, Jane and Joel. Annapolis, Md., Dec. 9, 1986.

Maloney, Purnell. Mebane, N.C., July 11, 1984.

McCrea, Bea and Ed. Memphis, Aug. 12, 1984.

McGill, Eula. Birmingham, Ala., July 24, 1984.

Orrell, Walter. Linwood, N.C., May 12, 1982.

Parker, Frank. Birmingham, Ala., July 23, 1984.

Payton, Boyd E. Charlotte, N.C., June 20 and 27, 1984.

Pedigo, Joseph. Charlotte, N.C., June 20, 1984.

Pierce, Jim. Charlotte, N.C., June 26, 1982.

Roehl, Lillian. Silver Spring, Md., March 16, 1984.

Rogin, Lawrence. Washington, D.C., Aug. 22 and 26, 1986.

Russell, John. Arden, N.C., March 12, 1983.

Schnell, Raymond J. Surf City, N.C., June 27, 1982.

Shankle, Bessie. Kannapolis, N.C., Nov. 6, 1986.

Slaiman, Don. assistant to the director of organization, AFL-
    CIO, Washington, D.C., March 14, 1984.

Sloop, Doris. Kannapolis, N.C., Nov. 6, 1986.

Smith, Stanton and Nancy. Chattanooga, Tenn., July 16,
    1984 (AFL).

Sneed, Geneva. Knoxville, Tenn., Aug. 14, 1984.

Starnes, Daniel and Sara. Oklahoma City, Aug. 10, 1984.

Strevel, Howard. Birmingham, Ala., July 24, 1984.

Thomas, John. Oak Ridge, Tenn., Aug. 14, 1984.

Thornburgh, Lucille. Knoxville, Tenn., July 15, 1984.

Touchstone, James. Meridian, Miss., July 27, 1984.

Trammell, A. G. Nashville, Tenn., Aug. 13, 1984 (AFL-CIO).
Weber, Palmer. Charlottesville, Va., April 15, 1984.
Weeks, Barney. Ala., July 26, 1984 (AFL, AFL-CIO).
White, Paul. Houston, July 30, 1984.
Williams, Herbert S. Nashville, Tenn., Aug. 13, 1984.
Wilson, Charles. Fairfield, Ala., July 25, 1984.
Wilson, Chuck. Kannapolis, N.C., Nov. 6, 1986.

II Secondary Sources

Proceedings

Amalgamated Clothing Workers of America. General Executive Board Report and Proceedings, Fifteenth Biennial Convention, Atlantic City, N.J., May 6–10, 1946.

Congress of Industrial Organizations. Final Proceedings, 1946, Eighth Constitutional Convention, Atlantic City, N.J., Nov. 18–22, 1946.

————. Final Proceedings, Ninth Constitutional Convention, Boston, Oct. 13–17, 1947.

Texas State Industrial Union Council. Proceedings. The Nineteenth Annual Convention, Austin, Oct. 19–20, 1946.

Textile Workers Union of America. Proceedings, First Constitutional Convention, Philadelphia, May 15–19, 1939.

————, CIO. Final Proceedings, Fourth Biennial Convention, Atlantic City, N.J., April 24–27, 1946.

United Furniture Workers of America. "Resume of Minutes of the General Executive Board Meeting," New York, Dec. 7–8, 1946.

Articles, Papers, Theses, and Dissertations

Adedeji, Moses "The Stormy Past: A History of the United Packinghouse Workers of America–CIO, Fort Worth, Texas, 1936–1956." M.A. Thesis, University of Texas, 1975.

AFL-CIO, Industrial Union Department. "The Southern Labor

Story." Publication No. 25. AFL-CIO pamphlet, Washington, D.C., n.d.

Barbash, Jack. "Trade Union Government: Concepts and Perspectives." In Proceedings of the Fourteenth Annual Meeting, Industrial Relations Research Association, (New York, Dec. 28–29, 1961.

Bellush, Bernard, and Jewel Bellush. "A Radical Response to the Roosevelt Presidency: The Community Party (1933–1945")." Presidential Studies Quarterly 10 (Fall 1980): 645–661.

Bloch, Joseph W. "Regional Wage Differentials, 1907–46: Long-Term Movement of Manufacturing Wages in the South, the Far West, the Middle West, and the Northeast." Monthly Labor Review 00 (April 1948): 371–377.

Bloomberg, Warner, Jr., Joel Seidman, and Victor Hoffman. "The State of the Unions." New Republic, (reprint, 1959), pp. 3–46.

Brody, David. "The Emergence of Mass Production Unionism." In David Brody, Workers in Industrial America: Essays on the Twentieth Century Struggle. New York: Oxford University Press, 1980.

―――. "The Expansion of the American Labor Movement: Institutional Sources of Stimulus and Restraint." In Institutions in Modern America, edited by Stephen E. Ambrose, Baltimore: Johns Hopkins University Press, 1967.

―――. "Radical Labor History and Rank-and-File Militancy." Labor History 16 (winter 1975): 117–126.

―――. "The Old Labor History and the New: In Search of an American Working Class." Labor History 00 (winter 1979): 110–126.

Burkart, Julia. "From Quarters to Castle: Home Ownership Among Black Sugar Cane Plantation Families." Ph.D. dissertation, Texas Women's University, 1983.

Cary, Lorin Lee. "Institutionalized Conservatism in the Early CIO: Adolph Germer, a Case Study." Labor History 13 (fall 1972): 475–504.

Chaison, Gary N. "A Note on Union Merger Trends, 1900–1978." Industrial and Labor Relations Review 34 (Oct. 1980): 114–120.

Critchlow, Donald T. "Communist Unions and Racism." Labor History 13 (spring 1972): 230–244.

Davenport, Walter. "Headache Down South." Colliers, July 13,

1946, pp. 13–16.

Davis, N. F. "Trade Unions' Practices and the Negro Worker: The Establishment and Implementation of AFL-CIO Anti-Discrimination Policy." Ph.D. dissertation, Indiana University, 1960.

De Vyver, Frank T. "The Present Status of Labor Unions in the South—1948." *Southern Economic Journal* 16 (July 1949): 1–22.

Dew, Charles B. "Disciplining Slave Ironworkers in the Antebellum South: Coercion, Conciliation, and Accommodation." *American Historical Review* 79 (April 1974): 393–418.

Dewey, Donald. "Negro Employment in Southern Industry." *Journal of Political Economy* 60 (Aug. 1952): 279–293.

Douty, H. M. "Collective Bargaining in Factory Employment, 1948." *Monthly Labor Review* 83 (April 1960): 345–349.

———"Development of Trade Unionism in the South." *Monthly Labor Review* 82 (June 1959): 555–582.

Emspak, Frank. "The Break-Up of the Congress of Industrial Organizations (CIO), 1945–1950." Ph.D. dissertation, University of Wisconsin, 1972.

Fenn, Elizabeth A. "Beyond the Bomb: Labor in Oak Ridge, Tennessee, 1942–1946." Unpublished manuscript, May 16, 1984.

Filippelli, Ronald L. "The United Electrical, Radio and Machine Workers of America, 1933–1949: The Struggle for Control." Ph.D. dissertation, Pennsylvania State University, 1970.

Fine, Sidney. "Frank Murphy, the Thornhill Decision, and Picketing as Free Speech." In *The Labor History Reader*, edited by Daniel J. Leab. Urbana and Chicago: University of Illinois Press, 1985.

Freeman, Joshua. "Delivering the Goods: Industrial Unionism During World War II." In *The Labor History Reader*, edited by Daniel J. Leab. Urbana and Chicago: University of Illinois Press, 1985.

Fuchs, Victor R., and Richard Perlman. "Recent Trends in Southern Wage Differentials." *Review of Economics and Statistics* 42 (Aug. 1960): 292–300.

Gabin, Nancy Felice. "Women Auto Workers and the United Automobile Workers Union (UAW-CIO), 1935–1955." Ph.D. dissertation, University of Michigan, 1984.

Gammage, Judie Walton. "Quest for Equality: An Historical Overview of Women's Rights Activism in Texas, 1890–1975." Ph.D. dissertation, North Texas State University, 1982.

Garrison, Joseph Yates. "Paul Revere Christopher: A Southern

Labor Leader, 1910–1974." Ph.D. dissertation, Georgia State University, 1976.

Gross, James Augustine. "Historians and the Literature of the Negro Worker." *Labor History* 10 (summer 1969): 536–546.

———. "The NAACP, the AFL-CIO and the Negro Worker." Ph.D. dissertation, University of Wisconsin, 1962.

Gutman, Herbert. "Working-Class Composition After the Civil War." Paper presented at the annual meeting of the Organization of the American Historians, Detroit, 1981.

Hall, Jacquelyn Dowd. "Disorderly Women: Gender and Labor Militancy in the Appalachian South." *Journal of American History* 73 (Sept. 1986): 354–382.

Hall, Jacquelyn Dowd, Robert Korstad, and James Leloudis. "Cotton Mill People: Work, Community, and Protest in the Textile South, 1880–1940." *American Historical Review* 91 (April 1986): 245–286.

Halpern, Martin. "The Disintegration of the Left-Center Coalition in the UAW, 1945–1950," vols. 1 and 2 Ph.D. dissertation, University of Michigan, 1982.

Hill, Herbert. "Labor Unions and the Negro: The Record of Discrimination." *Commentary* 1 (Dec. 1959): 479–488.

Hodges, James A. "The New Deal Labor Policy and the Southern Cotton Textile Industry, 1933–1941." Ph.D. dissertation, Vanderbilt University, 1963.

Homes, Michael S. "The Blue Eagle as 'Jim Crow Bird': The NRA and Georgia's Black Workers." *Journal of Negro History* 57 (July 1972): 276–283.

Hood, Robin. "The Loray Mill Strike." M.A. thesis, University of North Carolina, 1932.

Huntley, Horace. "Iron Ore Miners and Mine Mill in Alabama, 1933–1952." Ph.D. dissertation, University of Pittsburgh, 1977.

Jacobs, Paul. "Communists in Unions." *Commonweal*, Jan. 20, 1956, pp. 395–397.

Kassalow, Everett M. "Occupational Frontiers of Trade Unionism in the United States." In Industrial Relations Research Association, Proceedings of the Thirteenth Annual Meeting, St. Louis, Dec. 28–29, 1960, edited by Gerald G. Somers.

Kennedy, John Wesley. "A History of the Textile Workers Union of America, CIO." Ph.D. dissertation, University of North Carolina, 1950.

Klimmer, Richard. "Liberal Attitudes Towards the South,

1930–1965." Ph.D. dissertation, Northwestern University, 1976.

Knighton, Daniel Regis. "A Special Case of Union Influence on Wages: The Textile Workers Union of America." Ph.D. dissertation, University of North Carolina, 1972.

Koistinen, Paul A. C. "Warfare and Power Relations in America: Mobilizing the World War II Economy." In *The Home Front and War in the Twentieth Century: The American Experience in Comparative Perspective*, edited by James Titus. Proceedings of the Tenth Military History Symposium, Oct. 20–22, 1982. Washington D.C.: U.S. Air Force Academy and Office of Air Force History, 1984.

Korstad, Karl. "An Account of the 'Left-Led' CIO Unions' Efforts to Build Unity Among the Workers in Southern Factories During the 1940's." Paper presented at the Southern Labor History Conference, Oct. 1982, Atlanta.

Korstad, Robert. "Those Who Were Not Afraid: Winston-Salem, 1943." In *Working Lives: The Southern Exposure History of Labor in the South*, edited by Marc S. Miller. New York: Pantheon, 1980.

Kulik, Gary. "Patterns of Resistance to Industrial Capitalism: Pantucket Village and the Strike of 1924." In *American Working Class Culture* edited by Milton Cantor. Westport, Conn.: Greenwood Press, 1979.

Kuttner, Robert. "Can Labor Lead? *New Republic*, March 12, 1984, pp. 19–25.

Laurie, Bruce. "Nothing on Compulsion: Life Styles of Philadelphia Artisans, 1820–1850." *Labor History* 15 (summer 1974): 337–366.

Lawrence, Ken. "Roots of Class Struggle in the South." *Radical America* 9 (March–April 1975): 15-35.

Lenburg, LeRoy J. "The CIO and American Foreign Policy, 1935–1955." Ph.D. dissertation, Pennsylvania State University, 1973.

Levenstein, Patricia Hammond. "The Failure of Unionization in the Southern Textile Industry: A Case Study." M.S. thesis, Cornell University, 1964.

Linton, Thomas E. "An Historical Examination of the Purposes and Practices of the Education Program of the United Automobile Workers of America, 1936–1959," Ph.D. dissertation, University of Michigan, 1965.

Macdonald, Robert M. "Collective Bargaining in the Postwar Period." *Industrial and Labor Relations Review* 20 (July 1967): 553–558.

Mann, Arthur. "Gompers and the Irony of Racism." *Antioch Review* 13 (June 1953): 203–214.

Marshall, F. Ray. "Some Factors Influencing the Growth of Unions in the South." In Industrial Relations Research Association *Proceedings of the Thirteenth Annual Meeting*, edited by Gerald G. Somers. St. Louis: The Association, 1961.

———. "Unions and the Negro Community." *Industrial and Labor Relations Review* 17 (Jan. 1964): 179–202.

Martin, Charles H. "Southern Labor Relations in Transition: Gadsden, Alabama, 1930–1943." *Journal of Southern History* 47 (Nov. 1981): 545–568.

Mayo, Sez C. "Social Change, Social Movements and the Disappearing Section South." *Social Forces* 24–26 (Mar. 1946–May 1948).

McDonald, Joseph A. "Textile Workers and Unionization: A Community Study." Ph.D. dissertation, University of Tennessee, 1981.

McGovern, Reverend John J. "Philip Murray: An Analysis of His Activities and Economic Thought." Ph.D. dissertation, Georgetown University, 1964.

McPherson, W. K. "Industrial Trends in the Tennessee Valley." *Social Forces* 24–26 (March 1946–May 1948).

Mergen, Bernard. "A History of the Industrial Union of Marine and Shipbuilding Workers of America, 1933–1951." Ph.D. dissertation, University of Pennsylvania, 1968.

Mitchell, George Sinclair. "The Negro in Southern Trade Unionism." *Southern Economic Journal* 00 (Jan. 1936): 26–33.

———."The Working Classes of the Pre-Industrial American City, 1780–1830." *Labor History* 9 (winter 1968): 3–22.

Montgomery, David. "Gutman's Nineteenth Century America." *Labor History* 19 (summer 1978): 416–429.

———"To Study the People: The American Working Class." Labor History 21 (fall 1980): 485–512.

———"Violence and Struggle for Unions in the South, 1880–1930." In *Perspective on the American South: An Annual Review of Society, Politics and Culture*, edited by Merle Black and John Shelton Reed. London: Gordon and Breach, 1980.

Moore, Gilbert W. "Poverty, Class Consciousness, and Racial Conflict: The Social Basis of Trade Union Politics in the UAW-

CIO, 1937–1955." Ph.D. dissertation, Princeton University, 1978.

Morris, Bruce. "Industrial Relations in the Automobile Industry." In *Labor in Postwar America*, edited by Colston E. Warne et al. Brooklyn, N.Y.: Remsen, 1949.

Nelson, Daniel. "Origins of the Sit-Down Era: Worker Militancy and Innovation in the Rubber Industry, 1934–1938." *Labor History* 23 (spring 1982): 198-225.

Newman, Dale. "Work and Community Life in a Southern Textile Town." *Labor History* 19 (spring 1978): 204–225.

Nicholls, W. H. "The South as a Developing Area." *Journal of Politics* 26 (Feb. 1964): 22–40.

———. "Southern Tradition and Regional Economic Progress." *Southern Economic Journal* 26 (Jan. 1960): 187–198.

Olson, James S. "Organized Black Leadership and Industrial Unionism: The Racial Response, 1936–1945." *Labor History* 10 (summer 1969): 475–486.

Pashell, William, and Rose Theodore. "Anti-Communist Provisions in Union Constitutions." *Monthly Labor review* 77 (Oct. 1954): 1097–1100.

Polakoff, Murray Emanuel. "The Development of the Texas State CIO Council." Ph.D. dissertation, Columbia University, 1955.

Richards, Paul David. "The History of the Textile Workers Union of America, CIO, in the South, 1937–1945." Ph.D. dissertation, University of Wisconsin, 1978.

———. "The Textile Workers and Operation Dixie, 1946 to 1950." Paper presented at the Southern Labor History Conference, Atlanta, Feb. 23, 1976.

Rogin, Michael. "Voluntarism: The Political Functions of an Anti-Political Doctrine." *Industrial and Labor Relations Review* 5 (July 1952): 521–535.

Roper, Eugene Albert, Jr. "The CIO Organizing Committee in Mississippi, June 1946–January 1949." M.A. thesis, University of Mississippi, 1949.

Ryscavage, Paul M. "Measuring Union-Nonunion Earnings Differences," *Monthly Labor Review* 97 (Dec. 1974): 3–9.

Schatz, Ronald William. "American Electrical Workers: Work, Struggles, Aspirations, 1930–1950." Ph.D. dissertation, University of Pittsburgh, 1977.

Scherer, Philip M. "Rural Southern Residents and the Incentive to Work." Ph.D. dissertation, University of Missouri, 1972.

Selby, John G. "Industrial Growth and Worker Protest in a New South City: High Point, North Carolina, 1859–1959." Ph.D. dissertation, Duke University, 1984.

Shister, Joseph. "The Direction of Unionism 1947–1967: Thrust or Drift?" *Industrial and Labor Relations Review* 20 (July 1967): 578–601.

Shofner, Jerrell H. "The Legacy of Racial Slavery: Free Enterprise and Forced Labor in Florida in the 1940s." *Journal of Southern History* 47 (Aug. 1981): 411–426.

Simon, Hal. "The Struggle for Jobs and for Negro Rights in the Trade Unions." *Political Affairs* (Feb. 1950): 33–48.

Sloan, Cliff and Robert Hall. "It's Good to Be Home In Greenville . . . .but It's Better If You Hate Unions." *Southern Exposure* 7 (spring 1979): 83–93.

Streater, John. "The National Negro Congress, 1936-1947." Ph.D. dissertation, University of Cincinnati, 1980.

Suggs, H. Lewis, "Black Strategy and Ideology in the Segregation Era: P. B. Young and the *Norfolk Journal and Guide*, 1910–1954." *Virginia Magazine of History and Biography* 91 (April 1983): 161–190.

Sullivan, Patricia. "Gideon's Southern Soldiers: New Deal Politics and Civil Rights Reform, 1933–1948." Ph.D. dissertation, Emory University, 1983.

Tate, Juanita Diffay. "Philip Murray as a Labor Leader." Ph.D. dissertation, New York University, 1962.

Templeton, Ronald K. "The Campaign of the American Federation of Labor and the Congress of Industrial Organizations to Prevent the Passage of the Labor-Management Relations Act of 1947." Ed.D. dissertation, Ball State University, 1967.

Tobias, Sheila, and Lisa Anderson, "What Really Happened to Rosie the Riveter? Demobilization and the Female Labor Force, 1944–47." In *Women's America: Refocusing the Past*, edited by Linda K. Kerber and Jane De Hart Mathews, New York: Oxford University Press, 1982.

Tomlins, Christopher L. "The State and the Unions: Federal Labor Relations Policy and the Organized Labor Movement in America, 1935–55." Ph.D. dissertation, Johns Hopkins University, 1980.

Triplette, Ralph R., Jr. "One-Industry Towns: Their Location, Development, and Economic Character." Ph.D. dissertation, University of North Carolina, 1974.

Troy, Leo. "The Growth of Union Membership in the South,

1939–1953." *Southern Economic Journal* 24 (April 1958): 407–420.

Truchil, Barry E. "Capital-Labor Relationships in the United States Textile Industry: The Post-World War II Period." Ph.D. dissertation, State University of New York at Bimghamton, 1982.

Tuttle, William, "Cold War Politics, 1945–1961." In *A People and A Nation*, edited by Mary Beth Norton et al. Boston: Houghton Mifflin, 1982.

Urmann, Michael Francis. "Rank and File Communists and the CIO (Committee for Industrial Organization) Unions." Ph.D. dissertation, University of Utah, 1981.

Walkowitz, Daniel J. Review of Philip Taft, *Organizing Dixie: Alabama Workers in the Industrial Era*, edited by Gary M. Fink (Westport, Conn.: Greenwood Press, 1981). *Journal of American History* 68 (March 1982): 975–976.

Webb, Bernice Larson. "Company Town—Louisiana Style." *Labor History* 9 (fall 1968): 325–338.

Wiener, Jonathan M. "Class Structure and Economic Development in the American South, 1965–1955." *American Historical Review* 84 (Oct. 1979): 970–992.

Wolters, Raymond. "Section 7a and the Black Worker." *Labor History* 10 (summer 1969): 459–474.

Woodman, Harold D. "Sequel to Slavery: The New History Views the Postbellum South." *Journal of Political History* 43 (Nov. 1977): 523–554.

Worthman, Paul B. "Black Workers and Labor Unions in Alabama, 1897–1904." *Labor History* 10 (summer 1969): 375–406.

Books

Alinsky, Saul. *John L. Lewis*. New York: Putnam, 1949.

Belfrage, Cedric. *South of God*. New York: Modern Age Books, 1941.

Bernstein, Irving. *The Lean Years: A History of the American Worker, 1920–1933*. Boston: Houghton Mifflin, 1960.

———. *Turbulent Years: A History of the American Worker, 1933–1941*. Boston: Houghton Mifflin, 1971.

Betten, Neil. *Catholic Activism and the Industrial Worker*. Gainesville: University of Florida Press, 1976.

Brandfon, Robert L., ed. *The American South in the Twentieth Century*. New York: Crowell, 1967.

Brecher, Jeremy. *Strike!* San Francisco: Straight Arrow Books, 1972.

Brody, David. *Steelworkers in America: The Nonunion Era.* New York: Harper and Row, 1960.

Brooks, Thomas R. *Picket Lines and Bargaining Tables: Organized Labor Comes of Age, 1935–1955.* New York: Grossett and Dunlap, 1968.

Burtt, Everett Johnson, Jr. *Labor Markets, Unions, and Government Policies.* New York: St. Martin's, 1963.

Cantor, Milton. *The Divided Left: American Radicalism, 1900–1975.* New York: Hill and Wang, 1978.

Cash, W. J. *The Mind of the South.* New York: Vintage Books, 1941.

Caute, David. *The Fellow Travellers: A Postscript to the Enlightenment.* New York: Macmillan, 1973.

———. *The Great Fear: The Anti-Communist Purge Under Truman and Eisenhower.* New York: Simon and Schuster, 1978.

Christie, Robert. *Empire in Wood: A History of the Carpenters' Union.* Ithaca, N.Y.: New York State School of Industrial Relations, 1956.

Clark, Thomas D. *The Emerging South.* New York: Oxford University Press, 1961.

Cobb, James C. *Industrialization and Southern Society, 1877–1984.* Lexington: University Press of Kentucky, 1984.

———. *The Selling of the South: The Southern Crusade for Industrial Development, 1936–1980.* Baton Rouge and London: Louisiana State University Press, 1982.

Cochran, Bert, ed. *American Labor in Midpassage.* New York: Monthly Review, 1959.

———. *Labor and Communism: The Conflict That Shaped American Unions.* Princeton, N.J. Princeton University Press, 1977.

Conrad, David E. *The Forgotten Farmers: The Story of Sharecroppers in the New Deal.* Urbana: University of Illinois Press, 1965.

Cornell, Robert J. *The Anthracite Coal Strike of 1902.* Washington, D.C.: Catholic University Press, 1957.

Daniel, Henry. *The History of the Haymarket Affair.* New York: Farrar and Rinehart, 1936.

Daniel, John. *Labor, Industry, and the Church.* St. Louis: Concordia, 1957.

Dawley, Allan. *Class and Community: The Industrial Revolution in Lynn.* Cambridge, Mass.: Harvard University Press, 1976.

DeCaux, Len. *Labor Radical: From the Wobblies to the CIO, Personal History.* Boston: Beacon, 1970.

Dubofsky, Melvyn. *American Labor Since the New Deal*. Chicago: Quadrangle Books, 1971.

————. *Industrialism and the American Worker, 1865–1920*. New York: Crowell, 1975.

————. *We Shall Be All: A History of the Industrial Workers of the World*. Chicago: Quadrangle Books, 1969.

Durden, Robert. *The Dukes of Durham*. Durham, N.C., Duke University Press, 1975.

Dubofsky, Melvyn, and Warren Van Tine. *John L. Lewis: A Biography*. New York: Quadrangle Books, 1977.

Earle, John R., Dean D. Knudsen, and Donald W. Shriver, Jr. *Spindles and Spires: A Re-Study of Religion and Social Change in Gastonia*. Atlanta: John Knox, 1976.

Edwards, P. K. *Strikes in the United States, 1881–1974*. New York: St. Martin's, 1981.

Edwards, Richard. *Contested Terrain: The Transformation of the Workplace in the Twentieth Century*. New York: Basic Books, 1979.

Egerton, John. *Generations: An American Family*. Lexington: University Press of Kentucky, 1983.

Eller, Ronald D. *Miners, Millhands and Mountaineers: The Modernization of the Appalachian South*. Knoxville: University of Tennessee Press, 1982.

Fickle, James E. *The New South and the "New Competition": Trade Association Development in the Southern Pine Industry*. Urbana: University of Illinois Press, 1980.

Filippelli, Ronald L. *Labor in the U.S.A.: A History* New York: Knopf, 1984.

Fine, Sidney. *Sit-Down: The General Motors Strike of 1936–1937*. Ann Arbor: University of Michigan Press, 1969.

Fink, Gary M., et al., eds. *Biographical Dictionary of American Labor Leaders*. Westport, Conn.: Greenwood, 1974.

Fink, Gary M., and Merl E. Reed, eds. *Essays in Southern Labor History: Selected Papers, Southern Labor History Conference, 1976*. Westport, Conn.: Greenwood, 1977.

Fink, Leon. *Workingmen's Democracy: The Knights of Labor and American Politics*. Urbana: University of Illinois Press, 1982.

Flynn, Charles L., Jr. *White Land, Black Labor: Caste and Class in Late Nineteenth-Century Georgia*. Baton Rouge and London: Louisiana State University Press, 1983.

Flynt, J. Wayne. *Dixie's Forgotten People: The South's Poor Whites*. Bloomington and London: Indiana University Press, 1979.

Foner, Philip S. *The Fur and Leather Workers Union: A Story of Dra-*

matic Struggles and Achievements. Newark, N.J.: Norden, 1950.

————. *The Great Labor Uprising of 1877*. New York: Monad, 1977.

————. *Organized Labor and The Black Worker, 1619-1981*. New York: International Publishers, 1981.

————. *Women and the American Labor Movement: From the First Trade Unions to the Present*. New York: Free Press, 1979.

Foner, Philip S., and Ronald L. Lewis, eds. *The Black Worker from the Founding of the CIO to the AFL-CIO Merger, 1936–1955*. Vol. 8. Philadelphia: Temple University Press, 1983.

Foster, James C. *The Union Politic: The CIO Political Action Committee*. Columbia: University of Missouri Press, 1975.

Freidel, Frank. *F.D.R. and the South*. Baton Rouge: Louisiana State University Press, 1965.

Friedlander, Peter. *The Emergence of a UAW Local, 1936–1939: A Study in Class and Culture*. Pittsburgh: University of Pittsburgh Press, 1975.

Galenson, Walter. *The CIO Challenge to the AFL: A History of the American Labor Movement, 1935–1941*. Cambridge, Mass.: Harvard University Press, 1960.

Gilman, Glenn. *Human Relations in the Industrial Southeast: A Study of the Textile Industry*. Chapel Hill: University of North Carolina Press, 1956.

Ginger, Ray. *The Bending Cross: A Biography of Eugene V. Debs*. New Brunswick, N.J.: Rutgers University Press, 1949.

Goldman, Eric F. *The Crucial Decade—and After: America, 1945–1960*. New York: Knopf, 1966.

Goodwyn, Lawrence C. *Democratic Promise: The Populist Moment in America*. New York: Oxford University Press, 1976.

Gordon David M., Richard Edwards, and Michael Reich. *Segmented Work, Divided Workers: The Historical Transformation of Labor in the United States*. Cambridge, Eng.: Cambridge University Press, 1982.

Gornick, Vivian. *The Romance of American Communism*. New York: Basic Books, 1977.

Green, James R. *The World of the Worker: Labor in Twentieth Century America*. New York: Hill and Wang, 1980.

Guerin, Daniel. *100 Years of Labor in the U.S.A.* London: Inks Links, 1979.

Gutman, Herbert G. *Work, Culture, and Society in Industrializing America: Essays in American Working-Class and Social History*. New York: Vintage Books, 1966.

Hagood, Margaret J. *Mothers of the South: Portraiture of the White Tenant Farm Woman*. Chapel Hill: University of North Carolina Press, 1939.

Hamby, Alonzo L. *Beyond the New Deal: Harry S. Truman and American Liberalism*. New York: Columbia University Press, 1973.

Harris, Howell John. *The Right to Manage: Industrial Relations Policies of American Business in the 1940s*. Madison: University of Wisconsin Press, 1982.

Harris, William H. *The Harder We Run: Black Civil Workers Since the Civil War*. New York: Oxford University Press, 1982.

Herring, Harriet R. *Welfare Work in Mill Villages: The Story of Extra-Mill Activities in North Carolina*. Chapel Hill: University of North Carolina Press, 1929.

Hodges, James A. *New Deal Labor Policy and the Southern Cotton Textile Industry, 1933–1941*. Knoxville: University of Tennessee Press, 1986.

Hogan, Bernard, ed. *The Chicago Haymarket Riot: Anarchy on Trial*. Boston: Heath, 1959.

Hoover, Calvin B., and B. U. Ratchford. *Economic Resources and Policies of the South*. New York: Macmillan, 1951.

Howard, Sidney. *The Labor Story: A Survey of Industrial Espionage, 1619-1973*. New York: Praeger, 1974.

Huberman, Leo. *The Labor Spy Racket*. New York: Modern Age Books, 1937.

Hylan, Lewis. *Blackways of Kent*. Chapel Hill: University of North Carolina Press, 1955.

Jacobs, Paul. *The State of the Unions*. New York: Atheneum, 1963.

Jacobson, Julius, ed. *The Negro and the American Labor Movement*. Garden City,N.Y.: Anchor Books, 1968.

Jensen, Vernon H. *Nonferrous Metals Industry Unionism, 1932–1954: A Story of Leadership Controversy*. Ithaca, N.Y.: Cornell University Press, 1954.

Jones, Jacqueline. *Labor of Love, Labor of Sorrow: Black Women, Work, and the Family from Slavery to the Present*. New York: Basic Books, 1985.

Kampelman, Max M. *The Communist Party vs. the CIO: A Study in Power Politics*. New York: Praeger, 1957.

Kasson, John. *Civilizing the Machine: Technology and Republican Values in America*. New York: Penguin Books, 1977.

Kaufman, Stuart Bruce. *Samuel Gompers and the Origins of the American Federation of Labor, 1848–1896*. Westport, Conn.: Greenwood, 1973.

Keeran, Roger. *The Communist Party and the Auto Workers Union.* Bloomington and London: Indiana University Press, 1980.

Kennedy, Stetson. *Southern Exposure.* Garden City, N.Y.: Doubleday, 1946.

Kennedy, Susan Estabrook. *If All We Did Was to Weep at Home: A History of White Working-Class Women in America.* Bloomington: Indiana University Press, 1979.

King, Richard H. *A Southern Renaissance: The Cultural Awakening of the American South, 1930–1955.* New York: Oxford University Press, 1980.

Kornbluh, Joyce. *Rebel Voices: An IWW Anthology.* Ann Arbor: University of Michigan Press, 1968.

Kraus, Henry. *The Many and the Few: A Chronicle of the Dynamic Auto Workers.* Los Angeles: Plantin, 1947.

Laslett, John. *Labor and the Left: A Study of Socialist and Radical Influence in the American Labor Movement, 1881–1924.* New York: Basic Books, 1970.

Lembcke, Jerry, and William M. Tattam. *One Union in Wood: A Political History of the International Woodworkers of America.* New York: International Publishers, 1984.

Lens, Sidney. *The Crisis of American Labor.* New York: Sagamore, 1959.

————. *Left, Right and Center: Conflicting Forces in American Labor.* Hinsdale, Ill.: Regnery, 1949.

Leuchtenburg, William E. *Franklin D. Roosevelt and the New Deal, 1932–1940.* New York: Harper Colophon, 1963.

Levenstein, Harvey A. *Communism, Anticommunism, and the CIO.* Westport, Conn.: Greenwood, 1981.

Lichtenstein, Nelson. *Labor's War at Home: The CIO in World War II.* Cambridge, Eng.: Cambridge University Press, 1982.

Lindsey, Almont. *The Pullman Strike: The Story of a Unique Experiment and of a Great Labor Upheaval.* Chicago and London: University of Chicago Press, 1942.

Livesay, Harold C. *Samuel Gompers and Organized Labor in America.* Boston: Little, Brown, 1978.

Lynd, Alice, and Staughton Lynd, eds. *Rank and File: Personal Histories by Working Class Organizers.* Boston: Beacon, 1973.

Mandel, Bernard. *Samuel Gompers: A Biography.* Yellow Springs, Ohio: Antioch Press, 1963.

Marshall, F. Ray. *Labor in the South.* Cambridge, Mass.: Harvard University Press, 1967.

Martin, Andrew. *The Politics of Economic Policy in the United*

States. Beverly Hills, Calif.: Sage, 1973.

Mason, Lucy Randolph. *To Win These Rights: A Personal Story of the CIO in the South*. New York: Harper and Brothers, 1952.

Mathews, Donald G. *Religion in the Old South*. Chicago: University of Chicago Press, 1977.

McKinney, John C., and Edgar T. Thompson, eds. *The South in Continuity and Change*. Durham, N.C.: Duke University Press, 1965.

McLaurin, Melton. *Paternalism and Protest: Southern Cotton Mill Workers and Organized Labor, 1875–1905*. Westport, Conn.: Greenwood, 1971.

Meier, August, and Elliott Rudwick. *Black Detroit and the Rise of the UAW*. New York: Oxford University Press, 1979.

Michigan Labor History Society. *Sit-Down*. Detroit: The Society, 1979.

Montgomery, David. *Workers' Control in America: Studies in the History of Work, Technology, and Labor Struggles*. Cambridge, Eng.: Cambridge University Press, 1979.

Moreland, John Kenneth. *Millways of Kent*. Chapel Hill: University of North Carolina Press, 1958.

Morris, James O. *Conflict Within the AFL: A Study of Craft versus Industrial Unionism, 1901–1938*. Ithaca, N.Y.: Cornell University Press, 1958.

Mortimer, Wyndham. *Organize! My Life as a Union Man*. Boston: Beacon, 1971.

Newman, Dorothy K., et al. *Protest, Politics, and Prosperity: Black Americans and White Institutions, 1940–75*. New York: Pantheon, 1978.

Nicholls, W. H. *Southern Tradition and Regional Progress*. Chapel Hill: University of North Carolina Press, 1960.

Northrup, Herbert R., and Richard L. Rowan. *Negro Employment in Southern Industry*. Philadelphia: University of Pennsylvania Press, 1970.

Oates, Mary J. *The Role of Cotton Textile Industry in the Economic Development of the Southeast, 1900–1940*. New York: Arno, 1975.

Odum, Howard W. *Southern Regions of the United States*. Chapel Hill: University of North Carolina Press, 1936.

Payton, Boyd E. *Scapegoat: Prejudice/Politics/Prison*. Philadelphia: Whitmore, 1970.

Pessen, Edward. *Most Uncommon Jacksonians: The Radical Leaders of the Early Labor Movement*. Albany: State University of New York Press, 1967.

Pope, Liston. *Labor's Relation to Church and Community*. New York: Institute for Religion and Social Studies, 1947.

——.*Millhands and Preachers: A Study of Gastonia*. New Haven, Conn.: Yale University Press, 1942.

Preis, Art. *Labor's Giant Step: Twenty Years of the CIO*. New York: Pioneer, 1964.

Preston, William, Jr. *Aliens and Dissenters: Federal Suppression of Radicals, 1903–1933*. New York: Harper and Row, 1966.

Ransom, Roger, and Richard Sutch. *One Kind of Freedom: The Economic Consequences of Emancipation*. New York: Oxford University Press, 1977.

Raper, Arthur F. *Preface to Peasantry: A Tale of Two Black Belt Counties*. New York: Atheneum, 1968. (Originally published c. 1936.)

Rayback, Joseph G. *A History of American Labor* New York: Macmillan, 1959.

Record, Wilson. *The Negro and the Communist Party*. Chapel Hill: University of North Carolina Press, 1951.

Reed, John Shelton. *The Enduring South: Subcultural Persistence in Mass Society*. Chapel Hill: University of North Carolina Press, 1972.

——. *One South: An Ethnic Approach to Regional Culture*. Baton Rouge: Louisiana State University Press, 1982.

Renshaw, Patrick. *The Wobblies: The Story of Syndicalism in the United States*. Garden City, N.Y.: Anchor Books, 1968.

Rhyne, Jennings J. *Some Cotton Mill Workers and Their Villages*. Chapel Hill: University of North Carolina Press, 1930.

Rogers, Daniel. *The Work Ethic in Industrial America, 1850–1920*. Chicago: University of Chicago Press, 1978.

Rubin, Morton. *Plantation County*. New Haven, Conn.: College and University Press, 1963. Originally published 1951.

Ruchames, Louis. *Race, Jobs, and Politics: The Story of the FEPC*. New York: Columbia University Press, 1953.

Salvatore, Nick. *Eugene V. Debs: Citizen and Socialist*. Urbana: University of Illinois Press, 1982.

Saposs, David J. *Communism in American Unions*. New York: McGraw-Hill, 1959.

Schacht, John N. *The Making of Telephone Unionism, 1920–1947*. New Brunswick, N.J.: Rutgers University Press, 1985.

Schatz, Ronald W. *The Electrical Workers: A History of Labor at Gen-*

eral Electric and Westinghouse, 1923–60. Urbana and Chicago: University of Illinois Press, 1983.

Seaton, Douglas P. *Catholics and Radicals: The Association of Catholic Trade Unionists and the American Labor Movement, from Depression to Cold War*. London and Toronto: Associated University Presses, 1981.

Simkins, Francis Butler. *A History of the South*. New York: Knopf, 1963.

Smith, H. Shelton. *In His Image, but . . . . : Racism in Southern Religion, 1780–1910*. Durham, N.C.: Duke University Press, 1972.

Smith, Robert Sidney. *Mill on the Dan: A History of Dan River Mills, 1888–1950*. Durham,N.C.: Duke University Press, 1960.

Smith, Timothy. *Revivalism and Social Reform in Mid-Nineteenth Century America*. New York: Abingdon, 1957.

Stolberg, Benjamin. *The Story of the CIO*. New York: Viking, 1938.

Taft, Philip. *Organized Labor in American History*. New York: Harper and Row, 1964.

———. *Organizing Dixie: Alabama Workers in the Industrial Era*. Westport, Conn.: Greenwood, 1981.

Tang, Anthony M. *Economic Development in the Southern Piedmont, 1860–1950: Its Impact on Agriculture*. Chapel Hill: University of North Carolina Press, 1958.

Terrill, Tom T. and Jerrold Hirsch, eds. *Such as Us: Southern Voices of the Thirties*. Chapel Hill: University of North Carolina Press, 1978.

Tilley, Nannie. *The R. J. Reynolds Tobacco Company*. Chapel Hill: University of North Carolina Press, 1985.

Tindall, George Brown. *The Emergence of the New South, 1913–1945, vol. 10: A History of the South*. Baton Rouge: Louisiana State University Press, 1967.

Tippett, Tom. *When Southern Labor Stirs*. New York: Jonathan Cape and Harrison Smith, 1931.

Turner, Jonathan H., and Charles E. Starnes. *Inequality: Privilege and Poverty in America*. Santa Monica, Calif.: Goodyear, 1976.

United States Department of Labor, Bureau of Labor Statistics. *Labor in the South*. Bulletin No. 898. Washington, D.C.: Government Printing Office, 1947.

Walsh, J. Raymond. *CIO: Industrial Unionism in Action*. New York: Norton, 1937.

Warne, Colston E., et al., eds. *Labor in Postwar America*. Brooklyn, N.Y.: Remsen, 1949.

Weaver, Robert C. *Negro Labor: A National Problem*. New York: Harcourt, Brace, 1946.

Wilensky, Harold L. *The Welfare State and Equality*. Berkeley: University of California Press, 1975.

Wittner, Lawrence S. *Cold War America: From Hiroshima to Watergate*. New York: Praeger, 1974.

Wolff, Leon. *Lockout, The Story of the Homestead Strike of 1892*. New York: Harper and Row, 1965.

Wolman, Leo. *Ebb and Flow in Trade Unionism*. New York: National Bureau of Economic Research, 1936.

Yellen, Samuel. *American Labor Struggles, 1877–1934*. New York: Monad, 1936.

Zieger, Robert H. *American Workers, American Unions, 1920-1985*. Baltimore: Johns Hopkins University Press, 1986.

Index